Psalms for

the Soul

A SINNER MEETS
JESUS IN THE PSALMS

ROBERT WARRICK

Endorsement

I believe this devotional booklet is a series of divinely inspired reminders that our walk with God is not so much dependent upon our living as we should as it is a reminder that God is always there to offer support, encouragement, and guidance in the most difficult and trying times in our lives no matter how far we may have strayed.

As Gib speaks openly and honestly of his failures and how God used those mistakes to help him see more clearly his need for continual guidance and dependence upon God, it offers us the assurance that if we submit to God, He will use our mistakes and dependence on Him to mold us into becoming the person He created us to be.

—Larry Franklin
Author of: *The Lodge*

This book presents frank, honest, and spiritually challenging thoughts that, upon daily reflection, may help you to more fully understand Christ's ability to deliver you even from your deepest sin.

—Michael Larkin

ISBN: 978-1-998188-17-8 (paperback)
ISBN: 978-1-998188-18-5 (hardcover)
ISBN: 978-1-998188-19-2 (ebook)

Available in paperback, hardcover, e-book

Published by Reachout Publishing
PO Box 159, Clyde, Alberta T0G 0P0
www.reachloveconnect.com

Foreword

Following a deep moral and spiritual failure, the Lord took me through a deep work of restoration, which took six months to get through. During those months, the Lord used the book of Psalms to get me back in touch with the person of Jesus. What I found was that, though the gospels gave us the life, events, and teachings of Jesus, the book of Psalms gives us His inner, emotional life. I came to realize that, even though I knew Jesus, I really did not have a vital connection with the heart of Jesus. During those six months, I would face many anxiety attacks. Oftentimes, I would roll out of bed to my knees and pray myself up onto my feet to face another day. It was getting in contact with the heart of Jesus that made my restoration possible. As I read and reread through the book of Psalms, always reading them in order, a picture of Jesus emerged that I had never seen before. These devotionals chronicle much of that journey. They are written in the first person and usually addressed to the Lord Himself. The reader is brought into my thoughts and conversation with Jesus. Whereas most devotionals speak to the reader and present a challenge to the reader to implement in his life, this one does not. As you enter into my thoughts and experience, I ask you to see how that might apply to you and let the Holy Spirit change your life while He presents Jesus to you.

Dedication

This book is dedicated to my dear wife, without whom this book would not exist. It was her love and encouragement that gave me the impetus to write these devotionals, and her tireless typing, reading, and reflecting back a reader's perspective proved invaluable.

Psalm 1
The Secret of the Inner Life

Vs. 1—Blessed *is* the man that walketh not in the counsel of the ungodly, nor standeth in the way of sinners,
nor sitteth in the seat of the scornful. (KJV)

What is it that makes one's life blessed and another's humdrum?
What exalts one man's life while another's wallows in mediocrity?
This question can be answered by another one: In what do you
delight? For the Lord Jesus, it was amazingly simple: "My delight
is in Your Word." He only knew and taught what the Father had
taught Him; He only did what He had seen the Father do; His
sole joy, delight, and pleasure were in pleasing His Father and
accomplishing His will, His work. It is the inner life of Jesus that
produces the outer life that is seen.

Is the joy of your life to please God in all things? Do you see and
cherish God's word more than your necessary food? Do you have
meat to eat that others know not of? (John 4:32)? If so, then the
life of Christ is being realized in your life. Then your walking,
standing, and sitting will be those of the blessed man; your life
will be that fruitful tree planted beside the inexhaustible supply
of God's Holy Spirit; your life will be a joy and delight to the heart
of God. Never before in the history of all creation had there been
a man so blessed, so delightful, so pleasing to the heart of God as
the blessed Man, the Man Christ Jesus.

Psalm 1
Which Way

Vs. 2—But his delight *is* in the law of the LORD; and in
his law doth he meditate day and night. (KJV)

When all is said and done, there are only two ways. Jesus made
that clear: there is a narrow way leading to life and a broad way
leading to destruction. Jesus stands at the head of the narrow way,
proclaiming, "I am the way, the truth, and the life. No one comes
to the Father except through me." (John 14:6, NKJV). It is narrow
because it allows for only Himself and provides no room for self.
"Come unto me all that labor and are heavy laden..." (Matthew
11:28, KJV). (This is the way of deliverance, freedom, and rest
which yields a relationship of love, joy, and peace.) The righteous
are not righteous for what they have done; they do what they do
because they have been made righteous in Christ. They have a
right relationship and standing with God because of Jesus' work
on the cross.

Being on the way with Christ, we yield to Him so He can live His
life through us. Regardless of how outwardly upright they may
appear or outwardly degenerate they may live, the unrighteous
are on that broad way. Why so broad? Because there are many
lanes on that road: lanes for religion, philosophy, meditation, self-
help, self-actualization, and selfishness. Be one a philanthropist
or a profligate, humanitarian, or hedonist, that way will lead to
destruction. We must take hold of Jesus to live.

Psalm 2
The Inner Raging of Sin

Vs. 2—The kings of the earth set themselves, against the LORD… and against his anointed… (KJV).

Why these ragings within me? Why this striving and rebellion? Is it not the motions of sin in the members? Is it not my restless flesh? Jesus said, "That which is born of the flesh is flesh" (John 3:6, NKJV). He never hints at any attempt on God's part to change the flesh into spirit—it must be put to death. This is the ceaseless cry of our flesh, "Let us break their bonds in pieces."

All the restless energy of sinful mankind culminated in one fatal act against the Lord and His Anointed, Jesus. Man was fully exposed for what he is, what I am in myself—all at the cross. God allowed man to vent his full hatred and rage against Him on Christ. But, precious Savior, the very instrument of Your death becomes the source of life to me. I, who sought to break all bonds of restraint and act out my sinful pleasures, have been broken by Your loving hands.

What do I find when all of my sin is broken and all of my rage spent? A loving Savior who has endured it all, borne it all with me, broken my world as a dried-up piece of pottery, and beckons me to Himself. I kiss the Son out of love and gratitude, freely and spontaneously, not out of timidity or dread, not as one who merely wants to appease His wrath, but as one who is an object of His love. I am blessed.

Psalm 2
What Now?

Vs. 10—Now therefore… (NKJV).

Can life ever be the same as it was? After having been forgiven so much, could I just carry on with *business as usual?* Should not I be different after having received from you such grace. Did not Jesus condemn just that attitude in Matthew 18:21-35 that could receive such grace and then be unable to express it to others? Could Peter ever be the same after being on the Mount of Transfiguration?

If there is anything You have taught me, Lord, it is this: that my heart truly is deceitful above all things and desperately wicked. Let me not for a second think that my flesh has been the least bit improved, that my natural mind has learned a thing. It is only in my inner man that I have received from you as a consequence of new birth that I can live in the benefit of what your sovereign hand in my life in dealing with my sin has wrought.

I see a few things regarding what I should do in this Psalm. I need discernment to see my flesh at work and instantly judge it. I need to worship, to bask in your presence. I need to rejoice, to revel in what Your great grace has accomplished, but NEVER take it for granted. I need to show you homage to demonstrate your worthiness publicly.

Psalm 2
My King

Vs. 7—I will declare the decree; the LORD hath said unto me, "Thou *art* my Son; this day have I begotten thee" (KJV).

God has highly exalted the Lord Jesus and given him a name higher than all other names. All creation shall bow to His name and at His feet—whether willingly or unwillingly. A day will come when Jesus will be here on earth physically, visibly, and powerfully to rule over this earth with a rod of iron. But what about me now? Yes, I should pray: "Thy Kingdom come" (NKJV) for so it shall, and God will have Jesus reign from Zion, but I have the privilege of Him reigning as sovereign in my heart and life now. He has returned to heaven. He has received from His Father a Kingdom. He is reigning now, but we do not see it yet in its full expression in this world where Satan is still the god of this world. But He is to reign in me now!

By new birth, I "see the kingdom of God." By that same new birth, I "have been translated from the kingdom of darkness into the kingdom of His dear Son." I have been yoked to Christ, seeing it not as bondage to be broken but as discipleship to be accepted and growing thereby. I have kissed the Son, not in fear or dread, but from an affectionate heart. I own Him as my King and Sovereign now. Jesus told Pilate, "My Kingdom is not of this world." Though not of it, it is definitely in it and shall one day be over it.

Psalm 3
Hope Amidst Despair

Vs. 3, 4—But thou, O LORD, *art* a shield for me; my glory, and the lifter up of mine head. I cried unto the LORD with my voice, and he heard me out of his holy hill, Selah. (KJV)

To despair is terrible, and to believe that there is no hope in God is worse than death. You, Lord Jesus, understand what it is like. In your innocence, evil men would multiply and assail you, would hound and dog you every step of the way, opposing every word and deed done in Your Father's name. But all your hope was in God, not in this world or this world's men. Where evil would proclaim that you had no hope in God, faith would look up and see Him who is Your all in all. It was my sin, Lord, which has brought me low and left me in despair. And daily, my sin rises up against me to accuse, and all those accusations are true.

How hard it is to rise each morning, to face another day. How easy just to sleep and try to forget, but I cannot. I must rise for it is in rising that I meet you. I cry out to You, and You answer, beckoning me to Yourself. Yes, there is a lot of sin to deal with—the root and the fruit, but as I rise each day and commune with You in Your word You, bit by bit, refashion me from all of those broken pieces. Where there was despair, there is hope; where there was self-loathing, there is Your love; where there was fear, there is faith.

Psalm 3
Salvation Belongs to God

Vs. 8—Salvation *belongeth* unto the Lord; thy blessing is upon thy people. Selah (KJV).

Salvation is such a beautiful word and communicates so much of the heart of God. Upon Adam's sin, God would have been perfectly within His rights to condemn all of mankind immediately or even to have struck them both dead instantaneously. Such an action would have vindicated God's righteousness and satisfied divine justice. God was not obligated to do anything for man, yet He did. For God is more than righteousness, holiness, and justice; He is also love, mercy, and grace. Man's sin became the occasion for God to unfold His perfect plan. It was a plan conceived from eternity past and put in place, not as a contingency plan, but as the unfolding of His eternal purposes in grace.

Salvation belongs to God and was made possible solely through the act of love of Jesus on Calvary's cross who gave Himself for sin in fulfillment of the Father's will. Now, having won salvation, He can confer it upon all those who, by faith, accept the free offering of grace through confession, repentance of sin, and faith in the work of Christ. What an anchor for my soul, to have its eternal destiny founded upon nothing less than the work of Christ and to look unto Jesus, the author and finisher of my faith who in joy gave Himself.

Psalm 4
Relieved in Distress

Vs. 1—You have relieved me in *my* distress. (NKJV)

What a wonderful comfort there is in knowing that You do answer when I call. There are times, Lord, when the distress I am in is due solely to my own bad choices and decisions. Do you then leave me to stew in my juices and sleep in the bed I have made? You will use the misery that I have brought upon myself to help me realize to what extent I have dishonored and disappointed You. But in the midst of it is also the assurance that, with confession and repentance, restoration is there. The consequences of my failure may continue as Your principle of sowing and reaping is carried out in life, but through all of that, I now have the assurance of Your presence.

There will also be times when I am distressed due to my faithfulness to You. Indeed, that was the experience of Your Son, as He walked amongst sinners and bore their hatred and reproaches. And what was his resource? He had the complete assurance of your favor and love upon Him. He could draw upon that in prayer and receive from You the calming assurance that all things are in your hands and that nothing could happen to Him apart from Your will and plan. In so many ways, Jesus, You were perfected as my high priest through suffering. Now I can come to You, call upon You, and fully know that You understand what Life is like in this fallen world, to intercede for me before the throne of grace.

Psalm 4
The Lord Does Hear

Vs. 1—Hear me when I call, O God of my righteousness: thou hast enlarged me when I was in distress; have
mercy upon me, and hear my prayer (KJV).

No one suffered the contradiction of sinners as You did, Lord.
You, who came to live among sinful men and enter fully into our
life and feelings, experienced the full hatred of men. Yet You were
ever mindful of the presence of the Father with You even when
heaven seemed silent. You could call upon Your God, and He
would answer to give you comfort and relief amid Your distress.
Your confidence was ever in God, the full assurance that He is
there and hears.

It is to you I come, Lord Jesus, with all of my sin and failure and call
upon You who are full of compassion and grace. You are teaching
me to hate my sin the way You hate it. Though I deserve the distress, hatred, and scorn, You do not wish to leave me there. Little
by little, light is coming in; bit by bit, I am receiving Your forgiveness and experiencing the dawning of a new day. You are putting
gladness into my heart, and one day, You will grant me peace and
safety. Will I once again be able to offer You praise? Will there
again be sacrifices of righteousness to come from a life so marred?
As I come to the end of a day, I can lay down in peace and sleep
knowing that One is with me who knows me and understands.
Whatever may come and whatever I face in the morning, I am
not alone.

Psalm 4
Gladness in my Heart

Vs. 7, 8—Thou hast put gladness in my heart, more than
in the time *that* their corn and their wine increased. I
will both lay me down in peace, and sleep: for thou,
LORD only makest me dwell in safety (KJV).

What a wonderful realization that God wants me to experience
gladness, even now in this lost, sinful world. He has made us for his
pleasure, and He derives pleasure from seeing His children enjoying the life and world He has given to us. In a world full of so much
sin, sorrow, and suffering, God is able to put gladness in our hearts.
This is not circumstantial gladness, mere happiness due to things
going our way, but the joy of relationship and the gladness that
comes through it. This Psalm portrays anything other than an easy
life or a life of pleasure; the outward circumstances are difficult,
and inwardly, there is much distress.

Can we not sympathize with David as he pours out his heart in
honest confession and dismay at the apparent success of those
opposed to him? But he is always drawn back to God as we should
be too. It is so easy to quote Romans 8:28 when it is someone else's
distress, but it is an altogether different thing to trust God in the
midst of my own. But as we allow the Spirit of God to calm our
hearts and settle the ceaseless agitation within our minds, He can
minister His peace. Truly, we can then say as David did, "You have
put gladness in my heart more than in the season that the grain and
wine increased," more than the outward would explain, but that
full, inner gladness from God.

Psalm 5
In the Morning

Vs. 3—My voice shalt thou hear in the morning, O
LORD; in the morning will I direct *my prayer* unto thee,
and will look up (KJV).

What a blessing it was to Your heart, O God, to hear the voice of
Jesus ascend to you each morning. Early He would rise, while it
was yet dark, and seek Your face, seek Your will, meditate upon
Your wonder and greatness. And He knew You were listening and
had confidence in Your attentiveness; thus did Jesus direct His
thoughts upward. He was fully grounded in Your character, fully
persuaded of Your love, and He looked upward. "But as for me.."

You had to deal with me after the manner of my sins first; I had
to see my sin the way You saw it. You hate iniquity; You abhor
evil. It cannot stand in Your presence, and I had to have that same
attitude. "But as for me..." I, too, want to be a source of delight to
Your heart; I want to rise early and give You praise in the morning.
I want you to hear my voice, consider my meditations, heed my cry,
and be pleased. You have so blessed me to be concealed within the
person of Your beloved Son, to be hidden behind His blood, to
be so fully identified with Him that it is no longer I, but Christ in
whom I am complete. To meet with You and to please You each
morning is joy, and His joy is being made complete in me.

Psalm 5
I Will Look Up

Vs. 7—But as for me, I will come *into* thy house in the multitude of thy mercy: *and* in thy fear will I worship toward thy holy temple. (KJV)

What a comfort to be assured that You are attentive to my cry, interested in my needs, and responsive to my prayers. If I had not this confidence in You, then there would be no point in looking up. But when I look up, You are there; when I look around, it is Your presence that surrounds me; when I look within, it is Your Spirit who draws me. As I look up to You, I proclaim Your wonder, greatness, and glory. To You, I render my prayers and thanksgivings; to You, I direct my meditations and thoughts.

When I look unto Jesus, the author and finisher of my faith, I see Him who is the lover of my soul and bow in worshipful adoration. What a work You had to do in my heart to cleanse it from evil thoughts and inordinate desires to be purified. Your desire was always to have mankind in relationship with You. Your delights were with the sons of men, and as believers, we find our greatest delight and fulfillment in our relationship with You. So, we rejoice in Your presence, all those who have put their trust in You, whose hearts are full of gladness and whose mouths are full of praise. We joy in You, our King, our redeemer, and our God. We who love Your name and hope in You, look up to You to satisfy our souls.

Psalm 5
Where is Gladness?

Vs. 11—All who take refuge in Thee be glad... (NASB 1977).

How could You be glad in a world full of wickedness, a world so set in its animosity toward You? You have shown me the secret of Your joy and gladness—it is in taking refuge in God. It is only the perverseness of my sinful flesh that leads me to take refuge in God merely as *a last resort.* But You, Lord, have shown me to seek that refuge early and not attempt to handle things myself since I am so prone to come to You in prayer only *when all else fails.*

And what do I find now that I am coming to you early and often? I am finding joy; and rather than being a happiness born of circumstances which is easily understood, it is a joy despite circumstances which passes understanding. I find a song; there is rejoicing in Your presence because the heart and mind are relieved of their burden since it has been rolled onto your shoulders. I find exultation; I sense the rising within my spirit of rejoicing in Your presence. There is no longer condemnation from God and the condemnation from man recedes into the background. You have set me in a place of favor due solely upon Your work both for me and within me.

Psalm 6
Cleansing Tears

Vs. 6, 7—I am weary with my groaning; all the night
make I my bed to swim; I water my couch with my
tears. Mine eye is consumed because of grief; it waxeth
old because of all mine enemies. (KJV)

O Lord, You are angry. Dear Father, You are greatly displeased. My
course of sin that I pursued so long against all of Your conviction
has broken out upon my life. All around me, I see the wreckage,
the flotsam, and jetsam of a self-lived life. Be angry, be displeased,
but have mercy upon me, for I am weak. Punish me not to the level
that my sins deserve. If You were to punish me to that extent, then
I would never again see the light of day. How long shall this be? As
long as it needs to be to have its work in my soul, as long as it takes
for me to hate my sin and sinful flesh as much as You do. It is not
the consequences of my sin that I need to hate; it is the sin itself.

Lord, some days it takes all my strength just to roll out of bed
and right to my knees. The tears shed at night become my bath in
the morning. The sorrow and shame, the memories and regrets,
become the balm as each new day I rise and meet my Savior, and
I find that He is there waiting to receive me. He has borne all the
condemnation of God on Calvary already; He has taken the punishment that I could never bear. The punishment that is left for
me to bear is measured out by His mercy. Lord, You have heard my
supplication, received my prayers, and I am at peace.

Psalm 6
I Am Weak

Vs. 9—The LORD hath heard my supplication; the LORD will receive my prayer. (KJV)

Do we really have a sense of our weakness, or do we deceive ourselves into thinking we can handle our lives for the most part and only need God for the big issues? The apostle Paul recounts his *credentials* in II Corinthians 11, primarily in response to unfounded attacks and insinuations against him and his ministry. But, after laying out all of those things well known to the Corinthian saints, he tells them of his supreme experience—the most humbling of all: being brought into the presence of God. And what was the result of that experience? To learn that God's grace is sufficient and that His strength is made perfect through weakness. Paul would far rather boast of his weakness that the glory would be all of God rather than compare credentials and have something to boast before men.

Acknowledging weakness runs contrary to my pride, to the cultural messages I have been taught all my life, and to the myths of masculinity that permeate our society. But to acknowledge weakness, to admit to my dependency before God, to confess that I do not have all the answers (do I even have any?) and lack the power is to open my life up to divine answers and the Spirit's power. As paradoxical as it sounds, the path to strength lies through weakness.

Psalm 7
The Pleadings of Christ for Himself

Vs. 1—O Lord my God, in thee do I put my trust: save
me from all them that persecute me, and deliver me;
(KJV)

What great contradiction of sinners You endured, Lord. As You
walked this earth in perfect, loving obedience to Your Father, You
became the target of so much hatred and disdain. Why would one
who only did good and always sought the healing and benefit of
others become such an object of persecution? It is because evil
hates good. Evil is self-destructive and destructive of everything
around it. Evil hates good because it reveals the true condition of
evil and reminds it of its wickedness before God.

How You suffered, Lord, all throughout Your life. You, who could
have called down all the power of heaven, yet You relied fully on
God to deliver. As men would heap hatred and threats upon You,
surrounding You and threatening to tear You to pieces, Your
trust was fully placed in God. God allowed You to feel the full
measure of man's animosity against God, and He allowed man
to fully reveal the depth of his hatred toward God. Yes, I know
at Calvary You bore the full weight of God's wrath against sin on
Your holy soul, but I see so clearly also how You bore the hostility
of sinful man against Your holy person in Your life. You felt every
sting of hatred and rejection, yet You trusted in God, who is a just
God, to deliver You, and He did. May I understand Your heart of
sympathy.

Psalm 7
The Pleadings of Christ for Me

Vs. 6—Arise, O LORD, in thine anger, lift up thyself
because of the rage of mine enemies: and awake for me
to the judgment *that* thou hast commanded. (KJV)

You, God, have tested my heart and my mind. Your testing was
not so that You could see what was there, but to reveal to me what
You already knew was there. I, who had enjoyed my sin, indulged
my flesh, and denied You access to many areas of my life, have seen
You burst my life asunder. I have done this and have iniquity in
my hands, I have perpetrated evil where there was innocence and
deserve to be overtaken and trampled to the ground. How can I
plead to You when I deserve what is happening to me? Upon what
ground can I approach You for deliverance? You are a just God and
my sin demands justice.

Then I see Jesus approach Your throne. He presents Himself
before the Judge. I hear Him say that I am His, that He knows
all about my sin, and has taken the divine punishment for it. He
reminds the court that I am His, covered by His blood, protected
from wrath. There is mercy. Mercy has triumphed over justice!
What lies before me in reaping the consequences of my sin I know
not, but one thing I do know: I will not be alone. The One who
knows me best and loves me most will be with me all the way. The
throne is not a place of condemnation for me, but of grace. I know
I can come before God because I am accepted in God's Son. Jesus
found me in my sin, but He was not content to leave me there. He
has received more glory in forgiving than in judgment.

Psalm 7
What have I done?

Vs. 3—If I have done this...(KJV).

Lord, You were innocent of all of the charges that they brought against You. You never repaid evil for evil; on the contrary, You prayed for those who sought to destroy You. Even on the cross, You prayed, "Father, forgive them, for they know not what they do." You never plundered Your enemies (oh, how You were surrounded by them!), but rather, You blessed Your enemies. You gave them every opportunity to see the evil in themselves and deal with it. You were hated without a cause; they hated You because they hated Your Father. They hated You because Your life and words testified against them.

You always went about doing good; but as for me, what have I done? I have done plenty that deserves evil to be repaid to me, to have my freedoms taken away from me, to receive hatred, reviling, and punishment. But what did You do? Did You return to me all that You could mete out? No! Where I saw sin, You saw conviction. Where I saw evil, You saw contrite confession. Where I saw guilt, you saw repentance. Where I saw rejection, You saw reconciliation. O Lord my God, in You I have put my trust.

Psalm 8
What is Man?

Vs. 4—What is man, that thou art mindful of him? and
the son of man, that thou visitest him? (KJV)

Just what is man? What did You intend him to be? He was made in Your image and after Your likeness. He was to represent You in this world by exercising beneficent dominion over all creatures. He, of all creatures, was like You with moral capacity and the desire for spiritual fellowship with You. What a terrible thing sin has done to the crown of Your creation, and what shame I have brought to Your name through my sin. So, what is man? Weak, feeble, corrupt, evil, condemned. Whereas before all things were put under his feet, now You have placed the fear of man in the hearts of the animals.

But, where man has failed, God will still triumph, for You have introduced the Man, Christ Jesus. He has come in the likeness of sinful flesh and for sin, to put away sin by the sacrifice of Himself. What a distance He did come; from the heights of Godhead glory to be made a little lower than the angels, then crowned with glory and honor. Everything has changed now. It is no longer me standing alone in a place of judgment, but Jesus standing with me, pleading my cause, pleading His blood. Whereas I would have nothing to say other than "Guilty—I abhor myself." Jesus can say, "He is mine—I love him." God can now say, "justified," and I can now praise Him. Out of a heart of simplicity, out of a mouth of child-like dependence You bring forth praise to Yourself.

Psalm 8
It's All About God

Vs. 9—O LORD our Lord, how excellent *is* thy name
in all the earth! (KJV)

Ultimately everything that happens is under the Sovereignty of God. No action or event can occur unless God has explicitly allowed it. God is the center and focal point of all His creation. It is always about God. Even our salvation is about God. Why is salvation even available to man? Is it because man wanted it or deserved it? No. It is because God wanted it. God is the initiator, Jesus is the author and finisher of our faith who carries out the divine plan, and the Spirit brings that conviction without which we naturally would have no interest in God or His salvation.

Little wonder David extols the excellence of the name of God, the majesty of His nature. David wonders to himself, "What is man that God would take interest in him?" Yet God did, and He did solely as an expression of His divine love and not in response to man's felt need. The natural man loves his sin; he may not love the consequences of his sin, even though many of them he truly relishes, but he loves his sin. "But God..." Where would we be without that expression of divine interest? What God's love has conceived, God's power can execute, and His Sovereignty assures us that His will is done. How excellent You are, oh, our God.

Psalm 9
Forsaken?

Vs. 3—When mine enemies are turned back, they shall
fall and perish at thy presence. (KJV)

In Your times of distress, where did You turn, Lord Jesus? When
enemies would arise and seek Your destruction, where was Your
refuge? It was in Your God. In all of Your affliction and persecution from men, You could praise God fully and completely
because His presence was ever with You. Early You sought God,
often You fled to Him. Your confidence was always in Him, and
He was ever faithful. It is to this same God that I come. Though
full of sin and shame, where else can I go for You alone have life.

You are a merciful God ready to receive any who would forsake
their sin and seek You. Jesus showed me the kind of God You
are—a God of mercy and compassion. Jesus showed me on
Calvary the extent to which You were willing to go to have me for
Yourself. When my sin looked as if it would engulf my life, You
proved greater than my sin. When I would consider forsaking my
life, You showed that You had not forsaken me. Lord Jesus, when
all would forsake You and flee, Your God would send an angel to
strengthen You. Daily, Lord, I need Your strength so that I will not
be overwhelmed by much sorrow and grief; daily, I receive Your
grace and favor so that I might praise You, rejoice in You, and be
glad in Your presence.

Psalm 9
Maintained

Vs. 4—For You have maintained my right and my cause… (NKJV).

In all things, Lord Jesus, You were perfectly right and just. You were willing to suffer the reproaches of men against God, knowing that Your Father would sustain You. Even though they would hate You and revile You, yet You could weep over their city, Jerusalem, desiring that they would even in that late hour repent and accept You. In the title to this Psalm, it is inscribed to Muth Labben—death of the son. You, Lord Jesus, are the Son whose death was so unjust yet so necessary. Without Your death, none of the Father's plans for this world would ever have come to fruition. You made it possible for Him to have joy and rejoicing in this world. As You contemplated the cross, the joy set before You was of being received back into your Father's presence, having done all things to His satisfaction.

So I hear You say that if I would come after You, I must deny myself and take up my cross. And what is that cross? It is the instrument of my death! Am I now ready to die to myself for You? Am I finally thoroughly done with my past way of life and willing to see it all go? The flesh is a completely and utterly terrible thing that does not want to give an inch. Every day, may I, in Your strength, take up the cross and die to myself afresh. That is my choice now—either to let my flesh have the upper hand and rule my passions and lusts, or to see myself crucified with You daily and live for You in joy.

Psalm 9
Rejoicing in Salvation

Vs. 8—And he shall judge the world in righteousness;
he shall minister judgment to the people in upright-
ness. (KJV)

Do I really appreciate this great salvation of which I have become
a recipient? One principle of human behavior is that the value we
place on something is reflected in the price we are willing to pay,
what it shall cost us. Consider these three verses: "For the redemption of their souls is costly" (Psalm 49:8, NKJV). "You who have
no money, come, buy without money and without price" (Isaiah
55:1, NKJV). And "What will a man give in exchange for his
soul?" (Matthew 16:26, NKJV) They teach us of the high price of
redemption which is beyond our ability to pay. It costs too much,
but God paid the price. Do we, then, now value it as highly as we
ought? Do I? How can I show God how much I appreciate His
salvation? Through sacrifice! But what sacrifice is sufficient?

No sacrifice can ever be sufficient, but we can do what He asks:
"Present your bodies as a living sacrifice..." (Romans 12:1, NKJV).
Once that is done, then He has all of you. It is not that we are to
make a sacrifice in some Lenten fashion; rather, it is to be the sacrifice itself. Once we have given ourselves as a living sacrifice, then
"present(ing) ...your members as instruments of righteousness to
God" (Romans 6:13, NKJV) will be the most natural thing in the
world. Then you can "offer the sacrifice of praise, the fruit of our
lips giving thanks to God" (Hebrews 13:15, NKJV). As you rejoice
in His salvation, He is delighted.

Psalm 10
Forsaken

Vs. 4—The wicked, through the pride of his countenance, will not seek after God: God *is* not in all his thoughts. (KJV)

Lord, You have not been afar off in my time of trouble, but that is only because Jesus was forsaken of God on the cross. He experienced a separation that I never shall as He made His soul an offering for sin. He was forsaken so that I never shall be. It is a wonder of grace that I, so caught up in my sin and so deserving of condemnation and death, have such a Savior who doesn't stand afar off from me nor hide Himself in my times of trouble. He comes alongside of me through His Spirit to restore me to the Father.

It is something I will never understand how You, Father, allow evil and wickedness to continue in this world. Yet You are not willing that any should perish; You both allow the evil of men's hearts to be fully exposed for what it is, and You allow men to speak evil of You. You were merciful to me and brought my sin and rebellion to an end in Your perfect time. May I have faith in You to do the same with others, to believe that the same grace with which You dealt effectively with me can be effective in another's life too. Though evil appears to prevail, and it seems that You are distant, I now see Your mercy and grace acting in concert with Your justice to bring about glory to Yourself just as You did on the cross.

Psalm 10
Forgetting and Remembering

Vs. 11, 12—He hath said in his heart, God hath forgotten: he hideth his face; he will never see it. Arise,
O LORD; O God, lift up thine hand: forget not the
humble. (KJV)

Whenever we, in our Western cultural way, think of these two
concepts of forgetting and remembering, we see them as purely
cognitive functions, exercises of our mind's memory to recall
events. But that is not the biblical concept being conveyed by those
two words. God's infinite mind, which knew all things before
anyone ever existed to do any of them, does not lose His memory
of those events. He chooses to "forget," means that He ceases
to act upon those events as something to be taken into account
anymore.

Similarly, when God "remembers," it's not that it had slipped His
mind, and now He's got to *figure out* what to do about it. For God
to remember means that He begins to act out in time the eternal
purpose He had planned. When the wicked say, "God has forgotten; He hides His face" (verse 11), they are expressing their hope
that it doesn't matter to God anymore and that He won't act in
response to their wickedness. When God *forgets* our sins, He is no
longer acting toward us as sinners, seeing us in our sin as vessels
of wrath and holding those transgressions against us; but rather
is acting toward us in grace by the virtue of Jesus' shed blood. In
His *remembering,* He takes us up as His children to unfold His
purposes of grace in Christ Jesus.

Psalm 10
I am Caught

Vs. 2—"Let (me) be caught in the plots which (I) have devised..." (NKJV).

Little did I know that as I nursed and fed upon my anger, resentment, and bitterness, I was actually laying down the traps into which I would be ensnared. "How deceptive is sin, how it hardens the heart" (Hebrews 3:13). Satan comes along, sees what is in my heart, and then feeds it with gall and bile. Satan looks for opportunities to turn an event into another case to support the ugly narrative I am encouraging in my own soul.

Little wonder that Paul warns us about the root of bitterness that grows up and defiles many (Hebrews 12:5). And who was the first one defiled? It was me! All that wasted time, all that spent energy, all those opportunities that God gave me to have a way of escape, but I continued in my bitterness. Did I ever think that God could not see? Was I ever fooled into believing that God had forgotten? Did I conclude that, since God had not stopped me in my tracks, that He didn't really care? For me, it was not any of that; rather, it was simply that I grew to the point that I didn't care. One day, God asked me, "Are you ever going to come clean on your own?" When I said no to Him, I forced His hand to act. But despite my sin, I found a God that would judge me and yet be gracious to me.

Psalm 11
To Whom Shall I Go?

Vs. 1—In the LORD I put my trust: how say ye to my
soul, Flee *as* a bird to your mountain? (KJV)

Lord, I have put all my trust in You. Only You can make something beautiful out of the mess I have made of my life. My grief
and shame are so great that I can barely walk amongst people for
fear that I shall be exposed. It would be so easy to try to hide out
somewhere away from it all. Was that not Adam's first impulse?
But You will not have it so. You have told me that I am not merely
to survive but to thrive. For the suffering to accomplish its purpose
in me, I cannot and must not seek to artificially make it easier, to
either try to deaden the pain or to reduce it.

Proverbs 20:30 reads, "Blows that hurt cleanse away evil, as *do*
stripes the inner depths of the heart" (NKJV) Great evil comes
from a deep source, and an evil pursued for a long time makes deep
roots, so I must have faith in Your hand to fully deal with this sin
within me. Yes, I know there will be those who will glory in my
failure, and there will also be those who will never believe I can be
delivered completely from my sin, but I will not waver from what
You have assured me You shall do. You are watching, evaluating,
and measuring out what is needed to produce fruit, which will be
to Your praise and glory.

Psalm 11
The Foundation

Vs. 3—If the foundations be destroyed, what can the
righteous do? (KJV)

Regardless of how well the structure itself is built and how secure
and strong its walls are, nothing can compensate for a poor foundation. And what is our foundation? "For no other foundation
can anyone lay than that which is laid, which is Jesus Christ" (I
Corinthians 3:11, NKJV) The foundation of all the purposes of
God, the reason why everything God has in mind for us as believers shall come to pass, is because it is all predicated upon Jesus
Christ and His work accomplished at Calvary. God showed His
total satisfaction in that work by raising Him from the dead and
seating Him at His own right hand. To dare to secure my salvation
or my Christian life upon anything else is to besmirch His work.

For most true believers, the most seductive alternative is to fall into
the Galatian error, "Having begun in the Spirit are you now being
made perfect in the flesh" (Galatians 3:3, NKJV) Let us not add
anything to the work of Jesus made good to us through the Holy
Spirit, the most common thing being the Old Testament law. To
attempt to add law to grace for our life is like building half the
house upon the rock and the rest on the sand. When the storm
comes, and it shall, the part on the sand will collapse and take
much of the part on the rock with it. Thank God our foundation
rests secure.

Psalm 12
Purified Seven Times

Vs. 3—The LORD shall cut off all flattering lips, *and* the tongue that speaks proud things... (KJV).

Lord, You have brought me a long way. For many years, I resisted Your conviction and refused to let Your Holy Spirit search me out and reveal the evil that lay within. I built walls around areas of my life and said, "Stay out! Go no further!" To my shame I realize that I had made peace with my sin. I regarded it in my heart and nurtured it, indulging in it, yet not so much that it would break out like leprosy and become evident to all. But You finally broke all that down. You destroyed the stronghold in my heart and have dug deep. Your words are pure, and they are purifying. You have used Your pure word to purify my life, to bring me back into the right relationship with You.

Your word is like silver purified seven times. You have had to refine me seven times. There was so much to face, so many lies, deceits, hypocrisies, and overlaying justifications that needed to be brought to the surface, revealed, judged, and repented. I can look back and see Your hand of love as You broke me and remade me, removed each piece, cleaned it off, and put it back into place. How can I rejoice in Your work in my life? Though men may refuse me, reject me, and not believe in the work You have done, yet You shall keep me, and I shall keep close to You.

Psalm 12
Tried Seven Times

Vs. 6—The words of the LORD *are* pure words: as silver tried in a furnace of earth, purified seven times. (KJV)

What does it take to purify my heart? Here, we read that the purity of God's word is as silver after being purified in the furnace seven times. God's word is intrinsically pure, but my heart is not. We read here what God is willing to do in us to purify our hearts if we are willing. Do we have any idea how much dross is in us? Have we examined ourselves in the light of God's word as revealed in Jesus? As God begins the process of removing the dross, He knows the intensity of heat and the amount of affliction, tribulation, and suffering to use.

We become so accustomed to the dross in our lives, having lived with our thoughts, feelings, and behaviors so long, that we see them as *normal*. But God knows what is not of Jesus, what does not come from the new life implanted within us by new birth. But I resist, complain, squirm, and even beg God to take His hand away. Only He knows what He is after, only He knows what it takes, and my responsibility is to yield to His hands. We all want a sanctified life, but we are not always willing to pay the price. God has made it clear: we will have the spiritual life we want. His quantity is infinite, and our capacity is finite, but He will give us as much of Himself as we desire.

Psalm 13
The Sympathies of Christ

Vs. 2—How long shall I take counsel in my soul, *having* sorrow in my heart daily? how long shall mine enemy be exalted over me (KJV)?

How often it must have been, Lord Jesus, that Your soul was vexed and afflicted by the evil around You. How alone You must have felt as You walked through this world amid sinful men. I read in the gospels how Your heart sighed, how it was grieved, how it was stirred up to righteous indignation. As You met opposition, rejection, and misunderstanding on every side, from friend, family, and foe alike, did You sometimes feel that God had abandoned You, that He had left You on Your own and forgotten about You? As You had to experience life down here in this fallen world and feel the weakness and frailty of human existence, did You not wonder how long God could tolerate man's wickedness?

But Your God heard You as You went to Him in prayer, sometimes praying late into the night, other times rising early a great ways before dawn. You were drawn to seek out God, for You trusted in His mercy and rejoiced in His deliverance. Lord Jesus, You went through so much apart from the cross, preparing You to be a faithful and true high priest who can understand all of my confusion and all of my feelings and comfort me in all my distress. Thank You, Lord, for being there before God's throne for me, interceding for me, dealing bountifully with me, and causing me to rejoice in Your salvation.

Psalm 13
Bountifully

Vs. 6—I will sing unto the LORD, because he hath dealt
bountifully with me. (KJV)

Can we sing to the Lord amid the trial? Is our heart so narrow that
we only see deliverance from the trial rather than through the trial?
Here David trusts and sings even though there is no deliverance
in sight. So, will I walk by faith or walk by sight? The spiritual life
is a walk of faith, not measured by outcomes and prosperity but
by joy and nearness. It is only the one lying on the Lord's bosom
who can hear His most heartfelt, intimate thoughts. I must trust
in the character of God that He always acts consistently with
Himself. He doesn't act consistently from person to person as we
measure consistency. Hence, my eyes are to be upon Him rather
than others.

When I have fully grasped that I deserve none of God's goodness,
that there is nothing in myself to commend me to God's favor, I
can begin to acknowledge that He has surely dealt bountifully
with me. Every breath I take is a gift from Him: the warmth of the
sun, the refreshment of rain, the beauty that surrounds me, the
wonder of life. Bounty, an overflow of the abundance of God, is
what I have received. Do you feel it too? In Christ, we have love,
peace, joy; He has been made unto us all these things, and we have
received grace upon grace. Truly, He has dealt bountifully.

Psalm 14
The Foolishness of Sin

Vs. 1—The fool hath said in his heart, There is no God.
They are corrupt, they have done abominable works,
there is none that doeth good. (KJV)

The fool says in his heart, "There is No God." Is this a statement of atheism or one of rebellion? I believe the latter. The fool says, "There is no God over me." The fool tries to live his life as if there were no God, as if he were "free" from the restrictions of conscience and the shackles of morality so that he can give full expression to his wickedness and desires. This is the spirit of rebellion; this is the spirit of lawlessness, believing that God's morality does not apply to me. John writes, "Sin is lawlessness," (I John 3:4 NKJV). Sin is my will asserting itself against God's will. And where does this lead other than corruption, wickedness, iniquity, and judgment?

Is not that exactly what I did as I pursued my course of sin and self-indulgence? Did I not refuse to heed my conscience? Did I not reject the conviction of the Holy Spirit? Did I not tell God, "Stay out of that area of my life! You are not welcome there"? Did I not play Satan's fool? He knew my weakness, he knew my hurt, and he had his means by which I could assuage that hurt. When I needed to yield that area to God, I kept it closed off. All sin is self-destructive and demonstrates the spirit of rebellion. Lord, thank You for never giving up on this old fool and finally crashing through! It has come at a high price, but it is worth paying for this liberty.

Psalm 14
Foolish Heart

Vs. 4—Have all the workers of iniquity no knowledge?
who eat up my people *as* they eat bread, and call not
upon the LORD. (KJV)

The opposite of knowledge is ignorance. One who is ignorant has merely never had the truth, the knowledge put before him. This is how we view knowledge as a state of awareness and ignorance as being unaware. If we look at wisdom as the right application of that knowledge, then the opposite of wisdom is foolishness. The fool cannot be accused of ignorance, for he knows better and does not do better. Spiritually, God likens our growth in Christ to our maturity as humans. We begin life as babies, and the inexorable movement of life is toward growth and maturity—our very DNA is preprogrammed to this end.

We start our spiritual life as ignorant babes who earnestly desire the sincere milk of the word, the unadulterated truth of God. But if the mother eats onions, it comes out in her milk. If those who are teaching the word lust after the leeks, onions, and garlic of the world or try to inject law into grace, then the truth is adulterated. Lord, deliver us from being fools, from knowing the truth but not doing it. When Your Spirit brings conviction to my life, and I reject it, I am telling You that I don't want You. "No God for me." I make myself my god. The result will inevitably be corruption in my life and whatever abominable deeds my conscience can bear. Jesus told us that joy doesn't come from knowing the truth but from doing it (John 13:17). We are exhorted to have the obedience of faith and follow Christ, having denied ourselves, taken up the cross, and followed Him.

Psalm 15
To Abide Where Christ Dwells

Vs. 1, 2—LORD, who shall abide in thy tabernacle? who shall dwell in thy holy hill? He that walketh uprightly, and worketh righteousness, and speaketh the truth in his heart. (KJV)

To abide where Christ dwells is to desire to be in His presence and to enjoy fellowship with Him. Jesus spoke in John's gospel of His joy remaining in me and my joy being full. What was His joy? Was it not to complete the work the Father had given Him to do and to return to Him? Lord Jesus, this was the great motivating force of Your entire life and ministry—to please Your Father, to glorify Him, and to return to His glory. This has become my joy and passion—to enjoy Your word, commune with You in prayer, come into Your presence, and enjoy your relationship.

How could I ever have been so deceived for so long? How could I have ever thought that gratifying the flesh would ever ease the deadness and pain of my soul? Like a drug, its effects wear off, guilt and shame are added to it, and, like a dog returning to his vomit, I return to my sin. But praise be to God that He has broken that cycle, released the shackles, and freed my soul to rejoice in the God of my salvation. Who may abide in Your tabernacle? Who may dwell in Your holy hill? Only those who are in Christ. He has gone into the holy place not made with hands, He has made intercession for me, He has accepted me as forgiven and restored, and You, Father, have accepted me in the perfection of Your Son. Oh, to ever abide and to be satisfied by naught else!

Psalm 15
To Abide

Vs. 1—LORD, who shall abide in thy tabernacle? who shall dwell in thy holy hill? (KJV)

When Andrew and John first met Jesus, they asked him, "Where are you staying?" Jesus' reply was so simple, "Come and see." We must all be abiding somewhere; the only questions are where and with whom. David here answers those questions. He desired to dwell with the Lord, to abide in His tabernacle. Our privilege as believers is to abide in Christ. So, where is my home? Have I made Christ's heart my home? Do I see Him as the lover of my soul? I can have as much of Jesus as I want, for I have been given His life, born from above, of incorruptible seed. "For God does not give the Spirit by measure." (John 3:34, NKJV)

Do I believe that God is an extravagant or a reluctant giver? God wants me far more than I can begin to imagine, more than I could ever want Him. It is my privilege to abide in Christ, to experience that vital connection with Him, to feel His life force flowing through me by His Spirit, and to enjoy His presence. And what is the evidence of this abiding? Fruit, more fruit, then much fruit. We read in Galatians 5 what quality such fruit is: love, joy, and peace, to name three. As we love others as Jesus loved them, we show that we have His life in us.

Psalm 16
The Secret of the Inner Life

Vs. 7—I will bless the LORD, who hath given me counsel: my reins also instruct me in the night seasons. (KJV)

In one simple phrase, Lord Jesus, You have told me the secret to
Your entire life and walk, "I have set the Lord always before Me"
(verse 8). To live in the constant consciousness of Your intimate
relationship with the Father is the most sanctifying power on
earth. How could I entertain any lustful thought? How could
I harbor any resentment? Where would there be place for pride
or selfishness when I see myself having God always before me?
All those other things are idols, substitutes, hindrances and dis-
tractions to take my gaze off of Him who is always before me.
"Looking unto Jesus..." (verse 3).

Dear Lord I am so thankful that You have smashed all those idols,
those false pretenders which held my gaze for so long. Truly, Lord,
apart from You, I am and can do nothing; apart from You, nothing good is in me. Now that all these idols are gone, I have an
unobstructed view of my Savior's face. I am surrounded by light
with nothing to eclipse it, and I do not draw back in shame but
am drawn forward in worship and thanksgiving. Lord, You truly
are my portion; You are the very food and drink that sustains my
soul. It was ever Your joy to please the Father; it was Your great joy
to return to heaven to be there with Him. And so it is for me as I
see myself seated with You in heavenly places.

Psalm 16
My Delight

Vs. 11—Thou wilt shew me the path of life: in thy presence is fulness of joy; at thy right hand there are pleasures for evermore. (KJV)

God has let us listen in on a beautiful conversation between the Father and the Son. Jesus tells His Father that He delights in men. This is much the same feeling expressed in Proverbs 8:21. It helps us to understand the motivations of God. Just why did He create us? Because it delighted Him to do so; it gave him inexpressible joy to do it. He wanted to share Himself and share His love with a creature that would be like Himself, express part of His own nature, and be able to freely respond lovingly in return. And He did this fully knowing all the consequences of His creative act—the Fall, sin, death, violence, and all the terrible things man has done, what He would do for His creature and what the cost it would be to Himself.

But such is the heart of God, such is the depth of His love for us, and such is the extent of His grace. Our redemption is all about God; it expresses His will, His love, His desires, and His determination to have a people with whom He can share Himself. We are that people; we are the undeserving recipients of that love. Let me never for a moment cheapen the work of Jesus on the Cross by seeking to earn His favor or trying to make myself appear deserving; otherwise, grace is no longer grace. Let me bask in the warmth of His delight.

Psalm 17
The Testing of the Heart

Vs. 3—Thou hast proved mine heart; thou hast visited me in the night; thou hast tried me, and shalt find nothing; I am purposed that my mouth shall not transgress.
(KJV)

How Your heart was tested and sorely tried while here upon earth. In John 14:30, it is written that Satan came to you and assailed You repeatedly, but could find nothing—no access point, no defect, no hidden allurements, no means by which he could draw Your heart away from God. At Your most physically vulnerable, after 40 days in the wilderness, and Your most spiritually vulnerable, in the Garden of Gethsemane, Satan found no means to draw You away.

So Your God could say, too, that He found nothing—nothing to offend, nothing to divert, nothing to divide Your heart from His. But such was not the case with me. There was so much that had to be rooted out. It lay so well hidden beneath layers of religiosity and respectability. You tested my heart and gave access to Satan to sift and afflict it so all the ugliness could be brought to the surface and purged out. So, dear God, visit me in the night, continually test my heart, and let me never resist the probing light of Your Holy Spirit. I want to be precious to You as the apple of Your eye; You need to do in me whatever it takes to keep me supple and sensitive, attentive to Your still, small voice.

Psalm 17
Where is My Portion?

Vs. 7—Shew thy marvellous lovingkindness, O thou
that savest by thy right hand them which put their trust
in thee from those that rise up against them. (KJV)

Jesus said, "Where your treasure is, there will your heart be also."
So, which came first? Did I set my heart upon something and thus
placed my treasure there? Or did I treasure something, and thus
my heart was set? In the end, it doesn't matter; only the process
differs. I, as a believer in Jesus Christ, am in this world but no
longer of this world. I have been translated out of the kingdom
of darkness into the kingdom of the Son of His love. Such is the
effect of sovereign grace. My heart, my life can never again find rest
and satisfaction in this world because I no longer belong here. I
am a pilgrim and a stranger called to live the life of Jesus in a world
that would gladly kill Him if it had another chance. So, I have a
treasure.

Paul tells me in II Corinthians 4:7 (NKJV) that "We have this
treasure in an earthen vessel." We have the most precious treasure,
eternal life, in a most common vessel of clay. But this only allows
even more of the excellence of that life to show forth as being from
God. To love this world or the things of this world, to treasure
this world, is enmity with God, for it shows a preference for the
world over God and deprives me of the birthright I have by grace,
much as Esau did. Let me say, as Paul did, "Christ who is our life"
(Colossians 3:4, NKJV).

Psalm 18
He Heard

Vs. 3—I will call upon the LORD, who is worthy to be praised: so shall I be saved from mine enemies. (KJV)

Your love to the Father was not dependent upon Your circumstances but rather was the foundation of Your understanding and endurance through Your circumstances. Lord Jesus, You were fully persuaded of His love for You, His care for You, and You derived strength from that love. "Many waters cannot quench love" (Song of Solomon 8:7, NKJV). And what terrors You faced! Not only did You face the hatred of men, from us sinners who hated You because of Your goodness and how it exposed our vileness, but You faced the terrors of the wrath of God against our sins.

When I see You scourged, I can understand the physical pain and suffering it entailed and the dread of it You faced. But when I see the three hours of darkness, as Your soul is made an offering for sin, as You who knew no sin was being made sin for me, my mind cannot comprehend what that meant. Here I read of the pangs of death, the rebukes and taunts of evil men at the cross, the deep cry of anguish of being forsaken of Your God, the strong tendrils of death as they wrapped themselves about You as Your life's blood flowed out, and then the triumphant cry, "It is finished." As Peter would preach months later after Pentecost, it all happened according to the predetermined counsels of God. What humility! What agony! What love!

Psalm 18
He Heard (con't)

Vs. 6—In my distress I called upon the LORD, and cried
unto my God: he heard my voice out of his temple, and
my cry came before him, even into his ears. (KJV)

Your Father saw it all, heard it all, received it, and accepted it all.
In You, He had found all His delight and was fully satisfied. Lord,
You had said that You could have called ten thousand legions of
angels, and they would have been instantly ready to keep You from
Your sufferings. But where would that have left You? No triumph,
no people, returning all alone to heaven. The cross is both the measure of our hatred for God and the measure of the awfulness of sin.
You were to be delivered, though not from suffering but through
suffering. You went into death for us, were in the belly of the earth
three days and three nights, and then were raised by the glory of the
Father (Romans 6:4). God would deliver You from Your strong
enemy, and what was it? That strong enemy was death, the last,
greatest, and mightiest of all (I Corinthians 15:26). God did loose
the pains of death that could not hold you (Acts 2:24) and has
brought You into a large place.

Lord, how often do I want to merely be delivered *from* my circumstances rather than being willing to be delivered *through* the
circumstances? How much of You I would not experience if it
were not for the sufferings and Your presence with me through
them. Much of my suffering is because of my own sin; Your suffering was all because of our sins. Lord, let Your sufferings in me
have their perfect work, accomplish Your perfect ends, and deliver
me in Your perfect time.

Psalm 18
He rewarded

Vs. 17—He delivered me from my strong enemy, and
from them which hated me: for they were too strong
for me. (KJV)

Jesus, You have so pleased the Father that He has exalted You above all things. God has put all things under Your feet; He has given You a name above all other names. No other name under heaven is given among men whereby we must be saved. He has rewarded You, raised You, exalted You, and one day, You will return to exercise Your kingship authority from the very place that was the scene of Your rejection.

Dear Jesus, I confess You as my Lord, You are my King, You are the head, and I am one of Your members. You have saved me to Yourself, and I am Yours, seated with You now in heavenly places. Make my feet like hinds' feet. Give me that sure-footedness that they have to walk the high, elevated life. Not in the sin, self-will, and wickedness that was true of me before, but in sincerity and purity of spirit. May I eschew evil, hate every motion of indwelling sin in my flesh, and judge it before You. Might I neither fall into the trap of self-righteous legalism nor use liberty as a license for the flesh. You have seated me in Your heavenly places; may I walk here on earth in that realization, to be tender and sensitive to the leading of the Holy Spirit to please You in my life as You pleased the Father in Yours.

Psalm 18
He Delivered

Vs. 19—He brought me forth also into a large place; he delivered me, because he delighted in me. (KJV)

Surely, Lord Jesus, Your Father delighted in You. You were ever His delight from eternity past, and in Your walk here upon earth as a man, He could open up the heavens and proclaim His full delight in You. You were ever the dependent man praying to and trusting in Your Father's every provision. Such could not be said about me. In my flesh, I would pursue my own course, nurse my own grudges, and resist Your Holy Spirit's conviction. But because I am Your child, You brought me out of all of that and have set me in a large place. You were not pleased for me to remain in my sins. While I would resist You, You would pursue me. And why would You do that? Was I deserving of it? No! It would only be due to Your love for me and the grace You could pour out on my behalf.

Because of Your great work on the cross, love, mercy, grace, and forgiveness have been extended toward me rather than the wrath, judgment, and condemnation I deserved. What a revelation it is to me that, despite my sin, You still delight in me and are not willing to leave me in it. It is such a comfort for me to know that Your work on the cross, which is effective for my eternal salvation, is also powerful for my temporal salvation—to deliver me from the power of indwelling sin and set my life upon a new footing in a great expanse.

Psalm 19
Secret Faults

Vs. 12—Who can understand his errors? cleanse thou
me from secret faults. (KJV)

When I read this poem of praise and exaltation to You, O God, to Your greatness, majesty, and revealed truth *I wonder, "Why didn't the Psalm end at verse 11?"* But then I see it. What effect does this vision of God have on my life? How am I to personalize this revelation of Yourself both in the natural creation and in Your word? It is supposed to sink deeply into my heart, permeate every part of my being, and transform me from the inside out.

It is so easy to put on a veneer of sanctity and piety, yet to have that secret place where I keep my private sins, my hidden indulgences, those traces of bitterness that I nurse and periodically review to justify whatever attitude I harbor. All these things corrupt my soul and leech into areas of my outward life. No one can understand his secret faults: "The heart is deceitful above all things and desperately wicked. Who can know it?" (Jeremiah 17:9, NKJV) Lord, use Your word like a light to reveal what is there so that it can be judged in the light of Your word. Your law is perfect, Your testimonies sure, Your statutes right, and Your commandments pure. I have tasted and seen that the Lord is good; even in discipline, He is loving and faithful. May my words and my life be pleasing in Your sight, Oh, my God.

Psalm 19
Open Heart

Vs. 14—Let the words of my mouth, and the meditation of my heart, be acceptable in thy sight, O LORD, my strength, and my redeemer. (KJV)

Lord, You would go up into a mountain and pray all night. What did You hear? Could it be the sound of Your creation declaring Your creative glory? You would behold the beauty, the vastness, and the greatness of this world you created. You knew its order, had established its complexity and precision, and comprehended the amazing variety and diversity of all of the heavenly bodies. You would commune with Your Father and discuss the greatest task of all—the work of redemption and its wondrous implications in the whole realm of creation.

The sun would rise; You had prayed all night and contemplated with Your God the wonders of Your word, its power to bring light into a darkened soul. You would hear the Father's words and know how to convey the most profound truths in such terms as to make the simplest soul wise. You contemplated the moral code contained in Your word and how it brings order to a man's life and makes him right with God. As a man on earth, You understood the weakness and frailty of human existence, the restless, ceaseless struggle to strive and survive, and would call men to seek first the Kingdom of God, the sovereignty of God over the life and soul of the individual, and call us to lay hold of the fear of God which keeps and sanctifies. Nothing thrilled Your soul like fellowship with Your Father. Make it so in me.

Psalm 20
A Burnt Offering

Vs. 5—We will rejoice in thy salvation, and in the name of our God we will set up our banners: the LORD fulfil all thy petitions. (KJV)

Just who is this one the Psalmist is addressing? Who is the Lord to answer in the day of trouble? Who is looking to God to defend him? Is it not You, Lord Jesus, who endured such reproach from men? The very hatred that men hold against God was heaped upon You, Lord Jesus. Yet You would go on loving, continue to heal, teach, and minister to needs. Your entire life was wholly dedicated to Your Father's will. You were truly that burnt offering, placed upon the altar and totally consumed by the fire. But that burnt offering is a sweet-smelling savor to God. Of whom else could God say, "This is my beloved Son in whom I am well pleased?"

Your life was a continual offering to God, wholly dedicated to Him. No wonder He will grant You Your heart's desire. God would say, "Ask of me, and I will give You the nations for Your inheritance" (Psalm 2:8, NKJV). Can my life be an offering to You? Has my sin so offended You that there is no room for me? Or is the offering of Your Son, in fact, greater than my sin? You have shown me, thanks be to God, that the Lord saves. You brought up Jesus from the dead and exalted Him; You can bring me up from the dead as well. And I shall yet rejoice in Your salvation, Lord, which You won on Calvary's cross for me. My hope, my trust, and my acceptance are all in You.

Psalm 20
My Heart's Desire

Vs. 7—Some trust in chariots, and some in horses: but we will remember the name of the LORD our God.
(KJV)

This Psalm is written as a blessing being pronounced upon someone that the favor of God would rest upon him and be active in his life. So, when the Psalm asks that God grant you according to your heart's desire, I must ask myself, *Are my heart's desires such that God would be pleased to grant them?* God desires to bless us, derives pleasure from seeing our joy, and is magnanimous in His giving. Do I cherish the same things Jesus cherished? Has my heart been ravished by God's love and captivated by His Son? Does it show in my decisions, relationships, money and time management, attitudes, and actions?

To have a sanctified heart means that I have set it apart as Christ's dwelling place, not that I have furnished a space where He dwells while I run the rest. This Psalm also asks that God would fulfill all my purposes. What have I purposed in my heart? We read of how Daniel purposed in his heart, and God favored him. Is it my purpose to sanctify the Lord Jesus in my heart? Then, I shall show the same character of love, mercy, grace, and forgiveness that He showed even while on the cross. Remove the words, "Father, forgive them," and tell me what you have. Proclaim them in your life and you will be Christ to this world.

Psalm 21
His Heart's Desire

Vs. 5—His glory is great in thy salvation: honour and
majesty hast thou laid upon him. (KJV)

Before You became the lion, You were the lamb; before being king,
You came the servant. You so perfectly pleased the heart of Your
God and Father that all the riches of heaven are at Your disposal.
Now, as the exalted One, You have those blessings of grace to dis-
pense. While on earth, Your joy in the Father was Your strength; it
was the unshakable conviction that nothing could happen to You
apart from God's permission. So, now that You are exalted and
seated, what is Your heart's desire? "Father, I desire that they also
whom You gave Me may be with Me where I am, that they may
behold My glory which You have given Me for You loved Me..."
(John 17:24, NKJV).

Lord Jesus, this Psalm is so full of all the expressions of satisfaction of God in You and all honor and majesty, greatness and glory
heaped upon You. You, as king, shall be exalted above all things
and will subdue all enemies under Your feet. What a Savior I have
and what a salvation is mine. The measure of this great salvation
is the power of the Savior; the measure of the Savior is the glory of
His exaltation. To think that I, a wretched, vile sinner, could be
brought into such a relationship of joy and love is beyond human
comprehension; it is all grace. "Yes He is altogether lovely. This is
my beloved, and this is my friend" (Song of Songs 5:16, NKJV).

Psalm 21
They Have Intended Evil

Vs. 11—For they intended evil against thee: they imagined a mischievous device, which they are not able to perform. (KJV)

Just because you're paranoid doesn't mean people aren't out to get you. Many are set upon evil, who plot, plan, and scheme to perform it, and who enjoy their evil. It is not a question of them, for we know that man's heart is set upon evil from childhood. What does grace call me to be? Jesus says we should love our enemies. To do that, we must first identify someone as an enemy—i.e., a person set on our harm or destruction. Then, knowing and acknowledging that, love them—i.e., seek their good.

Seeking their good may mean frustrating their plans and actively working against the evil they are perpetrating, for we are called to oppose evil and to promote the good. But unless we also show them a spirit of love and grace personally—one by one as we encounter them—then the conviction of sin and the message of forgiveness in Christ will have no power. Evil can defeat evil, but it only results in replacing one evil with another. Only good can overcome evil and win a victory to dispel it so that good arises in its place. We can only do this if, as Jesus did, we fully accept the sovereignty of God over all of our circumstances and see that the battle is not with flesh and blood but against spiritual forces.

Psalm 22
The Question of Jesus

Vs. 1—My God, my God, why hast thou forsaken me?
Why art thou so far from helping me, and from the
words of my roaring? (KJV)

"My God, My God, why have You forsaken Me?" (Matthew 27:46, NKJV) Never a more poignant cry came from a man's lips; never before had there been a man on earth who could demand an answer. Would heaven be silent; would God not answer? As Jesus hung between heaven and earth, as he was lifted up to bear our sins, to make His soul an offering for sin; as He the sinless one was made a curse for us, He would utter these words, came this plaintive question, that demanded an answer. "But You are holy" (verse 3).

Jesus knew better than any man ever could the absolute holiness of God, the total hatred and abhorrence of God against sin, the huge weight of the accumulated wrath of God against sin, and now it was all being unleashed upon His holy person. "But I am a worm and no man" (verse 6). How could You say this about Yourself? You are the sinless man, the spotless lamb. You are altogether lovely. You always went about doing good, pleasing the Father, and bringing glory to God. Oh, I understand. I have done this to You. It is because of my sin that He has chosen to crush You. "You have been My God" (verse 10). And at this point of extreme suffering of body and soul, Your faith is firmly set upon Your God. You will not waver; You will accept and submit to the Father's will.

Psalm 22
The Answer of God

Vs. 2—O my God, I cry in the daytime, but thou hearest not; and in the night season, and am not silent. (KJV)

So much lay between the question and the answer. Initially, it seemed as if the only answer was silence. The three hours of darkness descended like a shroud as You poured Yourself out completely, like a drink offering that could not be collected back up. It was not to be that You would be delivered **from** suffering and death, but **through** them. And three days and nights later, God did answer dramatically in resurrection.

And now You are exalted, seated at the right hand of the majesty on high. Angels surround the throne and praise you. An entire redeemed company that You brought with You in resurrection surrounds You, raising praises to You. You lead the praise of heaven and are its subject as well. All Your people on earth adore You. As we gather to Your name, we experience Your presence; as we celebrate Your passion and death, You reveal Yourself in the breaking of bread (Luke 24:35). When we are in tribulation and suffer for our faith, we can "look unto Jesus, the author and finisher of our faith who for the joy set before Him endured the cross ..." (Hebrews 12:2, NKJV). You are the focal point of all of human history, the pivot upon which all events turn, the beginning and the end of all of the thoughts of God. When God answered, He said, "Arise," and nothing in heaven or upon earth ever will be the same.

Psalm 23
Shepherded by God

Vs. 1, 2—The LORD is my shepherd; I shall not want.
He maketh me to lie down in green pastures: he leadeth
me beside the still waters. (KJV)

What was Your experience upon earth as the dependent Man? Was it not the experience of the lamb of God shepherded by His loving Father? Before You ever declared Yourself as the good shepherd, You learned what it was to be shepherded. And what animal epitomizes meekness, dependence, and innocence more than a lamb? You were not only the lamb of God upon the cross bearing our sins, but You were God's lamb, the object of His care. When you were in the desert fasting, and Satan came to test You to turn stones into bread, You could be reminded of how You shall not be in want, that You could depend upon Your shepherd.

When the citizens of Nazareth attempted to cast You from the cliff, You knew that You needn't fear any evil. As You spoke to the woman at the well about living water, You spoke from experience of drinking deeply of those still waters Yourself. When you fed the 5,000 by having them sit down on the grass in groups, they looked like a flock of sheep as You fed them. But You knew the real food they needed for Your soul had been fed in God's pastures of truth. Even as You rode into Jerusalem, You knew the fear, weakness, and hatred that lay within the human heart and what awaited You. Yet as You rode through the valley of the shadow of death, You were not alone, for He was with You.

Psalm 23
My Shepherd

Vs. 4—Yea, though I walk through the valley of the
shadow of death, I will fear no evil: for thou art with me;
thy rod and thy staff they comfort me. (KJV)

You, Lord Jesus, are my shepherd. You told me You were my good
shepherd and proved it by giving Your life for me. When I feel in
want I recall to mind how "No good thing will You withhold." If
you were willing to give Your life, then Your love will provide for
my real needs. When I feel fearful, for so often this world feels like
walking through a valley of death where all around I feel danger
and threats, then I remember that Your presence is with me. It's
not that I am walking in Your presence as You view from far off,
but You are with me every step of the way, seeing all the real dangers. You have a staff to direct me (oh, please keep me guide-able)
and a rod to ward off attack. I am calmed and comforted by turning anxiety into prayers (Philippians 4:6).

No matter how awful a place I may be in, You can refresh me
from Your word, to quiet my anxious heart, and to give joy in a
place man has designed to deny it to him. Truly, Lord, You are a
great shepherd (Hebrews 13:20), exalted in resurrection glory yet
abiding and dwelling within by the Holy Spirit. He is able to do
abundantly above anything we ask or think, for all authority in
heaven and earth has been given to Him. Surely, Lord, goodness
and mercy flow from You to me, totally undeserved, only because
of how wonderful You are.

Psalm 24
Who May Ascend?

Vs. 4—He that hath clean hands, and a pure heart;
who hath not lifted up his soul unto vanity, nor sworn
deceitfully. (KJV)

Who may ascend? On what basis can one stand in the holy place? How can it be that we can come into Your presence, Father? It is all upon the basis of redemption; it is only because of what Your Son has done. Before He could ascend, He first had to *descend* (Ephesians 4:9–10). His first descent was incarnation. How could it be that the finite could contain the infinite? Yet it did happen. He did not become less God to become all of a man. The Word, which existed with God from eternity past, became flesh; God tabernacled in flesh and took to Himself our nature, sin apart. Such a descent! And then He went even further. He went into death for us; He descended into the lowest parts of the earth. He spent three days and three nights in the belly of the earth. Hallelujah! Death could not hold Him.

So, Lord, You ascended; first in resurrection, when You came up from the grave and out of death to show Yourself victorious over the enemy, and then 40 days later, You ascended back to the Father to take Your place on His right hand. Without Your ascension, there would be no way for me, no room or place for me, no standing before the absolute holy presence of God. But it's not me, is it? It's all You and I in You and You in me.

Psalm 24
The Earth is the Lord's

Vs. 8—Who is this King of glory? The LORD strong
and mighty, the LORD mighty in battle. (KJV)

There is this notion among some that in the Fall, Satan won the
title deed to the earth, which Jesus had to win back at the cross.
But, as we see here, "The earth is the Lord's and all its fullness."
Satan has no legal rights, otherwise he would not need to receive
permission to do what he does. Satan is a creature, a created being,
and as such, does not have absolute autonomy. Man, in Adam,
was given dominion and *stewardship* over the earth and all of its
creatures, but God retained *ownership*.

Man, in his sin and rebellion, has yielded himself and become
a slave to sin. Satan strives to exercise dominion over this earth
through man, but God retains the ownership. Satan tempted Jesus
by offering Him a shortcut to sovereignty that would bypass the
cross. But Jesus knew that "Ought not the Christ to have suffered
these things and to enter into His glory?" (Luke 24:26, NKJV)
Satan would offer Jesus all the kingdoms of the earth, for he is the
god of this world, and all of man lies under the wicked one. By our
sin and our love of it, we had made ourselves its slaves, but God is
still the Sovereign. Thanks be to God that Jesus refused the offer
both in the desert and at Gethsemane, accepting the cup from the
Father's hand—the cross. So, why do we think that it should be
different for us? "For this reason I also suffer these things; never-
theless I am not ashamed, for I know whom I have believed and
am persuaded that He is able to keep what I have committed to
Him until that Day" (II Timothy 2:12, NKJV).

Psalm 25
Why Should You Pardon?

Vs. 7—Remember not the sins of my youth, nor my transgressions: according to thy mercy remember thou me for thy goodness' sake, O LORD. (KJV)

If there were no forgiveness in You, there would be no hope. Without room for repentance, life would have no meaning; all would be futility. What use would there be in a few more years of misery in this life were there no means of pardon? And why should You pardon me for my sin when it is so great? You do so for Your great name's sake. You would have received glory through judging and condemning me because it would uphold Your righteousness and holiness. But You received even more glory by forgiving and pardoning me, for it displayed the greatness of Your sacrifice on the cross. It is not for my sake You do this; I am getting far less punishment than my sin deserves.

It is to You that I lift my soul; it is to You that I look with longing, hope, and expectation. Without Your favor, I could never again lift my head in the presence of men. My shame is so great. Why did it take this for me to see the awfulness of sin? But You, Lord, are the God of my salvation. According to Your mercy You have remembered me and acted on my behalf. Even amid my deepest affliction and despair, You were there, and I groped as one in great darkness and found You. Jesus bore all this pain and suffering for my sin and came through triumphantly. And He has brought me through with Him. Now my heart is enlarged by my troubles for "To whom much is forgiven the same loves much" (Luke 7:47).

Psalm 25
My Eyes

Vs. 15—"Mine eyes are ever towards the Lord…" (KJV).

Lord, You have taught me that my initial point of departure was getting my eyes off You and looking to myself. If I had only truly understood what You meant when You said that I should have no confidence in the flesh, then I would have seen that "in me, that is my flesh nothing good dwells" (Romans 7:18, NKJV). But Lord, what about my bible knowledge? What about all the verses I had memorized and could quote? What about my personality, my temperament? What about my education? I had to come to realize that all of these are part of the flesh that I thought had some good to it.

How humiliating it was to realize, as Paul did in Philippians 3:7, that everything I had to offer the Lord was actually of no value to Him. All of these assets under my control are of no value to You. I must come to You as a pauper and then let You transform these natural abilities of mine into spiritual use for You. One may be a fine violinist, but if she plays the notes when she thinks she should rather than when the conductor says she should, then all of her playing is discordant and offensive. Teach me to look unto Jesus (Hebrews 12:1); teach me what it means when Jesus says, "Without me you can do nothing" (John 15:5, NKJV). Remind me—whenever amid any struggle or conflict, to not turn inward to find my resources in myself, my flesh; but rather to turn to You and set my eyes upon You to receive the guidance, insight, and direction I need. So much heartache can be avoided by looking to You.

Psalm 25
Be not Ashamed

Vs. 20—O keep my soul, and deliver me: let me not be ashamed; for I put my trust in thee. (KJV)

The apostle Paul said that he was not ashamed of the gospel of Christ, for it was the power of God. But why would one be ashamed of the gospel? For starters, in Paul's day, he proclaimed a Savior who had been hated by His own people and executed as a criminal by the State. He had been shamed, humiliated, beaten, stripped naked, nailed to a cross, and lifted up so that He could be on public display, His shame for all to see. Yet this great shame only all the more enhanced His glory that followed.

Since Jesus took all that shame upon Himself, any selflessness in serving Him is a measure of my devotion to Him. As I step out in faith, God gives the assurance of His presence and favor. So, why would I be ashamed in this life of faith? Sometimes, God doesn't come through quite the way I expected. Sometimes, my exuberance outstrips my faith. Sometimes, God's ways just don't make sense, and I feel put on the defensive by those who want to use human tragedy and suffering as an opportunity to accuse God of indifference. Sometimes, God allows me to suffer in the short term so that it appears as if He has forsaken me. But He has always the end in view (Job 23:10). God is in it for the long haul; He has proven that by giving His Son. I am not called to understand His ways, only to trust and wait on Him. In that, there is no shame.

Psalm 26
Living Openly

Vs. 2—Examine me, O LORD, and prove me; try my reins and my heart. (KJV)

Lord, You lived Your life in absolute transparency and openness before Your Father and the world. You could even challenge Your enemies: "Which one of you convicts Me of sin?" (John 8:46, KJV) You had no hidden area of Your life that told God "Keep Out." There was no shadow of turning with You. You walked so totally in the truth that Your life was constantly being sanctified. You could welcome God to examine You, to prove You, to put every thought, desire, and motivation under His microscopic scrutiny, and find only what pleased Him.

Lord, You were that blessed man from Psalm 1. You lived in total consistency throughout every area of Your life. I want to live like that. I want my life to be animated by the love of God. I want to live without fear, knowing that nothing can harm me apart from Your will. I want to experience what it means: nothing can separate me from God's love. I want to love You and Your things, Your interests, Your desires, Your favor, and Your presence more than anything else. I know this is possible because Jesus did it, and the very life of Jesus lives within me. This new creation life longs only to please You and to behold Your glory as Moses yearned to do. Make me open. make it so. May I yield.

Psalm 26
Hating the Assembly of Evildoers

Vs. 5—I have hated the congregation of evil doers; and will not sit with the wicked. (KJV)

This is the challenge of grace: to hate the sin yet love the sinner. Many are willing to love the sinner after his repentence and cleaning himself up. We find it possible to accept him after he is "seated, clothed, and in his right mind," but don't ask me to love him while he's still a demoniac, still possessed by his sin. "But God commendeth His love to us in that while we were yet sinners, Christ died for us" (Romans 5:8, KJV). To one who is totally spotless and pure, even the slightest taint is abhorrent.

Only we who are already spotted argue over degrees of sin. We become comfortable with our level of sin (greed, envy, lust, avarice, gluttony) and only deplore the sins of others we label too egregious (abortion, abuse, or homosexuality). I am to hate sin, but I can never hate sin properly until I hate the sin in me. I must hate my sin so much that plucking out my eye is preferable to using that same eye to sin. If I do not hate the sin in me to that extent, then I will look self-righteously at your sin while I excuse my own. Because Jesus purely hated sin, He could go wherever He needed to meet with the sinner and bring him out of his sin. If, like the Pharisee, he chose to stay with his sin, then Jesus would leave him to it. Or, as the publican who asked for mercy, Jesus could lead him out to liberty.

Psalm 27
My Heart Will Not Fear

Vs. 3,12—"Though a host should encamp against me,
my heart shall not fear: Deliver me not over unto the
will of mine enemies" (KJV).

Your word tells me that I should be anxious about nothing, but;
that I should be in prayer and supplication to combat the fears that
arise within me. But Lord, what about that host that is encamped
against me? What about all those enemies that are seeking my
destruction? I have found, Lord, that amid great failure there are
so many who are cheering for my demise. There are so many who
are ready to heap onto and increase the condemnation and self-
loathing I already feel. Why are so many otherwise well-meaning
believers so motivated this way?

Lord, I don't know why so many are cheering for my judgment,
but I know that You are planning my deliverance. Your word tells
me to not receive the grace of God in vain. Though my sin has
exasperated You and has resulted in my well-deserved judgment;
even there I see Your heart ready to forgive, Your hand ready to
deliver. Your word tells me that "perfect love casts out all fear." I
rely upon that love to heal me; I rely upon it to sustain me. I rely
upon your love to lift up my head so that I don't live in defeat. It is
so hard because all around me is judgmentalism. But Your love will
not take me where your grace cannot sustain me. Truly, knowing
Your goodness keeps me from despairing.

Psalm 27
Seek My Face

Vs. 8, 9—When thou saidst, Seek ye my face; my heart said unto thee, Thy face, LORD, will I seek. Hide not thy face far from me; put not thy servant away in anger: thou hast been my help; leave me not, neither forsake me, O God of my salvation. (KJV)

Do I actually hear what I think I hear? Is it actually the still, small voice of God beckoning me to seek His face? Could it be that His grace is actually greater than my sin? Can the love of God reach farther down than even my sin to lift me back up? Unless I believed that in this life, not in some great hereafter, I would still experience the goodness of God, there would have been no reason to go on. But Your Spirit, through Your word, brought Your Son fresh to my eyes, and faith arose, and hope sprang up.

I see Jesus whose trials were so great, the pressure so intense, yet He was sustained in joy and hope. You said, "Seek My Face," and my heart responded, *Yes Lord*. When I look up, I see Your face turn toward me, smile upon me, accept me, and restore me. I feel Your divine favor and, once again, Your pleasure. How can one have joy amid their despair? By seeing Jesus. He alone can deliver me from all my fears because perfect love, His love, casts out all fear (I John 4:18). Where once there was darkness, now there is light. One phrase I shall contemplate but never fully comprehend: to behold the beauty of the Lord. It is the beauty of love, of grace, of forgiveness, of joy, of hope, of favor, and of holiness. Thou art all together lovely and I will spend eternity in wonder.

Psalm 27
One Thing

Vs. 4—One thing have I desired of the LORD, that will I seek after; that I may dwell in the house of the LORD all the days of my life, to behold the beauty of the LORD, and to enquire in his temple. (KJV)

Can I reduce my life down to one thing, one primary motivation? Make a list of all the things that constitute the superstructure of your internal and external life, and then consider this: which things are for comfort and which are essential? Now, how would Jesus answer this? It's simple: I always do those things that please the Father. He had only one thing, and that one thing constrained Him, focusing all of His energies and simplifying His life. Here in this Psalm, David tells us what his one thing is: to abide. He wanted a relationship with God characterized by abiding. For him, his entire spiritual life was consumed by this passion for closeness.

Let us not substitute anything else for personal closeness. Knowledge and doctrinal purity are no substitute for personal closeness—just ask the church at Ephesus who heard this indictment, "You have left your first love." Let me ask a question, "What one thing does God want from you?" Simply put—absolute devotion! What one thing motivated the life of the Son of God? The Father's will. Only two men have ever lived who had a free will—Adam, who used his to rebel, and Jesus, who chose to not use His prerogative at all but said, "Not My will, but Thine be done." Just read the blessing of the one who has just one thing: he dwells in God's presence, he beholds the beauty of God, he offers sacrifices of joy, he sings praise, and seeks God's face—i.e., His gracious favor. What more could your soul desire?

Psalm 28
What If Heaven Is Silent?

Vs. 1—Unto thee will I cry, O LORD my rock; be not silent to me: lest, if thou be silent to me, I become like them that go down into the pit. (KJV)

What does it mean when heaven seems silent? What am I to do when there seems to be no answer? Psalm 19 tells me that even nature cannot be silent, that it is pouring out declarations of Your power, wisdom, greatness, and glory as energy pours out from the sun. There was one time when heaven seemed to not answer You, Lord, as You cried out, "My God, My God, why have You forsaken Me?" But God did answer You, and so God will answer me.

My Father, I have nowhere else to go, no one else to supplicate. Teach me in these moments of silence to wait patiently for I know You will answer. I am Your child; You cannot forsake me. By faith, I seize the truth that "He has heard the voice of my supplication" and that You are teaching my heart to trust. I want You to hand me a flashlight to illuminate my next several steps, but You are handing me a lamp to show me *only the next one.* I lived my life for so long in self-will, following my thoughts and my agenda. What a mess I made of it! You are teaching me to walk by faith, to listen for the still small voice telling me the way I should walk (Isaiah 30:21). Now I am learning to accept Your silence, to keep listening and walking. Your voice and presence will be there; You are shepherding me and I am slowly learning.

Psalm 28
God's Silence

Vs. 7—The LORD is my strength and my shield; my heart trusted in him, and I am helped: therefore my heart greatly rejoiceth; and with my song will I praise him. (KJV)

Have there been times when heaven has been silent, when God's ear seems deaf, and you have no indication that He is attentive to your cry? Even in those times, we can take heart—we are His child, the object of His love, one for whom He gave His Son; He has not forsaken you. Job wondered over the silence of God. He accepted quietly from the Lord's hand the loss of his wealth, his children, his livelihood, his reputation, and even his health. However, as time passed, the seeming pointlessness of life and existence descended upon him as a layer of dust settled out of the air.

For animals, existence is the only purpose and meaning they grasp; they do not search beyond that, but it is not that way for us. We, being in the likeness of God, search for meaning, and that meaning is ultimately bound up in God. When God is silent, it doesn't mean He's not listening. Sometimes, heaven seems deaf to our prayers because the noise in our head is drowning out God's still small voice. Other times, heaven seems silent because it is. He may want to stretch you, move you from one level of faith to another, or show you that *something* that you see as essential is not at all but is only a prop, a crutch. He wants us to depend solely upon Himself.

Psalm 29
The Beauty of Holiness

Vs. 2—Give unto the LORD the glory due unto his name; worship the LORD in the beauty of holiness.
(KJV)

Beauty is an enhancement; it is not the substance itself. The substance is holiness. I am called to worship the Lord in holiness—in the conscious recognition that He is holy, and to stand in His presence requires holiness. But how can I, who am a sinner and fallen, ever attain to that standard? It is only through the redemptive work of Christ. I, who have no righteousness in myself, am made righteous in Christ; I am given a garment of righteousness. He has been made unto me righteousness (I Corinthians 1:30). It's not that I have Christ's righteousness conferred upon me, but Christ himself is my righteousness. How precious, how comforting to know that my acceptance before the Father is the acceptance of Christ Himself!

So, what effect should that have on me? Holiness. Now that I am righteous in Christ and have His life with me, I should find a growing abhorrence of sin. And just as God who hates the sin and has compassion upon the sinner, so shall grow that same compassion for sinners in me. So, what is the beauty of holiness? Surely, it refers to the character of life and walk that God is producing in me, which is practical righteousness. But about worship there would be humility, meekness, lowliness of mind, sensitivity to the Holy Spirit, compassion for others, and a host of characteristics reflecting the life of Christ.

Psalm 29
Everything says Glory

Vs. 9—…and in his temple doth every one speak of his glory. (KJV)

What a sight Isaiah had when he heard the voice of the seraphim declaring,"Holy, holy, holy." Uzziah, who had been king for 52 years, had recently passed. For most Israelites, including Isaiah, he was the only king they had ever known. But this vision would remind Isaiah that, though circumstances on earth change, God is unchanging. At a time when things seem uncertain, God reminds us that He is still there. Joshua learned this when Moses died. Though the man God had used to deliver the people from their bondage and lead them through 40 years in the wilderness was now gone, God was still there!

In times like these, we need to go into God's presence and get our eyes back on Him. There I see that the wondrousness of Your character is unimaginable. And what was Isaiah's response? He immediately felt his sin and unworthiness. But You were not pleased to leave him in that condition and sent a seraph with a coal from the altar to purify him. So it is with You. You wanted to share Your greatness and glory with creatures that could experience and appreciate You. And though my sin would drive me away from Your presence, You would seek me out and bring me to Yourself. You have brought me into your family, Your house, so that I can behold Your glory. Jesus prayed for this in John 17—that I should behold His glory the glory He had with You before the world was. Everything around me cries out "Glory" and evokes a response of "Praise" from within me.

MARCH 8

Psalm 29
Give Unto The Lord

Vs. 11—The LORD will give strength unto his people;
the LORD will bless his people with peace. (KJV)

What a privilege it is to give to the Lord glory, to extol His name, His work, His ways. But why is it so important that we give Him glory? Isn't God able to glorify Himself well enough? Think of all the glory God receives from His creation. In Psalm 8, David's contemplation of the vastness of the starry canopy he beheld each night caused him to ask, "What is man?" Given the myriads of worlds God has created and how all creation declares His glory, what could puny man add to the heavenly proclamation? When God confronts Job, speaking to him out of the whirlwind, God speaks to Job of the order, variety, and complexity of the world around him that he takes for granted yet is sustained by the mind and will of God entirely apart from his apprehension of it.

Amid all this marvelous glory that creation proclaims, what difference could our small voice of praise make over creation's cacophony? *Plenty.* We can give God glory in acknowledgment of His great love gift Jesus; we can praise Him for the forgiveness that is available in Him; we can proclaim thanksgiving for the gift of eternal life; we can exalt Him for reconciling us to Himself and making us sons and heir with Christ; we can glorify Him by consecrating ourselves to Himself and dedicating ourselves to His will. Where sin had abounded, grace has super-abounded and reigns victorious over sin. We can give God glory like no other part of creation can.

Psalm 30
To Mourn or to Dance

Vs. 3—O LORD, thou hast brought up my soul from
the grave: thou hast kept me alive, that I should not go
down to the pit. (KJV)

Ecclesiastes 3:4 tells me that there is a time to mourn and a time to dance. But You have also taught me that You could turn my mourning into dancing. Could it possibly be that the very thing that would be the occasion for all my mourning would also introduce me to dancing? It all begins with the crying out to God and Your answering that cry with healing. When I cried out, I wasn't crying out to receive anything; it was the crying out of a broken soul groping to find itself with You. At first, my life looked like death and the future as black as the grave. But You held me up, helped me up, and gave me light and life. Yes, You were very angry about my sin and my stubborn pursuit of it, and You made me feel the horror of what I had done and the great shame I had brought upon Your name.

In Your mercy, I did not receive the measure my sins deserved. In the depths of that darkness, I found that Jesus was there. He had borne the full weight of the judgment due for my sins. My every thought, every action had added to the burden He had borne on the cross, and the awfulness of that realization was crushing at times. But in that dark place, where it seemed there was only sadness and despair, I also found the assurance of a life to follow. That I would not just survive but thrive; that the old life was dead and gone, but a new one would open up for me, and I would once again have joy, celebration, and dancing. I knew I would put off my sackcloth and wear garments of gladness one day. Truly His anger was for a moment, for Jesus hath borne it all, and joy awaited me in the morning.

MARCH 10

Psalm 30
Clothed with Gladness

Vs. 11—Thou hast turned for me my mourning into dancing: thou hast put off my sackcloth, and girded me with gladness... (KJV).

In Oscar Wilde's book, *The Portrait of Dorian Gray,* the protagonist, admiring himself in his youthful vigor in the portrait, asks that it would bear the scars of his life rather than him. Having received his wish, he enters upon a hedonistic life, his portrait reflecting back to him the true condition of his inner life. What garments would we wear if our outward garb could display our inward, spiritual life? David sets before us a picture of a man whose rich inner life stands in stark contrast to his outer circumstances. When foes sought his harm, God gave him healing; whereas they clamored for his death, God granted life. His enemies had caused much weeping, but God gave him joy. Even in his prosperity, he acknowledged it was solely because of God's favor.

That is why God could change the sorrow of mourning into a celebration of dancing. Habakkuk, in his great prayer of praise to God, could say, "Though the fig tree may not blossom, nor fruit be on the vines...yet will I rejoice in the Lord, I will joy in the God of my salvation" (Habakkuk 3:17–18, NKJV). When all the world around you is falling apart, every human support is swept away, and sackcloth seems to be your outward circumstances, it takes faith to be clothed with gladness and wear garments of praise, but such is our calling and what the Holy Spirit can do.

Psalm 31
Into Your Hands I Commend My Life

Vs. 5—Into thine hand I commit my spirit: thou hast
redeemed me, O LORD God of truth. (KJV)

Just how far am I willing to go with trust? Isn't that the problem—my will? It was certainly not with You; but I fear how things might turn out, that they won't end up the way I want them to, that I will be embarrassed in the end. But You, Lord Jesus, went all the way. You gave Yourself completely, unreservedly, with total abandonment of any say-so whatsoever, and God was faithful. What a dreadful way it was, but I triumphed in that You could pronounce with Your dying breath, "Into Your hands I commit my spirit." The terrors of the cross lay behind You, death and the grave yawned before You, but Your confidence in God overcame all.

This Psalm recounts how much You endured at the hands of sinful men and at the end of it all say, "My times are in Your hand" (verse 15). Dear Lord what a wonderful promise and prospect! When I first encountered this, I wept for joy. I had made such a mess of my life and had brought about the ruin of years of hard work with nothing to show for it, or so it seemed. But I had You. My times, however many they may be, are all in Your hands. Into Your hands, I can commit my life. I know not what lies ahead, though certainly much sorrow and pain shall, but the most important fact is that You are utterly faithful. No matter what lies ahead or what befalls me, no matter the hatred or reviling I endure due to my sin, I have this calm assurance.

Psalm 31
My Times, Your Hands

Vs. 15—My times are in thy hand: deliver me from the hand of mine enemies, and from them that persecute me. (KJV)

Do you really believe your times are in His hands, or are you still holding onto the reigns of control? Do you truly accept God's providence or believe it still all depends upon you? The providence of God is neither fate nor karma. Fate was the Greek pagan notion that your destiny was predetermined and that nothing you did or said could do anything about it. Fate was an impersonal, unfeeling force that acted in the lives of men, dictating the course of life. Providence is the execution of the Sovereignty of God in the lives of men; that as a man lives his life and makes his decisions, it all happens within the sovereign care of God, within the scope of His will, to bring about His purposes and plans. Far from being an impersonal force, providence is the outward expression of His intimate love for us.

Karma, in pagan religion, is the great equalizer; that as one sows seeds of strife and discord, an equal level of evil eventually comes back on him, either in this life or a reincarnation life. But God, in His infinite power and foreknowledge, has already incorporated everything into His vast, providential plan from eternity past. It includes all of His interventions into each person's life in all of human history and all the decisions that each person makes at each juncture in his own life. He establishes His plan to unfold His purpose in grace, which reflects His love. Nothing ever takes Him by surprise; nothing can derail or deter its unfolding; with God, there is no randomness. All is in His control, and I can rest in that security.

Psalm 32
The Blessed Man

Vs. 1—Blessed is he whose transgression is forgiven,
whose sin is covered. (KJV)

In Psalm 1, You showed me the blessed man, Jesus, who was blessed in His life lived perfectly for You. But where does that leave me, one who is a sinner? Blessed forgiveness! His perfect life, without spot or blemish, qualified Him to be that perfect sacrifice for me. I am that man who is so blessed by God and by Jesus, who paid the price for my sin on the cross and blessed by the Holy Spirit who did a work in me to bring me to conviction and repentance.

Why did I keep silent for so long and continue in my sin so carelessly? Even as it sapped the vitality out of my life, I persisted in it. As I became an empty shell, still You did not forsake me. Now, day and night, Your hand of conviction is heavy upon me; now I see how dried up my life truly was, now "I acknowledge my sin to You" and am no longer hiding from You. To have been such a fool, yet You take me up! Now, "You are my hiding place." The one whom I have offended so greatly and against whom I have sinned is the one to whom I flee for protection and care. I can rejoice and shout for joy for He has restored me, He has lifted me up, put my feet upon the rock, and is guiding me with His eye being upon me. May You have pleasure from my life and may Christ be glorified.

Psalm 32
The Contemplation of Forgiveness

Vs. 5—I acknowledge my sin unto thee, and mine iniquity have I not hid. I said, I will confess my transgressions unto the LORD; and thou forgavest the iniquity of my sin, Selah. (KJV)

Have you ever contemplated forgiveness? Have you ever considered how unnatural it is? Whenever anyone is offended, sinned against, or harmed in any way, is forgiveness the immediate reaction? No. Every fiber of our being screams for justice, for the other party to suffer at least as much as we have, if not more, to seek revenge and maybe even vengeance. That is the natural response of our heart. And what of God? Our sin is such an offense to His holy nature. His sense of righteousness, that divine justice rises up to punish sin. But another, even stronger impulse steps forward that is greater, stronger, and runs deeper than divine justice: that is divine love. Thanks be to God that justice and peace kissed each other at the cross.

Do you want to be like God, to act as His nature does? Then, hate the sin, love the sinner, and forgive in Jesus' name. Is anyone even remotely capable of offending your sensibilities more than you have offended His? Has anyone's sin been as egregious against you as yours has been against Him? Yet God has called us to be like Him, to show love and grace to the undeserving, to put aside our natural impulse, and to forgive. My ability and willingness to forgive others is the single greatest indicator of just how much blessing God's forgiveness of me has been in my life (Luke 7:47).

Psalm 33
The Song of Redemption

Vs. 5—He loveth righteousness and judgment: the earth
is full of the goodness of the LORD. (KJV)

When Moses led the children of Israel across the Red Sea, he
led them in a song of deliverance. Here, God is inviting me to
rejoice and praise Him and sing unto Him a new song—a song of
redemption. The redemption I have in Christ Jesus has not only
redeemed my soul from the penalty and condemnation of sin, but
now I gloriously know that He has redeemed me from the power
of sin in my flesh. As the blessed man who has received forgiveness, God has brought me into such a wide place of enjoyment
of His goodness and has given me a spirit of praise and a song to
sing. My heart is now free, free from the guilt and consciousness
of regarding sin in my heart and doing nothing about it, and full
of thanksgiving, adoration, and praise. "He fashions their hearts
individually" (verse 15).

Lord, You knew what I needed; You knew that I had crossed a
line and would not confess on my own. I gave You no option but
to expose me Your way. You have marvelously measured out the
sorrow, grief, and pain and have given me the opportunity to
respond, confess, repent, and be restored. You knew exactly how
to deal with me to bring me to this point where I can rejoice in
all my circumstances, and in Your mercy, for Your eye is on me to
keep me.

Psalm 33
The Goodness of God, the Evil of Man

Vs. 10—The LORD bringeth the counsel of the heathen to nought: he maketh the devices of the people of none effect. (KJV)

When you consider the world, do you see it as full of the goodness of God or full of the evil of man? This is not a glass-half-full or half-empty kind of question, nor is it seeking to see if your outlook is optimistic or pessimistic. Man has undoubtedly filled this world with violence, greed, and avarice. We plunder this earth as if it were ours to do with as we wish. Sin permeates all human activity and death hovers over all creation. But this Psalm declares that the earth is, in fact, full of the goodness of God; that despite all that man in rebellion has wrought, God is still here, this is still His world, and His love has won.

The natural world testifies to the goodness of God; He sends it the warmth of the sun and the life-sustaining rain. The earth still brings forth life; the fields, the seas, the skies teem with its bounty and diversity. The world groans and travails, awaiting the revelation of the sons of God. When you look at life, do you see what sin has done or what grace can do? When you consider the world with all of its suffering and pain does your heart soar, thinking how it doesn't even compare to the glory that is to come? Where sin abounds, grace superabounds; where death reigns, life and immortality have come to light. It is only because of the work of Christ that all of God's purposes and glory will come to pass. And that is a certainty. In this, we rejoice and have hope. That is why we can see the goodness of God.

Psalm 34
Deliverance from Fear

Vs. 7—The angel of the LORD encampeth round about
them that fear him, and delivereth them. (KJV)

John writes in his epistle that "Perfect love casts out fear" (I John 4:18). Do I have a consciousness of His perfect love for me? Do I have a sense of the depth of His love for me? The cross is the measure of God's love for me. So, I shall bless the Lord and will be continually taken up by His awesome wonder and will exalt You marvelously. Lord, You knew the extent of my fears being rejected by my family, losing my good name, my business, my future, being alone, having no friends, fear abounding,…, and on and on it goes. Bit by bit, You taught me to rely upon Your perfect love—not my love for You, but Your love for me. Oh that I would seize hold of that love!

You are teaching me to trust in Your provision, that nothing can happen to me unless You allow it. In every place that I go, You shall have angels to protect me. Lord, You are showing me just how good You are, and I taste the sweetness of relationship every day. Lord, You knew that You had to break me in order to remake me: that rather than being soft, pliable clay, much of me had become baked hard by sin. You broke my stubborn heart and will, taught my spirit to be contrite and sensitive to Your Spirit again, and are delivering me from all my fears and troubles.

Psalm 34
The Value of a Broken Heart

Vs. 18—The LORD is nigh unto them that are of a broken heart; and saveth such as be of a contrite spirit.
(KJV)

In Proverbs, wisdom calls out to see if anyone is eager after her or if there is any sorrow and mournfulness over the sin of the people. God is looking for someone who is in sympathy with His feelings, who sees things the way He does, and who is broken over that condition. Before I can see it rightly out there in the world, I must first see it rightly in here, inside of me. God is looking for a heart broken over its own sin, willing to come to God with all that he is and making no excuses, no justifications, and no minimizations. It is only the broken heart that God can heal. As long as I hold on to any part, I limit the scope of God's activity in my life.

But there is another side to this. Often it is God who breaks the heart Himself. He knows how fickle our hearts are; He knows how prone to wander our minds are, and how our own lusts draw us out to unhealthy things. So, He, at times, allows us to suffer disappointments, heartaches, and setbacks to teach us that apart from Him, we can do nothing. Have I given my allegiance to anything else? He will need to remove it. Have I given my heart to something? He will have to break it. He wants to have the preeminence; He deserves it.

Psalm 35
Speak to My Soul

Vs. 17—Lord, how long wilt thou look on? rescue my
soul from their destructions, my darling from the lions.
(KJV)

Who was there to sympathize with Jesus in His passion? When
You faced Your greatest test of all, You made only one request of
Your disciples, "Stay here and watch with Me." Once again, those
about You could not give to You the human companionship and
comfort You so much desired. But where man failed, Your God
was there to speak to Your soul's deepest need. The clouds of man's
hatred gathered around You. The religious officials plotted Your
hurt, sought Your life, and without cause, tried to entrap You. But
angels came to strengthen You so God would speak to You. As
You would plead before God, You showed how lovingly You had
cared for humanity as You taught them, fed them, healed them,
and raised their dead. You pleaded and interceded for them, and
they returned evil for good. God would speak, "My will be done."

Jesus, what can I say in the face of such love? What can I do to
ever deserve anything from Your hand? I hear Your plaintive cry, I
hear God's simple reply, and my heart bows in adoration because
it was for me. How can it be that You could reward me for such
indifference to Your suffering to so continue in my sin, but it is all
of love and grace. I hear God speak to my soul, "I am Your salvation." You, Lord Jesus, were delivered through death that I might
never taste that forsaking. How can I do anything other than praise
You all day long!

Psalm 35
Rejoicing at My Distress

Vs. 26—Let them be ashamed and brought to confusion together who rejoice at mine hurt... (KJV).

When the Pharisees and Sadducees finally had You before Pilate, they thought they were so clever to have finally outmaneuvered everyone and gotten their way. They even got the crowds behind them to plead for the release of a criminal rather than You, the Prince of Life. And who was this Barabbas, whose name means "son of the father?" He was the leader of an insurrection and rebellion against Roman rule in which both thievery and murder were committed. He was an opportunist seeking to add the patina of respectability and religious fervor to his criminal enterprise. As odious and repulsive such an opportunist must have appeared to the religious officials, he did not represent the threat to their power as You did. They reveled and gloried in your defeat, little knowing that everything they were doing was according to the predetermined will and counsels of God (Acts 4:28).

Lord, You understand the feelings of my heart as I suffer the shame, humiliation, and consequences of my own sin. And even though I deserve much of the reproach I am receiving, there are so many who want me to never forget what I have done. They want my failure to be ever before me. They desire that I would never again be able to lift my head or to be used by You. Yet, just like Moses, David, and Saul of Tarsus, who were all murderers, You were able to use them, so I know that You have work I must do for You. May I see your grace triumph over both my sin and the desire of those who would wish me to be on the shelf—unused, unseen. I don't know what is in store for me, but I know your grace is greater than my sin.

MARCH 21

Psalm 35
His Footsteps Our Pathway

Vs. 27—Let them shout for joy, and be glad, that
favour my righteous cause: yea, let them say continually, Let the LORD be magnified, which hath pleasure
in the prosperity of his servant. (KJV)

Do you hear God speaking to your soul? If He did, then what
would He say? What He says falls into two large categories: He
tells your soul what He is to you and He tells your soul what you
are to Him. Do you hear His still small voice whisper, *I am here?*
Let Him tell you, *I am the lover of your soul.* Do you believe it, or
do you discount it? In this Psalm, He says, "I am your salvation."
Do we only accept that for eternity, but for tomorrow, do we
think, *No way?* I wonder if one of the greatest insults we give to
God daily is that we just don't believe what He tells us.

Has He told you, "Be careful for nothing."? So, we tell Him: *You
just don't understand the pressures of life, the sorrows and disappointments I have suffered.* But hear what Jesus says, *I became
one of you so that I could know through personal experience and
not by divine omniscience what your life is really like. And you
mean more to Me than all the splendor of heaven, more than the
glory and comfort of divine existence. I made you, I formed you,
and I have had my eye upon you all your life. You are cherished,
precious, unique, and wonderful. Do you have any idea how beautiful you are? I have made you with outward beauty, but that was
only intended to enhance and display your inward beauty. If you
could only see yourself as I see you.* Quiet your restless mind, turn
off the voices of your own discounts in your heart, and listen to
what He is saying to your soul.

Psalm 36
Could That Be Me?

Vs. 1—The transgression of the wicked saith within my heart, that there is no fear of God before his eyes. (KJV)

How deceptive sin is, how it blinds the eyes to the reality in our life. Did I really have no fear of God? Had I allowed sin to take root so deeply within me that it didn't fill me with fear and dread? Unfortunately, I must answer, "Yes". I had gotten to the point where I was nearly impervious to conviction, and what little I did feel was nothing to the sinful pleasure I enjoyed. I now see how truly wicked I had become though all these other areas of my life wore a garment of respectability. Now, as I look back, I hate the thing I had become and abhor the things I did, but then it was not so.

Oh, how God had to bring that to an end, and what an awful end it was. Yet even in His judgment upon me, there was mercy. You allowed me to confess out loud to You that I would never confess on my own, and then You brought me low. In those depths of facing my own wickedness and abhorring myself, Your loving faithfulness could reach me even there and lift me ever so slowly up. You did not allow my sin to utterly crush me, though for a fleeting moment, suicide didn't look all so bad. Little by little, you drew me in under the protection of Your wings and bore me up. I again found the source of joy in You, the fountain of life. May I drink deeply and never depart again.

Psalm 36
Thy lovingkindness ...Thy faithfulness

Vs. 5,7— "Thy faithfulness reacheth unto the clouds…
How excellent is thy lovingkindness. O God!" (KJV)

Such a contrast, Lord, between my sin, its deceitfulness, and Your mercy, lovingkindness, and grace. How am I to know that I can approach You with all of my sin? My expectation is that You could never accept me, that I need to do something about my mess first to show You how sincere I am and try to fix all the problems I have caused. But that is not your approach at all. When the overwhelming weight of my sins fell hard upon me, I fell to Your feet. It was Your mercy I sought. I knew that there was nothing I could do to make anything right, nothing I could do to mitigate the effects of my sin, nothing I could do to take away the sting of its shame. All of that had to come from You.

It is easy to understand Your lovingkindness toward those who are faithful to You, those who look to You and call out to You. I have now also come to see what Your lovingkindness is to the fallen saint; how You go out to seek him, how You wait and watch for him, and how You run to and receive him once he has turned to You in repentance. You have shown me that no sin is so great that the cross cannot handle it. Even though there are life consequences for my sins, there is eternal acceptance with You.

MARCH 24

Psalm 36
The River of His Pleasures

Vs. 8—They shall be abundantly satisfied with the fatness of thy house; and thou shalt make them drink of the river of thy pleasures. (KJV)

All things have existence and were created for the pleasure of God. His desire to bless us and endow us with pleasure is beyond our comprehension. Why do we think that pleasure is sinful or wicked? Only the perversion of pleasure and the misuse of our senses result in sin. God made us sensual and to experience a world of beauty and wonder through our senses. Our eyes take in the grandeur, wonder, color, and beauty of this marvelous creation from the minutest of bacteria with its structures and complexity that defy science to replicate it to the most immense galaxies He spun off in creation's fourth day. With our ears, we are moved by the sounds of music that speaks to our hearts on a far deeper level than words could ever do.

But the rivers of His pleasures are not only in the natural realm; they are also in the spiritual realm. He longs for us to enjoy His peace. Jesus has made peace for us with God through the blood of His cross; how much He wants to share His peace and rest with us. He wants us to share in His joy; He wants His joy perfected in us. His peace passes all understanding and is joy outside of our circumstances. To the woman at the well, He said, "If you only knew..." That can be said for us as well. If we only knew what we have in Christ, we would drink deeply of the river of His pleasure, and He would take pleasure in us.

Psalm 37
What is my Delight?

Vs. 4—Delight thyself also in the LORD: and he shall give thee the desires of thine heart. (KJV)

My soul will feed upon something. Either it will feed upon life's worries, doubts, fears, and anxieties or it will feed on God's faithfulness. Either I will fret, wearing myself down emotionally and spiritually, over what man will think and do, or I will be built up in Christ, trusting in Him, delighting in Him. To delight in the Lord is not to be giddy, to feel tingles up and down my spine. Still, rather it is the settled disposition of a heart that is rejoicing in its relationship with God, finding its satisfaction in fellowship with and obedience to Him, yearning every day to enjoy meeting with Him over His word, and thirsts after times of prayer drinking in His grace and love.

When my delight is in the Lord, His delight becomes my delight, His will becomes my will, and what I desire for myself is a reflection of His desire for me. It becomes easy to commit my ways to the Lord, for I know His love will not allow anything to come into my life for which His grace is insufficient. I may have my idea and my goal, but I want Him to have His way. Trust in the Lord is an extension of His love for me; my trust in the Lord is a measure of how much I have laid hold of the reality of His love.

MARCH 26

Psalm 37
Resting and Waiting

Vs. 7—Rest in the LORD, and wait patiently for him:
fret not thyself because of him who prospereth in his
way, because of the man who bringeth wicked devices
to pass. (KJV)

Jesus calls us to rest. He bids us to come unto Him and find rest
for our souls. Rest from the ceaseless agitation of our lives. We
all know that rest is good and necessary but difficult to achieve.
And why is that? Because to rest requires faith. When everyone
around me is railing, circumstances are all against me, and I feel
powerless in the face of events, the word bids me, "Do not fret—
it only causes harm." To release and cede control of my life to
the One who knows me best and loves me most takes faith, but
results in rest. Resting and waiting go hand in glove. If I am not
resting, I cannot wait. If I am not waiting, then I am agitated and
not resting.

They are also not passive. It is far easier for the flesh to be doing
something, anything other than waiting; waiting seems like such
a waste of time and opportunity. Resting and waiting takes tremendous spiritual energy. Notice how we are exhorted to wait
patiently, —not in agitation that is, without rest. Whatever level
of fasting, whatever amount of prayer, and whatever degree
of searching the word are all involved in the spiritual exercise
of one resting and waiting. Just ask Saul about the disastrous
consequences of not resting and waiting on Samuel (I Samuel
13:8–14). Lord, You know the restlessness of my heart; make me
feel the peace and security of Your love. May I relax my neck,
accept Your yoke, and learn of You.

Psalm 37
Do not Fret

Vs. 8—...do not fret– it leads only to evil. (NIV)

Just how dangerous is worry and anxiety? You have taught me that worrying means that I am looking to myself and my own resources to solve my problems rather than relying upon your strength. You showed me that it was only those things I perceived were outside of my control that I worried or was anxious about. So, You taught me the simple principle: if it is worth worrying about, it is worth praying about. So, now, anytime I sense worry within, it is a sure signal that I should pray. But what happens if I ignore your Spirit and continue to seek to solve it in my own strength? Then I find that it consumes an ever increasing amount of my time and energy—both spiritually and emotionally. I also find that I become more obsessive about the problem, brooding over it again and again. As I brood over it, it doesn't take long before I am angry about it, angry at myself for getting into the mess in the first place, and finally angry at You because You could have prevented the whole thing.

Lord, deliver me from this fretfulness. Deliver me from thinking that I have any strength in myself to take care of things so that I learn to rely upon Your strength and not lean upon my own resources. Keep me from getting so caught up in my fretfulness that I begin to be consumed with anger and lash out in either word or deed. If I begin to act upon my fret-induced anger, then You will need to chastise me. Teach ever to rely upon You and pray so that You can show me what You would have me to do.

 MARCH 28

Psalm 37
God Delighting in Me!?

Vs. 23—The steps of a good man are ordered by the
LORD: and he delighteth in his way. (KJV)

It is so easy to understand how my delight is in You, but is it possible that Your delight could be in me? Your word says, "His delight was with the sons of men" (Proverbs 8:31, NKJV). How could it be that I, fallen and sinful though I am, could be Your delight? Yet Your word says it. It is only because of what You have wrought in my innermost being through the work of redemption and new creation that anything good is there for You to delight in. "In me, that is in my flesh, dwells no good thing" (Romans 7:18, NKJV). It could only be that You see the life of Jesus within me that there is anything in which to delight. Christ is being formed in me by redemption and the power of Your Holy Spirit.

You know that in this life I shall never achieve moral perfection, that indwelling sin in the flesh will ever be a present source of problems, and that I shall fail and disappoint; yet You shall not let me be utterly cast down but shall uphold me for I am Your child. You are always there to comfort, correct, or chastise as the need demands. But the relationship is always there for You never forsake Your saints. How wonderful to know that You delight in me, Your relationship with me is all based upon the perfect work of Your Son; that I am accepted in Him. It causes my heart to exult in You and bask in the warmth of Your love.

Psalm 38
My Sin His

Vs. 3—There is no soundness in my flesh because
of thine anger; neither is there any rest in my bones
because of my sin. (KJV)

What does it mean when we read: "He was made sin for us who
knew no sin?" (II Corinthians 5:21) This is not high-sounding
theology, but deep experience for Jesus. My sin became His sin; He
was punished as if He had done it Himself. Lord, I read this Psalm
and hear the depth of your anguish. Bearing the sorrow, shame,
and punishment for my own sin as I have is little in comparison
to your righteous soul taking it upon itself. And it was God who
was afflicting You. He poured out His hatred and wrath against
my sin on You. What a tremendous burden You bore, and it was
not just mine, but the whole world's. Could anyone bear such a
burden? Could any man endure such suffering? Only You, Lord.
You had a joy set before You, so You endured the cross—with all of
its terror, pain, and rejection—and thought nothing of the shame.
Three and a half years of pouring Yourself out as a drink offering,
which cannot be gathered back up. So few stayed with You in Your
trial, as You were deserted by disciples, family, and friends. You had
a joy set before You, and though forsaken of God as You became
my sin-bearer, my sin offering, You knew He would take You up
in resurrection glory. Had it not been that You had so fully identified with my sin and made it Your own, I would have no hope. But
instead, I have a Savior.

Psalm 38
All My Desire is Before You

Vs. 9—Lord, all my desire *is* before thee; and my groaning is not hid from thee. (KJV)

How much we need to live transparently before God and then
others. It's not as if we can hide anything from Him, yet we try
anyway. Everything is open and naked before Him with whom we
have to do. So, we accomplish nothing by seeking to hide anything
from Him; we just put ourselves in denial and defer the inevitable
day of reckoning. But it is not enough to admit this cognitively;
we must act on it experientially. Let us bring before our God everything: the good, the bad, and the ugly. If I'm angry, talk to the Lord
about it, resolve it, and sin not.

Have I been offended, seek comfort from Him and not vengeance.
Give place for God's wrath for our vengeance does not do His
work. Has someone hurt me? Then I forgive him for I, too, have
hurt others and need forgiveness. Where there has been weakness,
sow encouragement and grace. Where there has been rejection, be
accepting; in place of hatred, be loving. God knows all the needs
and desires of my heart. He knows all that we have been through
and hears every sigh. He does not reject us for our weakness but
gives us grace as we need it, for His strength is made perfect in our
weakness. As we are honest with God, we will drop our false faces
and our masks, be more genuine with others, and have a richer life.

Psalm 39
What is My End?

Vs. 4—Lord, make me to know mine end, and the measure of my days, what it *is: that* I may know how frail I *am.* (KJV)

Lord, You have awakened me. While I was pursuing my sin, it didn't matter where all of that would lead. I did not guard my ways but followed after my lust. But now You have awakened me to make me to know my end. You are now my end, the direction all my thoughts go in; You are the terminus of all my activities and desires. If I had only seen that it was always that way, that You would not let my sin define me but had already mapped out how You would bring good out of all my evil. You have exposed tremendous weakness, but I look to You.

The fear of what awaits is ever with me, yet You give peace each day. It is You I wait on; You I look to every morning, with face up and mouth open, to receive Your food just like a baby bird. As fear besets me, I know that You will deliver me from my transgressions and protect me from some of its consequences; only what Your love allows will befall me, and grace will cover the rest. Since it is You who has done this, I have no complaints; it is only because of Your love that my sin and sorrow does not consume me. Even in Your rebuke is love. "Hear my prayer, O Lord, and give ear to my cry; do not be silent at my tears" (verse 12). You have brought me nigh by the blood of His cross and call me Your child, Your son.

Psalm 39
A Stranger with God

Vs. 12—Hear my prayer, O LORD, and give ear unto my cry; hold not thy peace at my tears: for I *am* a stranger with thee, *and* a sojourner, as all my fathers *were*. (KJV)

Is it possible that God is a stranger in His own world, that man in his rebellion has moved so far from Him that He is a stranger? Paul tells us that Satan is the god of this world (II Corinthians 4:4), this age, and that man prefers what Satan has to offer—sin and bondage—to what God has to offer—life and liberty. Jesus calls Satan the ruler of this world (John 14:30). Satan had offered to Jesus all the kingdoms of the world and their glory in exchange for worship. In Isaiah 14, Satan's fall is described, and he is linked with Babylon; in Ezekiel 28, he is associated with the prince of Tyre. Man has so fallen under the spell of Satan's lies that God is a stranger to him.

So what am I called to do? "To go forth unto Jesus without the camp bearing His reproach" (Hebrews 13:13). Moses faced this same dilemma. Is it better to enjoy the privileges and benefits that Egypt (a type of the world in its glory) offers or to esteem the reproach of Christ as greater riches? (Hebrews 11:25–26) Even though Jesus was Son and heir the workmen cast Him out of the vineyard and killed Him (Mark 12:7). So, dear Christian, if you feel like you just don't quite belong here, that the world around you doesn't share your values and priorities, then take heart. You are a pilgrim, stranger, and sojourner here. The time of Jesus' visible reign is coming, but until then, let us be strangers with Him in this world bearing His reproach.

Psalm 40
What did God desire?

Vs. 8—I delight to do thy will, O my God: yea, thy law
is within my heart. (KJV)

What did God desire? What was it finally going to take? How
would the sin question finally be settled? If sacrifices and offerings
were what it took, then they would have ceased long ago. A body
had to be prepared, ears dug by an awl. You, Lord Jesus, had to step
out of eternity into time, shed the infinite, and be clothed within
the finite, and as a man, the second man, the last Adam, satisfy
God's desire. Your delight was ever the Father's will.

Even at twelve, Your young heart was awakened and your tender
conscience touched by the inexorable call of God upon Your life.
You ever declared the word and will of God, gave a perfect display
to His love and righteousness, and even amid such hatred and
opposition did not withhold any of God's mercies. While You
did good, men wished evil upon You; while You offered life, men
sought Your destruction. And heaven was silent when God could
have spectacularly delivered You from the cross. My sins became
Your sins, and they seemed to almost overwhelm You. But Your
cry of triumph rang out, and God answered with an earthquake
and a rending of the veil. What did God desire? He desired a man
whose only thought was to please Him, would do His will without
reservation, would perfectly display Him to a lost world, and find
all His delights in Him. Jesus fulfilled God's deepest desire.

Psalm 40
What has Christ wrought!

> Vs. 12—For innumerable evils have compassed me about: mine iniquities have taken hold upon me, so that I am not able to look up; they are more than the hairs of mine head: therefore my heart faileth me. (KJV)

I know this Psalm is primarily about You, Lord, but I hear echoes of my own experiences written there. From the depth of my sin and shame, I cried unto You, and You heard. I didn't despair but waited patiently for You and You looked my way. You delivered me out of the filth and mire of my own life and gave my life back to me again. I now have this wonderful song of redemption to sing to Your glory and praise. May others take heart that You are loving and able to deliver them, too. There is fear and dread on the dark side, but let them trust in You and see light.

Now I know the tender mercies of the Lord, now I have felt so intimately His love, now I have received grace upon grace and cannot cease to proclaim Your wondrous work. You did not ask of me any great thing, but as Naaman, I had to humble myself, accept Your conviction against me, make confession to You of all I'd done, and repudiate it absolutely in repentance. Now You are my delight, not my sin; daily may it be Your will, not mine. What would compel the Samaritan woman to announce, "Come see a man who told me everything I ever did" (John 4:29, NIV). She found a love greater than her sin, grace greater than shame. Have no fear, dear sinner; seek Him and you, too, can rejoice in forgiveness and have the joy of relationship. It is true, grace is greater than all your sin.

Psalm 41
On being triumphant

Vs. 2—The LORD will preserve him, and keep him alive; *and* he shall be blessed upon the earth: and thou wilt not deliver him unto the will of his enemies. (KJV)

If one were only to look at the cross from a human perspective, the conclusion would be this: You had nothing to show for all Your love, for all Your ministry of good works, for all the wonderful words of grace You spoke, and for the incomparable life You lead. You sought to deliver the poor yet died penniless. You sought to save others but could not save Yourself. You sought to free man from tyranny yet died at the hands of a tyrant. And many rejoiced at Your death, reproached You in Your suffering, and reviled You for Your faith in God. Even one of Your most trusted disciples was a party to Your demise.

When it looked as if hatred had prevailed and Satan had triumphed, You could declare, "It is finished." For God was beholding; You had triumphed. By death, You defeated death; by being made sin, You broke sin's dominion over us. Your God was merciful, and He would vindicate You and glorify You by raising You up from the dead by His own glory—a glory He said He would never share with another (Isaiah 42:8), but will gladly share it with You (John 17:5). God is well pleased, wondrously delighted and has received You into glory as well as every soul You call Your own. Blessed be the name of the Lord God Almighty forever and ever.

Psalm 41
Heal My Soul

Vs. 4—I said, LORD, be merciful to me: heal my soul;
for I have sinned against thee. (KJV)

In salvation, our spirit, formerly dead in trespasses and sins, is quickened and made alive in Christ for God. Our soul, formerly a slave to sin and under its dominion, is set free and made a slave to righteousness. Our flesh, our body, is not redeemed until death and resurrection. Until then, we struggle with the effects of indwelling sin. Paul even goes as far as to say, "It is no longer I who do it, but sin that dwells in me" (Romans 7:20, NKJV). Now, as a believer, I am to present myself (my entire being) as being alive from the dead (Romans 6:13). Though sin is in my mortal body, it is not to reign there. Because sin still moves within my flesh (and I must have flesh to live in this world), it is in constant enmity against my spirit and God's indwelling Spirit.

The effect of this struggle with indwelling sin is the scarring of my soulish life. Desires for love, affection, beauty, joy, pleasure, and the whole plethora of sensations that constitute my soulish life are all liable to being twisted and perverted to satisfy sinful desires. Paul assures us that "To him who is pure all things are pure" (Titus 1:15, NKJV). God desires to purify our souls through His word so that our lives and desires will be pure and satisfying. He can deliver from all those negative consequences of sin: rejection, bitterness, resentment, abuse, fear, and a whole host of soulish (psychological) problems. He can bring healing both from those which are a consequence of my own sin and those inflicted upon me by others. Let God heal your soul.

Psalm 42
Deep Calls Unto Deep

Vs. 7—Deep calleth unto deep at the noise of thy water-spouts: all thy waves and thy billows are gone over me.
(KJV)

When we are going through deep waters, be they persecution, tribulation, or trial of difficulty, our soul looks for a kindred soul with which it can find comfort. We are not looking for platitudes or pious phrases, canned spiritual answers to our soul's deep need, but we do look for another soul to come alongside us, sometimes just to be there, sometimes to encourage or comfort us, certainly to empathize with us. Deep calls unto deep and asks if there is anyone there who understands. Jeremiah certainly felt this way. He pours out his soul in the book of Lamentations, giving expression not only to his own sorrow and pain but prophetically giving voice to God's as well. Can anyone read Lamentations 1:12 and not hear echoes of our Lord's heart?

We also see this in Hosea. God has been cuckolded. Israel has played the harlot, betraying the sanctity of their love relationship with God. God's heart is broken over what they have done and what He shall do in response. He finds in Hosea a man who can sympathize with Him, so God calls him to be His prophet to display in his life and marriage with Gomer all that He, as God, is going through with Israel. When deep calls unto deep, it is listening for an answer. May we be in a condition of heart "that we may be able to comfort those who are in any trouble, with the comfort with which we ourselves are comforted by God" (II Corinthians 1:4, NJKV).

Psalm 42
The Thirsty Soul of Jesus

Vs. 2—My soul thirsteth for God, for the living God:
when shall I come and appear before God? (KJV)

"Give me to drink," You would say to the Samaritan woman and then unfold to her the living water You had flowing out of Your belly. You knew from experience what it meant to thirst after the living God as a man here below, to know that nothing else can satisfy the soul's longing other than a close encounter with God. Others could not understand You, Your passion for lost souls, the sorrow over how we accepted such levels of sin in our lives as normal. You poured Yourself out for us, pleading with us, seeking to deliver us from our blindness. When You wept over Jerusalem, did any weep with You? Did any sympathize with You in Your deep exercises of soul?

You were so misunderstood that Your own family thought You were unstable. Your own disciples were so slow to understand, so dull of hearing. And after doing all the good, healing all their diseases, and meeting so many needs, who was there to recognize You, to minister to You? Then enters Mary of Bethany with her precious spikenard ointment. Your Father knew what You needed; He was a rock for You and a constant presence. Lord, You felt the frailty of our human flesh and all the vicissitudes to which we are subject and showed us how, though cast down and disquieted, we can hope in God, who will always satisfy.

Psalm 42
What Do I Thirst For?

Vs. 11—Why art thou cast down, O my soul? and why art thou disquieted within me? hope thou in God: for I shall yet praise him, *who is* the health of my countenance, and my God. (KJV)

Precious God, I come to you in desperate need, knowing that only You can satisfy. I have tried other cisterns, but they offer nothing but sorrow and disappointment. In Your mercy and grace, You have taught me, lovingly, that all my springs are in You, and I thirst for You. But there was a time when my sin was so fresh, the horror and awfulness of what I had done so great that my bed drank up my tears, and I was utterly cast down. I afflicted myself and cried out to You, wondering what would become of me. So, I poured out my soul to You, and little by little, Your love and grace penetrated my darkness. I was so cast down and disquieted, yet You called to me every morning, beckoning me to meet with You.

The very one I had offended the most was the only one who could lift me up. You taught me to hope in You. Yes, I must be chastened; yes, I shall be punished, but though I know much suffering awaits me, there is no condemnation. I could never warrant anything good from Your hand; that is why it is all of grace. You were my only hope; I cast myself upon You, and You caught me and lifted me up. I can never be satisfied apart from You again, for You are my all in all. My soul thirsts for You, for the living God.

Psalm 43
God my Joy

Vs. 4—Then will I go unto the altar of God, unto God my exceeding joy: yea, upon the harp will I praise thee, O God my God. (KJV)

Precious Savior, when You asked to be vindicated, it meant resurrection. God was not going to deliver You from the cross but through the cross, through death, all the way to resurrection. Man thought they were rid of You, Satan thought he had won. Then, after three days and three nights in the belly of the earth, You rose victorious over Satan's most potent weapon—death (Hebrews 2:14). Peter speaks this way in his Pentecost sermon showing from scripture that resurrection was Your vindication. So, Lord, I come to You asking, "What of me? What of my sin?" But Your word to me is that You have not cast me off, though I am chastened for a time.

Though I mourn now because of my sin, there will be joy. For You desire to have me, You send out Your light of forgiveness and lead me back through repentance to restoration. And when I return, I find that You have no second-class citizens; You have no back-row saints. You have restored me to fellowship and love. Now I can come to Your altar, fellowship at Your table, remember You in the breaking of bread, and rejoice in my God. Father, You have made me exceedingly joyful and I praise You for Your mercy and grace. Whenever I get down and feel disquieted in my soul, I remember that it is no longer I, but Christ, who lives in me.

Psalm 43
Light and Truth

Vs. 3—O send out thy light and thy truth; let them lead
me; let them bring me unto thy holy hill, and to thy
tabernacles. (KJV)

The Psalmist asks for God's light and truth to lead him, specifically
to lead him to a closer relationship with God. Light reveals what is
there, and it exposes the reality of the situation or circumstance.
While in sin, we actually live our lives in darkness. Jesus, who is
the light of the world, brings life and immortality to light. In the
absence of light we have, at best, a vague notion of what is around
us, what we face, and we consequentially use the lack of light as
an excuse for our failure. But as Jesus made plain in the healing of
the blind man, "If you were blind, you would not be guilty of sin;
but now that you claim you can see, your guilt remains" (John
9:41, NIV). In the presence of light all pretext for excuse is gone.

But Jesus is also the truth; He did not just speak the truth but was
the living embodiment of the truth. The truth reveals to us the
hidden things of God, things that we could not know apart from
God's revelation of it. As the light, Jesus made clear those things
that had already been revealed that should have been known. As
the truth, He revealed the new way of coming to God through
faith apart from the law. As a saint, I need both. I need the Holy
Spirit to reveal the truth to my spirit as it is in Jesus and I need the
light of the Holy Spirit to show me my path day by day so that I
can walk and live in the truth I've been shown. As Jesus said, "If
you know these things, happy are you when you do them."

Psalm 44
Favored by God

Vs. 3—It was not by their sword that they won the land, nor did their arm bring them victory; it was your right hand, your arm, and the light of your face, for you loved them. (NIV)

How wonderfully comforting it is to know, Lord, that any benefit and blessing I receive is due to Your favor, not my worthiness. If it depended upon me, there would only be judgment and condemnation for "In me that is in my flesh dwells no good thing." The giving of Your Son was "while we were yet sinners." Divine favor rests upon me not because of what I am but because of who He is. I am a recipient of grace and never an earner of it. Being on the ground of grace, I can praise You and worship You for all that I am, and all that I have comes from Your hand. But Lord I still sin, I still fail, I look within and still find that sin dwells in my flesh and erupts in wicked deeds and evil thoughts. My sin brings dishonor upon Your name and shame into my life.

Sometimes, I wonder within myself if people really knew what I thought and everything I had done, then would anyone want anything to do with me? But then I am reminded that "There is no condemnation to those who are in Christ Jesus." You had to deal with me, chasten me, and even afflict me to bring me to the point of conviction, confession, and repentance. Lord, You know the secrets of my heart; nothing is hidden from You. You know the evil that lurks there through indwelling sin and the good that is there is only by the power of Your Holy Spirit. Have Your way with me.

Psalm 44
But...

Vs. 9—But thou hast cast off, and put us to shame; and
goest not forth with our armies. (KJV)

This little word "but" indicates a contrast between what precedes it and what follows it; it causes us to pause and reflect on
the difference between the two conditions and assess the transi-
tion. Sometimes it indicates to us great grace such as in Romans
5:8, NIV "But God demonstrates His own love toward us, in that
while we were yet sinners, Christ died for us." Here in this Psalm,
Korah is experiencing something very different and is struggling
with it. The sons of Korah were spared from judgment when their
father rebelled against God in Numbers 16. He looks to the past,
recounts the favor of God displayed toward them, and acknowledges the source as from God and not themselves But now he sees
a different condition. He feels cast off, rejected, defeated, forsaken,
scattered, enslaved, and dishonored. That was a bitter pill to swallow for, "In God we boast all day long." Why all of this shame
when we are trying to be faithful?

But faith rises up to say, "All this has come upon us, but we have
not forsaken You." I do not need to understand what God is doing
to trust Him for what He is doing. If I could readily see how the
thing worked out for good, then where is the faith? "Our heart has
not turned back...but You have severely broken us." This Psalm
shows us how honest we can be with God—to pour out all of our
sorrow, pain, and confusion. God has not called us to stoicism,
pretending that what is hurting us doesn't, nor has he called us
to wallow in self-pity, whining, and complaining to Him. He has
called us to this level of honesty with Him so He can succor and
comfort us.

APRIL 13

Psalm 44
Not Forgotten

Vs. 17—All this is come upon us, but we have not forgotten thee… (KJV).

As I pursued my own path in life and made decisions to satisfy whatever agenda I had set for myself, little did I realize what would come upon me. Satan was so clever at presenting sin to me, so masterful at hiding from my sight what the end result of all of it would be, that I could justly be called a brute beast. I thought that I was doing so well for myself, that I was handling everything so well, but little did I acknowledge that the secret sins that I hid from everyone else would eventually be my undoing. God could countenance it for only so long; He could not continue to suffer with my continual hardening of heart.

Since I refused Your gentle hand, You had to turn me over to the hands of men. As I read the deep exercises you brought this Psalmist through: the feelings of rejection, being exposed to the ravages of others, and suffering reproaches, scoffing, and derision. I acknowledge that it was all under the control of Your love for me to bring about a deep work in my heart. And amid dishonor, humiliation, revilings, and reproaches, I was brought back to my senses and recalled to mind all the greatness of Your mercy and grace. I have not forgotten You because You remembered me and upheld me even as I was being chastened. Though painful, You have proven that all You have given me in the new covenant is more certain than the sun rising in the morning.

Psalm 45
A Heart Taught to Praise

Vs. 1—My heart is inditing a good matter: I speak of the things which I have made touching the king: my tongue *is* the pen of a ready writer. (KJV)

Lord Jesus, You have captivated my heart. I am overwhelmed at the extent of Your grace, the measure of Your forgiveness, the power of Your love. Who could have known that a God of such holiness would want a relationship with one so undone with sin, yet You did. And now I have an irrepressible theme of praise to declare Your goodness and grace. Isaiah wrote "There is no beauty that we should desire (You)," but that was with the eyes of flesh. Truly, You are the altogether lovely One, who fully gave Himself to God for me that I might be Yours forever.

One day, You will reign over this earth and subdue all enemies beneath You. Until then, reign in my life and subdue all the motions of sin in the members beneath Your righteous love. Bring humility and righteousness out of my life. Your life has been born in me. Now, I long to see what You will do in me to bring out of my life an expression of Your life. You are my Lord. You I worship.

Psalm 45
Forget Your Own People

Vs. 10—Hearken, O daughter, and consider, and incline thine ear; forget also thine own people, and thy father's house... (KJV).

As children, we grew up saying The Pledge of Allegiance every morning without seeing any conflict with our allegiances to God and country. We grew up being taught that we were founded upon Judeo-Christian ethics and that we were a Christian nation blessed of God. But eventually, we came to see the chinks in that armor and the reality that our country had feet of clay. Only God can demand our unqualified allegiance, and where our country diverges from God's ways, we must stand for God.

Peter and John faced this within months after Pentecost. In Acts 4:19, they saw the issue clearly: do I listen to God or to country? He chose to listen to God and accept the consequences of that choice. Notice Peter's response to those consequences, "they spoke the word of God with boldness" (Acts 4:31, NIV) while praying for their enemies. Imprisoned again shortly after that, he was threatened and beaten. His response: "rejoices that they were counted worthy to suffer shame for His name" (Acts 5:41, NIV). We have an allegiance that exceeds allegiance to our country and even to our families. Our devotion to Christ must exceed that to family. We are not to reject our families, but they might reject us, Jesus warns. We are not to reject our country, but it might oppose and oppress us as the disciples found. Our allegiance must ultimately be to Christ.

Psalm 46
Stillness

Vs. 1—God *is* our refuge and strength, a very present help in trouble. (KJV)

How readily do fears beset me, assail me, overwhelm me, but You tell me that I need not fear. Your word tells me, "Perfect love casts out all fear." It is Your perfect love for me anchoring my soul, causing me to see that the resources are all on Your side. I can rely upon You as my refuge and strength because You have proven Your love to me at the cross. If You would not withhold Your Son while I was a sinner, then how much more so is it for me now that I am one of Your saints?

Though the entire world is falling apart around me, though my carefully constructed life has proven to be a house of cards, yet You remain constant and unshakable. Amid upheaval, I see that You have provided an oasis, a well of water, an ever-flowing stream of spiritual and emotional refreshment that is a source of joy and relief. You are teaching me to look beyond the circumstances to see the God of those circumstances, and You bid me be still. You teach my anxious heart to trust and relax. You show me how to keep my mind fixed on Christ as the evidence and source of love so that I can bring all thoughts into submission to His mind and will. My restless energy wants to do something, anything, but You whisper to me, *My ways are not your ways.* I never realized how much spiritual energy went into being still, but as I meet You in stillness and quietness, I find peace, and it does truly pass understanding.

Psalm 46
Gladness

Vs. 5—God *is* in the midst of her; she shall not be moved:
God shall help her, *and that* right early. (KJV)

Such beauty there is in the relationship between stillness and gladness. How can I be glad if I am not still? How can I rejoice in the relationship I have with God in Christ if I am not resting in all that Jesus has done? If I am agitated about the circumstances around me or by the uncertainties within me, then my life, my inner self cannot rejoice. In Ezekiel 47, the prophet was caused to see a most marvelous thing. God brought him back to the threshold of the temple and there he saw a river flowing out that was for the refreshment and healing of the entire world. Ezekiel heard the depths of the water as it was being measured. It began at the ankles, then touched the knees, then up to the waist, and finally deep enough to swim. David contemplated a river whose streams made glad the city of God.

If God can do this for a city and for the whole world, then just imagine what He can do for me. If even for a moment I believe that my joy and gladness are due to the circumstances of my life, then I have made myself, my talents, and my resources my refuge. But, if by faith, I have made God my source of joy and gladness, then circumstances will not overwhelm me. When part of the ocean floor drops a huge amount of water drops with it and causes a massive wave to begin. Way out to sea that wave moves and is barely detectable. But as that wave moves inland toward shallower waters it becomes a mighty tsunami. Circumstances are like that. If I am in the depths of God's love, then the violent circumstances of life will ripple me and I ride them out. Lord, cause me to swim in the depths of your love.

Psalm 47
He will Choose

Vs. 4—He shall choose our inheritance for us, the excellency of Jacob whom he loved. Selah. (KJV)

When it comes down to matters of the will we can become very sensitive. We want to be able to exercise our own wills and the choices we make reflect a lot about the inner workings of our souls. It would be safe to say that we make hundreds of decisions every day from choosing whether to hit the snooze button on the alarm for ten more juicy minutes in bed to whether we will open up to our spouse about what is really going on inside us. We make choices ranging from the mundane to the major. Many of the choices we make are so automatic that we scarcely know or are aware that we have made them. There is a danger in placing more and more of our lives on autopilot so that we no longer have any heart in it anymore. How many of our conversations and interactions with others have become superficial and perfunctory due to that condition?

Eventually we shove God out of our practical lives so that even our relationship with Him is routine. Once this happens there is little room left for God's will to be exercised in our lives. But God has a lot to say about our daily lives and He has a lot at stake in how we conduct ourselves. We need to lay more and more of our lives in His hands and let Him do the choosing. He is interested in every facet of our lives. Do we just not trust Him or do we just not care? Yield more room to the Lord and His things, let Him speak to you and show you the choices to be made, the life He has planned for you. Lay aside the mindless, joyless, faithless life, and open up to the possibilities He has in store.

Psalm 47
Rejoice

Vs. 6—Sing praises to God; sing praises: sing praises
unto our King, sing praises. (KJV)

What praise, exaltation, and rejoicing breaks forth from a soul which is still. Do not mistake stillness with passivity, inactivity, or quietness. Stillness is all about a soul settled, stable, and dependent upon God. When the soul is that way it is set free from the worries, doubts, and fears of the flesh and released to exult itself in the Lord and exalt His wonderful name. As my spirit soars in wondrous awe for who God is and what He has done, my heart expands in love, adoration, and appreciation. My body responds to shout, to clap, to sing, to shout out and declare the wonders of my God and King. Jesus sits at the right hand of the majesty on high. He reigns in heavenly places over His people, both those in glory with Him now and those of us here on earth who are in the Kingdom of God's dear Son.

We look forward to and declare the day coming when He will return, put down all enemies, and sit upon David's throne ruling over all the kingdoms and peoples of the earth. Let the praises begin even now, Lord Jesus, for the suffering is behind You. You are in glory now, and soon every knee shall bow and every tongue confess that You are Lord to the glory of God our Father.

Psalm 48
Thinking on His Lovingkindness

Vs. 9—We have thought of thy lovingkindness, O God, in the midst of thy temple. (KJV)

"As a man thinks in his heart so is he," it says in Proverbs. Our thoughts both reflect the current state of our hearts as well as set the course for our lives. This is why we must do thought intervention. Are you worrying about something; is your life's energy being consumed by doubts and fears? Then avail yourself of God's remedy: pray. He wants us to turn our anxieties into prayers; for with prayer will come God's resources and thanksgiving. So many believers only worry and fret, then, when it *works out* where is the glory to God, the acknowledgment of His providential grace, the realization of His lovingkindness? Many will pass it off to luck, chance, fortune, fate, probability, or their own efforts and lose the spiritual blessing. Then, when the next circumstance arises (and it surely will) their reflex response is again to worry and the cycle continues.

But for those who, by faith, have prayed and seen God's hand move, they have an entire history of His faithfulness upon which to draw strength and resolve. They can think upon all of His past loving kindnesses and, knowing the heart of God experientially, trust Him for what comes. This is not a psychological ploy or the power of positive thinking, but the real way God makes an imprint of faith upon the soul.

APRIL 21

Psalm 48
Exaltation

Vs. 14—For this God *is* our God for ever and ever: he
will be our guide *even* unto death. (KJV)

Lord, You are having more and more control of my life as my will
yields and cedes more of my life's reins to Your Lordship. It is
as if my soul is becoming Your Kingdom. The worry, fear, stress,
and fretfulness are being replaced by faith, peace, joy, and stillness.
What a wonderful transaction. One day, this world will experience
Your Lordship. Satan will be deposed as god of this world, and You
will be enthroned in Zion, on David's throne. You will have put
down your enemies under Your feet, and Your reign will begin. It
will be a great and glorious day, to have Your personal presence
and rule with a rod of iron over the nations, to have them bring
their glory and tribute to you, and to honor You as King of Kings.

Such a joy we as saints shall experience to see Your vindication in
this earth. They said, "Away with him. We will not have this man
reign over us" (Luke 19:14), but now You are here. The nations
shall either willingly submit to You or be destroyed. The world will
begin to experience what I am beginning to experience now – the
joy of submission. When I think of how kind and loving You are
I am ashamed of how long I pursued my own way. But blest be to
God You hounded me down to submission, broke my will, and
raised me up. Walk around Your Kingdom, Lord, and enjoy being
my Lord, my head.

Psalm 49
Should I Fear?

Vs. 5—Why should I fear in days of adversity... (NASB).

The Lord has given me a wondrous confidence—my sin is not the end. Dark days will come, struggles, sorrow, and pain will be there, but so shall He. This is wondrous news, and I will be able to share and comfort those who are in affliction. But this message was told me in evil days, when the enormity of my sin and failure weighed so heavily and pressed me down. All those other things I had used to define myself and my life—my education, my success, my reputation—all were stripped from me. If there were anything I was relying upon humanly, it was gone. But then I realized that I didn't need them after all because I had You.

How silly we as men are, to heap up treasures on earth, to build our empires and pretend that they will actually endure when nothing does. Every investment in this world system is ultimately futile; only God is eternal. You have redeemed my life, You have lifted it up, and You are the only one that gives it worth and meaning. Why did I have to suffer the loss of all to realize this grand truth? Thank You for meeting me in my need, for giving me a hope and a life. May my gratitude never cease; may I never take it for granted. May it never seem common, but may I ever live in the realization of what You did and the grace You showered out. Hear this, O people, that with the Lord are grace and redemption; you have no need to fear.

Psalm 49
Their Inner Thought

Vs. 11—Their inward thought *is that* their houses *shall continue* for ever, *and* their dwelling places to all generations; they call *their* lands after their own names. (KJV)

We, each of us, have an inner thought life that we rarely let others know about. In our private thoughts we make plans, lay schemes, justify and rationalize all sorts of things, and nurse resentments and hidden grudges. We have to be very wary of our inner thought life for it can become the seedbed for all sorts of evil. And even if we do not carry out any of our plans, yet they can poison our outward life. "The heart is deceitful above all things and desperately wicked" (Jeremiah 17: 9, KJV). This is why we need to live our life in complete openness before God so that His Holy Spirit can take the light of God's word to every corner and nook to expose what is there. Then, once the light of God's word has shined upon it, let the truth of God's word do its work.

We are told in Hebrews that the word of God "is a discerner of the thoughts and intents of the heart." Allow the Holy Spirit to bring to light what is there and then don't hinder the process of conviction. Avoid blaming others to avoid responsibility, using what others have said or done to you to justify, minimizing the consequences of what we have done to others in their lives, or filtering out what we don't want to deal with. As we open the windows and let fresh air in, our inner thought life will be as a garden, blooming to the Lord and a place where He can go to speak with us.

Psalm 50
A Sacred Gathering

Vs. 5—Gather my saints together unto me; those that have made a covenant with me by sacrifice. (KJV)

How wonderful to be part of God's gathering. One day He will come forth and gather His people from the four winds of heaven, but even now we are able to gather unto His name and own Him in the midst. You told us that where two or three gather to Your name, You come into their midst. We could never deserve this blessing on our own; it is all because of Your sacrifice on Calvary's cross and faith in Your finished work that has brought us into such nearness. You have made a covenant by sacrifice, the new covenant instituted by Your shed blood bringing to us life and immortality by Your gospel. There was nothing we could have done, nothing that would have satisfied the demands of a holy God except Your sacrifice, Lord Jesus.

All those offerings of the old covenant, as good as they were for cleansing one to the purification of their flesh, could never make them perfect, and never purge the conscience. But You have done it and brought me into this gathering of Your saints, a sacred gathering, to worship You in the beauty of holiness, clothed in Your righteousness, and perfect before Your Father. Oh, what grace has brought, what sin seeks to destroy, and forgiveness has wrought! May Your name be praised.

Psalm 50
All its Fullness

Vs. 12—"… for the world *is* mine and the fulness thereof." (KJV)

Since it is a self-evident truth that You do not need anything, that You are perfectly content and satisfied within Yourself, then why do you want me? I can add nothing to Your existence nor would my non-existence produce a lack in You. Yet it remains that You did and do want me. Is that not the essence of divine love? You love purely from Yourself; Your love does not require a response from me in order for it to be complete. When trying to explain why You chose Israel to be Your people (Deuteronomy 7:7), Your answer was, "Just because the LORD loves you." For You, love is its own explanation.

What a relief it is to my soul that that remains the explanation for why You love me. "Just because." There was nothing I could do to warrant or merit Your love, no way that I could earn or deserve Your love. Since I can do nothing to deserve it, then I can do nothing to undeserve it; since I can do nothing to earn it, then I can do nothing to lose it. What peace this gives to my soul; just knowing that my gathering to You never depends upon myself. It is totally, utterly upon the merits of Jesus. He who perfectly satisfied Your heart has captivated mine. Truly, Father, You have shown me the salvation of God.

Psalm 50
Gather Together to Me

Vs. 15—And call upon me in the day of trouble: I will
deliver thee, and thou shalt glorify me. (KJV)

The church is the gathering of called out ones to assemble. We by
faith have been called out from this world and the world system
to be gathered to Christ. One of the great practical issues of our
life once we are saved is that though being in the world we are no
longer of the world. However, we have not only been called out of
something, but we have been called to someone. Paul writes to the
Thessalonians, "You turned to God from idols" (I Thessalonians
1:9, NIV). If all a person does is to turn away from one kind of sin
or error they might just turn toward another kind of sin or error.
However, if they turn toward God, then of a necessity they must
turn from sin and error. It's not the leaving behind of the world's
things that results in the sanctified life; any ascetic can do that.

It is the gathering to Jesus and following after Him that results in
the leaving behind of the world's things. Much of what the world
seeks to offer us is designed to distract us from our need for love,
joy, and peace by satisfying those needs the wrong way: selfishly. By
gathering to Christ, He satisfies these pressing needs of our hearts
so that the world's offerings fall by the wayside or into their proper
place. Let us look unto Jesus and gather to Him.

Psalm 51
Thoroughly Cleansed

Vs. 2—Wash me thoroughly from mine iniquity, and
cleanse me from my sin. (KJV)

Sin does not only include the actions which comprise the deed, but it also involves the thoughts of the mind, the motivations of the heart, and the lusts of the flesh. And even when the conviction of the Holy Spirit finally breaks through showing me my awful state and leading me to repentance, I must deal with the sin and the iniquity. Lord, you had to cleanse me from my sin so that I would no longer have any desire for that awful thing. But You also had to cleanse me from my iniquity, for that sin had left behind a lot of defilement in my life.

I realized that sin had been like a dirty, mangy, flea-infested dog which had made its way into my house and settled in. Now, even though I've dealt with the dog, I find there remains a lot of cleaning up to do. I need so much help with the iniquity of my sin as well and the house of my life needs a thorough cleaning. Everywhere I look I see another manifestation of the same attitude, rationalization, and justification that allowed sin to take up such residence before. Now it must all go! No more excuses, no more pity parties, no more hypocrisy; You, Lord, have judged, Your judgment is true, and I am so thankful that You have the keys to my house and are applying Your blood to every room, with hyssop. Just as the blood was sprinkled upon the door post and lintel for the first Passover, so You are sprinkling my soul to the sanctification of it for You.

Psalm 51
Made Clean

Vs. 12—Restore unto me the joy of thy salvation; and
uphold me *with thy* free spirit. (KJV)

Lord, thank You for Your cleansing work. It sure has taken some
strong chemicals, some coarse abrasives, and a lot of elbow grease,
but You have been both strong and gentle with me. But You knew
what You were about and I had to yield to Your hands and trust in
Your love. You would not cause more pain than was needed nor
did I shrink from the suffering You brought. You have cleaned
my heart and made it truly Your home. Thank You, Lord, for
the calming assurance that You would never leave me nor forsake
me—that You would never take Your Holy Spirit from me, for
He is the sealing of my salvation; the guarantee of my redemption.

When they offered a sin-offering, they would lay the animal open
and wash all of its inward parts. Now I understand what You were
portraying to me—to deal with inward sin it has to all be exposed
so it can be thoroughly washed. Now that the work is done I can
experience the joy of my salvation once again, like I did when I
was first saved only more so. Only Your grace could do this, for if
even a bit of this work depended upon me it would fail—what I
had to do was yield. You have broken my spirit, crushed the will
which sought to assert itself, and produced contrition in my heart.
Keep me this way Lord; I ever want a broken will, a contrite heart,
a cleansed life.

Psalm 52
A Green Olive Tree

Vs. 8—But I *am* like a green olive tree in the house of God: I trust in the mercy of God for ever and ever.
(KJV)

Lord, You are that man who is a tree planted beside the rivers of water producing that fruit. Psalm 1 describes You so much like the tree of life in Revelation 22. It is from You that I receive life and sustenance. Now I see what You want me to be. You want a green olive tree in Your house. What are You trying to tell me? An olive tree is not large and stately, but "giving my oil with which they honor God and man" (Judges 9:9, NASB). Highly valued, highly prized, with much labor and attention lavished upon them, when a crop is born. The olive tree communicates so much about how You are toward me. You want to get some blessing out of my life; You want Your life reproduced in me and the blessing of the Holy Spirit to flow from it. You expend so much effort for Your glory. And when a crop of olives is born You gather them and crush them, squeezing the precious oil out under pressure.

But isn't that how You deal with me, applying that pressure needed to draw out the precious oil? That oil then is used for light, for testimony. The light was never to go out on the lampstand in the holy place, nor should mine. Oil speaks of consecration, anointing and my life is to be dedicated to You. Oil reminds me of the Holy Spirit and how I have an "anointing from the Holy One" (I John 2:20, NASB) and have been "anointed in God" (I Corinthians 1:21, NASB). Green is the color of life, life in Christ. You, Lord, have accomplished all this, all is to Your glory; I will praise You forever.

Psalm 52
The Boasting of Evil Men

Vs. 1—Why boastest thou thyself in mischief, O mighty man? the goodness of God *endureth* continually. (KJV)

Just what is it about evil men that they need to boast? One thing that we learn about evil is that it provides a short-term advantage and appears to benefit the perpetrator. Take for example, cheating. Rather than invest the time and energy into doing the research and preparation or following the rules, cheating provides an effort free, painless way to get to the same end only get there quicker. Of course, then the cheater just has to tell someone how *smart* they were by being able to game the system to their advantage. In this way, they are glorying in their sin, lording your goodness over you, and looking for others' approval of their actions. But such gains are illusory, and eventually they find that their reach has exceeded their grasp and are found out or exposed.

The shortcut often looks so appealing, that is why Satan used that same approach on Jesus. Why wait upon God to meet your (legitimate) need for bread, just do it yourself? Why walk the miles preaching to ignorant, unappreciative people when one big, dramatic event will surely capture their attention and admiration? Why go through all the pain and shame of the sufferings of the cross when I can give you the kingdom now? Let us not envy the boaster after evil or its results, but heed Jesus' example, "Get thee behind me."

Psalm 53
On Being a Fool

Vs. 1—The fool hath said in his heart, *There is* no God.
Corrupt are they, and have done abominable iniquity:
there is none that doeth good. (KJV)

The fool says in his heart that there is no God for him; that he will live his life any which way he desires. It's not just the atheist being described here. I, too, have played the fool, for sin has made a fool out of me. And how did it do this? Because when I pursued my sinful course, I had no fear of God. I gave little thought to how my sin was such an offense to God. So many other areas of my life seemed just fine. I wasn't swearing, or stealing, or beating anyone so I was able to hide it for so long. How I deceived myself, heaping up judgment to myself. I told God, "Leave that area of my life alone, that's my little private thing." I would not have Christ reign over my life.

So as I turned away from God's conviction, my life became more and more corrupt. If my outer appearance had reflected my inward life I would have been like Dorian Gray in all my hideousness. There was no fear of what God would do, though I knew that He had to bring this wayward path to an end. It just didn't matter. Convincing myself that my life was pointless so what difference does it make? Oh, but it made a huge difference. You have now delivered me, brought me back from being captive to sin for, as I yielded myself to it, so was I its slave (Romans 6:16). But, thanks be to God, You have brought me out of that and given me beauty for ashes, rejoicing for sadness.

Psalm 53
When God Looks Down

Vs. 2—God looked down from heaven upon the children of men, To see if there were *any* who understand; who seek God. (KJV)

When God looked down to see if there were any who understood, who sought after Him, He was not surprised by what He found. He knew better than Adam what the universal consequences of sin would be on the human race and how thoroughly corruption would result. Nothing would be spared the effects so all creation became subject to futility on man's account. When Jesus came, God, for the first time, could again look down from heaven and see a man who would please Him in everything. Rather than use His will in rebellion as Adam did, Jesus chose to submit His will to the Father's.

God was so excited by what He saw in Jesus during His first 30 years of life that at His baptism the Father became exultant and declared His great pleasure in Him. The thing that pleasures the heart of the Father is when He looks down from heaven and sees His Son in me, in each of us. We have been born of incorruptible seed (I Peter 1:23) through the word of God, born from above, partakers of the divine nature (II Peter 1:4), having the life of Christ in us by the Spirit. Let our hearts desire to be such that we would not live to please ourselves, but to please Him who has called us out of darkness into His marvelous light.

Psalm 54
The Ziphites in My Life

Vs. 3—For strangers are risen up against me, and oppressors seek after my soul: they have not set God before them: Selah. (KJV)

In I Samuel 23 and I Samuel 26, we read how the Ziphites would betray David to Saul. Why would the Ziphites turn David in? After all he had done why would they betray him? Fear! Fear of King Saul, fear of his wrath, his retaliation, the total destruction they thought he would wreak upon them. So, David had to flee. David had no one to whom he could turn, no one that would risk himself for him. When Ahimelech had spoken up for David all the priests of Nob were cut down at Saul's command; such was the level of hatred and fury marshaled against David.

So David turned to You, God, cast himself completely upon Your name, prayed to You knowing that You would hear, and looked up. Sometimes I feel there are Ziphites in my life, that there are those (even in the body of Christ) whom I thought I could depend upon but cannot. Yes, I know that my decisions and choices brought this upon myself, but even after repentance and Your restoration, there are those voices—of doubts, rumors, and accusations—that I hear said of me. Like David of old, I cannot obsess about that; people shall think what they do and speak as they wish. Lord, keep my eyes fixed upon You, my heart set on You, my hope in You. You have brought me so far; let me not be discouraged with what people think or say, but let my praise be directed to You, my desire toward You.

Psalm 54
God My Helper

Vs. 4—Behold, God *is* mine helper: the Lord *is* with them that uphold my soul. (KJV)

It is a consistent principle in scripture that God will not do for you what you are supposed to do for yourself. Accordingly, we should not try to do for ourselves what only God can do. The farmer can only plow, plant, sow, and reap, but he cannot make it rain or make the seed germinate. However, God will not sow your field for you when it lies within your power. When God commanded Moses to fight the Amalekites Joshua mustered an army and fought in the plain while Moses stood upon the mountain overlooking the plain with the rod of God in his hand. Joshua prevailed whenever Moses held the rod out over the plain, but when his hands fell, the Amalekites prevailed. In this we see a picture of the believer doing what he is called to do and engaging the enemy arrayed against him while at the same time God is doing what only He can do sovereignly, coming to the aid of the believer in power for victory. (It is also a beautiful picture of intercession and the value of intercessory prayer.)

Before Jesus' passion and death He promised to send another helper. Jesus would be in heaven before the throne as our high priest making intercession for us while the Holy Spirit would dwell within us as our helper here on earth taking the things of Jesus and making them good practically in our lives. In this way, we can engage in spiritual warfare.

Psalm 55
Echoes of Gethsemane

Vs. 1—Give ear to my prayer, O God; and hide not thyself from my supplication. (KJV)

On the night of Your betrayal, meeting in the upper room to celebrate Passover, knowing all that lay ahead, You washed the disciples feet. Was there anyone on earth of Your intimates who was concerned after You? Was there anyone to sympathize with You in Your sufferings? Your heart severely pained, the terror of death beginning to crowd in upon You, the immensity of the work of redemption weighing upon You. And in Gethsemane, all You asked was for someone to watch and pray with You for one hour. It seems effortless to read the latest bestseller or watch a favorite movie for an hour; why is it so hard to pray for a whole hour? Wouldn't You have loved to have been able to dodge this one? Hadn't You suffered enough reproach, insult, and hatred of man? If man is so determined to stay lost, then so be it, those ungrateful creatures!

But love would have it no other way. The Father so loved and so did You. Therefore, rather than making like a dove, You faced Your destiny as a man. Judas, Your companion and acquaintance would turn You over to the hands of sinful men, but You knew that You were always in God's hands. You could place Yourself in God's hands for You knew that all was according to the counsel and foreknowledge of God. The victory of Calvary was won in the trenches of Gethsemane.

Psalm 55
As For Me

Vs. 16—As for me, I will call upon God; and the LORD shall save me. (KJV)

As those who are in the world but not of the world, we are called to live above our circumstances. Paul wrote of this when he told the Philippians that he had learned to be content whether in plenty or want. Now Paul's contentment was due neither to a passive resignation to his circumstances nor a stoic acceptance of them. His contentment sprang from his confidence in the love, providence, and sovereignty of God who engineered all of his circumstances. This gives the soul peace and rest. In this Psalm, David is contemplating the difficult circumstances of his life, then says, "As for me…" And what does David do? First he mentions that he calls upon God in whom is all his confidence, hope, and strength. Now that his attention is directed properly, he next says that he will pray and cry aloud. This is an impassioned pray, one that honestly lays before God the depth of his feeling and need. And what is his expectation? "He shall hear my voice."

This is spiritual confidence in the nature of God, not wishful thinking. If I live most of my life as if it is all up to me and scarcely let the Lord affect the way I live, then will I know what to say or what manner of God I am addressing? But let me come after with all my need to learn the heart of my God. This is why David exhorts us to "Cast your burden on the Lord." This is not the casting of a fishing line that lets you reel it back in, but a casting that requires relinquishing control to God. Let Him show Himself faithful.

Psalm 56
What Can Flesh Really Do?

Vs. 4—In God I will praise his word, in God I have put my trust; I will not fear what flesh can do unto me.
(KJV)

Did You feel like a silent dove in a distant land? You were so pure, so innocent, so gentle, and strong, yet Your words were powerful. Your presence could intimidate; Your jealous guard over God's honor stirred You up so that none could stand before You. So far away from Your true home, walking amid those who desired to devour You, did You have fear when the citizens of Nazareth strove to cast You from the cliff? Or when the soldiers came to arrest You in the temple? Or when Herod threatened Your life? Then You would trust in God—for what can flesh really do? They could beat You, pluck Your beard, revile You, spit in Your face, pierce You through and kill You. But all that was as nothing compared to what God could and would do to you.

You heard the snide words, the innuendos, the accusations and threats and felt them all so deeply—such was the tenderness of Your heart, never hardening Yourself against man's abuse. Your Father treasured every tear You shed and stored them up in a bottle, recording every act of love and devotion—so pure was Your heart. Lord, give me this same spirit, this same strength of heart, resolve of will. Though my sufferings originate from my sin, yet there will be those who will wish to multiply them. May I always put my trust in You as Jesus did. For really, what can flesh do? Only what You allow.

Psalm 56
Whenever I am Afraid

Vs. 3—What time I am afraid, I will trust in thee. (KJV)

Fear is a legitimate emotion that reflects our perception of vulnerability, dread, or powerlessness. To deny the reality of our fears would be to discount our own emotional makeup, would be schizophrenic. To succumb to our fears and to descend into mindless powerlessness is to deny the reality of our God. We must come to the realization that any sense of control we have in our lives is an illusion. Only God is in control, and I must cultivate a sense of His sovereign hand in my life, a faith in His providence, and a reliance upon His love (Romans 8:28). When I am fully grounded in the character of God, then I can prove the truth, "Perfect love casts out fears" (I John 4:18, NKJV).

When David faced his fears in Gath, he had to trust in the character of God and His love. Notice that as he placed his trust in God he found that he was able to praise Him. He then asks the question, "What can flesh do to me?" Flesh can do plenty, but it cannot do anything outside of what God's will permits. Jesus said to not fear those who can kill the body, but not the soul (Matthew 10:28). That is a tall order and a point to which He can bring us to only through faith. But rather than wondering if we will ever be called to that, let us seek to live fearlessly for Him every day.

Psalm 57
My Heart is Steadfast

Vs.1—Be merciful unto me, O God, be merciful unto me: for my soul trusteth in thee: yea, in the shadow of thy wings will I make my refuge, until *these* calamities be overpast. (KJV)

Lord, You have been merciful to me. You have not dealt with me after the manner of my sin for You have extended mercy and grace beyond anything I could have conceived. My soul trusts in You that whatever trials, afflictions, or chastening come to me, it is tempered by Your love. One day these calamities shall pass (and I must confess that many of them are of my own doing, reaping what I have sown) and I shall see Your faithfulness through it all. Whenever I cry out to You, You always hear and answer; You are teaching me to trust day by day.

Though I am often surrounded by those who hate me, despise me for what I have done and who believe that my sin defines me as who I am, yet You know all about it and preserve me. This is why my heart is steadfast because I have learned the character of the God with whom I have to do: one of justice, righteousness, and holiness who has taught me to have His same hatred for sin, and one of grace, mercy, and love who has forgiven my sin and restored me to a right relationship with Himself. Steadfastness does not come from any exertion of willpower on my part, but from drawing upon the deep resources of relationship and knowing the heart of my God.

Psalm 57
My Soul Trusts

Vs. 6, 7—They have prepared a net for my steps; my soul is bowed down: they have digged a pit before me, into the midst whereof they are fallen *themselves*. Selah. My heart is fixed, O God, my heart is fixed: I will sing and give praise. (KJV)

What a life of faith You showed us, Lord, from beginning to end. You knew how awful this world was, how committed to sin the human heart is, the level of hatred and animosity we held against God, and all about what You were going to face; yet You came. The plan of salvation and the road to the cross was laid out from eternity past, yet You came as a helpless baby, dependent upon Your very creatures for Your care. Your soul always trusted in God, always relied upon His mercy and grace. You would not use Your divine powers to even feed Yourself, much less defend Yourself, apart from the Father's express will. You sought refuge under the shadow of God's protection and cried out to Him in Your need rather than use Your divine resources for Your own self-aggrandizement. Your help, Your hope, Your deliverance was all in God.

So what I see in You is a man who showed me how to live and walk by faith. As Your life, Lord, was a life of dependence—so can mine be. Your life was a life of prayer—so can mine be. Your life was based in and centered on God's truth—so can mine. Your Father is my Father; Your God is my God. The same Spirit that animated Your life dwells within me. My soul is among lions who would love to tear me up, but You showed me how to live ... by faith. I praise You and exalt You for You have done all things well.

Psalm 58
Surely There is a Reward.

Vs. 11—So that a man shall say, Verily *there is* a reward
for the righteous: verily he is a God that judgeth in the
earth. (KJV)

In this world where wickedness seems to triumph, a day is coming.
Evil can only be tolerated for so long; the evil of man's heart will
only have room for expression for a little while. The deception
of sin is that one feels that since God isn't doing anything about
it then He doesn't care. And each act planned, perpetrated, and
enjoyed emboldens one to commit the next. I know this vicious
cycle for it has been mine, but You in Your grace brought it to an
end rather than let it go on and on. Sin deceives us into enjoying its
pleasures, thinking they will continue unabated, but they are only
for a season. Then the guilt settles in, and I find myself hating the
sin, enjoying it at the same time, miserable and wretched.

Thank You, Lord, for bringing it finally, mercifully to an end. Sin
is a taker—taking your time, your family, your money, your life,
your future, anything that you value—and gives sorrow and death
in return. Thank you, Lord, for redemption. Where would we
be without Your perfect, complete atonement, the propitiation
for my sins to give me love, life, joy, and peace again? Whatever
sin has taken, You can restore in Your way, Your time, for no one
can outgive God. May I walk daily in the newness of life You have
given, for You have reconciled me to Yourself by Christ's blood
and want to bless me.

Psalm 58
Silent Ones—Be Silent No More

Vs. 1—Do ye indeed speak righteousness, O congregation? do ye judge uprightly, O ye sons of men? (KJV)

Why are we silent when we should speak and speak when we should be silent? Is it not because it suits our purposes and coddles our flesh? If we do not speak righteousness, then who will? Is it because of fear of man, what he may do to us, the repercussions we might suffer that hinder us or intimidate us into silence? Perhaps, as is suggested in this Psalm by David, we remain silent to cover up our own sin; we look at the things in our life and remain silent so that we don't feel like hypocrites when our own sin is exposed. If that is the case, then let us get right with God. He does not expect moral perfection from us, but He does expect continual growth and maturity. The mature man in Christ doesn't regard iniquity in his heart but confesses it as soon as he recognizes the conviction of the Holy Spirit to receive forgiveness.

As believers, we are a living testimony to the grace of God. As I speak out for righteousness and someone points to something I have done in my past, I can testify to God's grace and forgiveness and offer to them that same grace and forgiveness that I received. If they point out something I am doing, I can confess it, repent of it, thank God for the conviction, and be a living testimony to the active power of grace and forgiveness in my life to change me and how it can change them, too. Let us not shrink in fear but be bold for Him.

Psalm 59
No Fault of His Own

Vs. 3—For, lo, they lie in wait for my soul: the mighty are gathered against me; not *for* my transgression, nor *for* my sin, O LORD. (KJV)

Why did Jesus have enemies? Why would there be any who would rise up against Him? Why would anyone want to destroy one who only went around doing good and speaking the truth? Because we don't want the truth! We can't handle the truth! His goodness highlighted our lost, wicked, decrepit condition and we hated Him for showing us what we really were. It was through no fault of Your own, blessed Savior, that You became the object of such animosity; the fault is all ours. Man hounded You, sought to catch You in Your words, ensnare You in some trap to have ought to accuse You of for Your goodness drew out our hatred. Such is the principle of sin. It is not merely actions that transgress Your holy standards, but an actual mind of animus and resentfulness against all that is good.

If I had only understood, if I had only cared, that each sin I committed added to Your suffering, Your pain. I was too bent upon self-satisfaction, but You were totally bent upon God-satisfaction. Your Father heard You, and until Your time had come, He delivered You. Lord, I look to You for deliverance from the power of sin within me so that I can sing aloud of Your mercies every morning, meet You in prayer, and rejoice in my salvation.

Psalm 59
Sing of Mercy

Vs. 16—But I will sing of thy power; yea, I will sing aloud of thy mercy in the morning: for thou hast been my defence and refuge in the day of my trouble. (KJV)

We have a song to sing the words of which the world can barely conceive. In several Psalms, we read of singing a new song — a song of deliverance. And what strains does that song contain? Certainly, it contains one of love, the great love of God that saw us in our need and acted on our behalf even while we were actively opposing Him. It also contains one of forgiveness, for we have sinned against a holy and righteous God who cannot accept us in our sin, so He offers forgiveness and cleansing. It also contains one of grace, for there is nothing we could do in even the slightest degree that could merit us an audience before God's throne whereby we could plead our case or absolve ourselves of our guilt. And it would also contain a strain of mercy, for we desperately needed it, and God proffered it. And not only were we objects of His mercy in salvation, but there is also the daily deliverance from trials and difficulties.

Each morning, we are encouraged to sing aloud of His mercies, His provisions for the day that is past, and expectation for what lies ahead. We live our Christian life amid a hostile world. If God opened our eyes, as those of Elisha's servant, so that we could see not just the forces arrayed against but also the spiritual forces available to us and the help God gives daily, then our song of His mercy would be even sweeter.

Psalm 60
Jehovah Nissi

Vs. 4—Thou hast given a banner to them that fear thee;
that it may be displayed because of the truth. Selah.
(KJV)

Lord, it must grieve You to show us hard things, but we don't give You much choice. You must chasten for You love me. And though I suffer for it, I know it is working the peaceable fruits of righteousness. Though You had been displeased with me, You sought to restore me. You worked in me through conviction, confession, and repentance, leading to restoration, and I praise You for it. You have set up a banner, a rallying point to which I gather. It is a call to holiness, and Jesus is my banner. In the wilderness journey, each tribe had its own banner. We now are Your people; You are our head, and Your banner over us is love.

The word fear has so many connotations, usually associated with feelings of dread, doom, danger, or impending destruction. Yes, we should have a fear of God as the righteous Judge, and part of my failure was due to not having that idea of "falling into the hands of the living God." That kind of fear will deter sin, but will never motivate to do good. To have that awe and respect for the greatness and majesty of God, to accept His authority in my life, and to hold what He says as authoritative truth is also involved in this. "Sanctify them by the truth. Thy word is truth," Jesus prayed. We love to gather to You and around You.

Psalm 60
Hard Things

Vs. 11, 12—Give us help from trouble: for vain *is* the help of man. Through God we shall do valiantly: for he *it is that* shall tread down our enemies. (KJV)

Has God ever shown you hard things? When you saw and experienced them, how did you respond to them? What effect did they have on you? Some believers cannot accept that God will send hard times and hard things to discipline and train His people, but there are lessons to be learned through them. This world is an evil place reflecting the hatred of and rebellion from God characteristic of sin. There is so much sorrow and suffering in this world; it is a creation groaning while it awaits redemption. Jesus lived and walked amongst such situations to bring the light of God's love to those in such conditions.

Do we, in our comfort and complacency, want to avoid such people and situations because they are hard things? Can we take Christ's love, grace, and forgiveness to them or will we be repulsed by what we see? Sometimes, the hard things He shows us relate to the evil that is within us. Until the day of our deaths, we will contend with the flesh and indwelling sin. God will allow situations to come into our lives to expose this. We must go through hard times and be shown hard things so that we can put to death the deeds of the flesh. These hard things will result in some confusion, for we will doubt how God could ever make such a thing work for our good, but He can. As we respond properly, as Joseph did, to these hard things we won't be hardened by them but should be softened and made tender and compassionate toward others.

Psalm 61
Overwhelmed No More

Vs. 2—From the end of the earth will I cry unto thee, when my heart is overwhelmed: lead me to the rock *that* is higher than I. (KJV)

Dear God, You are so gracious to hear my cry. Thank You, Lord, that no matter how far away I seemed, how distant I thought You were, You were waiting, watching, and listening. No well of sin so deep, no depth of hurt so great that You could not span the gap and bring me into Yourself. Even when my heart is overwhelmed with my sin, my circumstances, or my self-pity, You are there to respond when I call to You. And Your response is not halting, hesitant, begrudging, scolding me for having been gone so long, but welcoming, restorative, and rejuvenating to take me to a place of greater intimacy with and appreciation of You. Why would You want to answer such a cry? Only because You love.

Firstly, Your love for Jesus, who died for me and who imparted life to me, and then Your great love for us. Jesus knows and understands what life is like in bodies of clay in a fallen world. When You take me up, You lead me to a place that is higher than I am now; You draw me up to heavenly places where I am identified with Christ and seated in Him there. You have no illegal immigrants, no secondhand citizens of heavenly places, only true sons and daughters. You are my shelter, my strength, my security and my home. You have put praises into my mouth, a song on my lips.

Psalm 61
Lead Me Higher

Vs. 5—For thou, O God; hast heard my vows: thou hast given *me* the heritage of those that fear thy name. (KJV)

So many believers want a "mountaintop" experience of being closer to the Lord. But why does God give us a mountaintop experience? It is so that when we come back down into the valley where people live their lives, we can minister the grace of God to them. Many want the mountaintop experiences for themselves, almost like they see it as a fill-up station to bolster themselves for the week. But such is not the mind of God. God wants us close to Him; He wants a relationship with us far more than we want one with Him. He plans times of refreshing and strengthening for us; He knows we need them. And what is to be the result of these times? Greater faithfulness.

Two words are used to describe the relationship of the saint from these times: abiding and trusting. The saint sees himself abiding in Christ, as a branch abides in the vine and draws from it life and sustenance for fruit bearing. To abide also implies rest, the rest of enjoyment in Christ. These twin thoughts of fellowship and fruitfulness characterize abiding. Trusting is the complacency of the soul, which depends upon God's provision. It is not a complacency of inactivity in which the individual uses false spiritual reasoning to remove their responsibility. "I can do all things through Christ who strengthens me" is a statement of fact that I am empowered and responsible to do all things that He sets before me, trusting in His strength, not my own.

Psalm 62
How Long Will It Last?

Vs. 4—They only consult to cast *him* down from his excellency. they delight in lies: they bless with their mouth, but they curse inwardly. Selah. (KJV)

Jesus, You were so patient, enduring so much at our hands. Silently, You accepted so much suffering from our hands. Was there anyone to whom You could confide? Did any of Your disciples ever ask You what You were going through? Did they understand how it hurt when Your own family tried to divert You from Your ministry? Did they stop to wonder what it meant to Your loving heart when the citizens of Nazareth wanted to kill You? As for Capernaum, they had seen so many works in their midst that You declared that Sodom would have repented in the face of such witness! Who was there for You to receive comfort from rather than always giving comfort? Only Your Father.

So You silently bore all of it in Your precious heart. You could commune with Your Father, sometimes praying all night while other times rising early to receive what You needed as a man upon earth. As the pressure intensified, as the hatred mounted, it culminated in the cross. When will enough be enough? Another hair plucked; another scourge of the whip. Weave another thorn into the crown—press it down just a little harder! Why does man hate You so much? When will enough be enough? God replies, "You only have three more hours of darkness to go, and it will all be finished."

Psalm 62
How Long Will You Attack a Man?

Vs. 11—God hath spoken once; twice have I heard this;
that power *belongeth* unto God. (KJV)

The day is quiet and I am here with my thoughts. You are teaching me, Father, to trust You with my fears, my future, and my life. It has been a hard lesson to learn because I had spent a lifetime mostly caring for everything myself. I thought I was so "with it" when, in reality, I was completely fooled. The knockdown was a long time coming, and come it did! But You have been gracious with me the entire way, and in this stillness and quietness, I have learned that You are God.

However, though Your dealings in chastening have accomplished "the peaceable fruits of righteousness," there are so many that cannot forgive and believe I have not suffered enough. And I agree that I have not suffered to the degree that I deserved, but "You have not dealt with (me) after the manner of (my) sin," and I am thankful. So, I come to You as I learned, as You have taught me, to leave it with You. I wait silently; teach me not to complain but to confide. You are my source; my destination and expectation are all bound up in You. My heart is open; let it never be closed or hardened, but ever tender. Give me the heart of Jesus.

Psalm 63
Feasting In the Wilderness

Vs. 1—O God, thou *art* my God; early will I seek thee:
my soul thirsteth for thee, my flesh longeth for thee in
a dry and thirsty land, where no water is... (KJV).

This world is a wilderness. Look around. There is nothing to satisfy, nothing to fill the empty soul, and no means to satisfy the thirsty longing of the heart. No one knew this better than You, Lord. I must confess that I still feed from the world's troughs and drink from its cisterns, but always, ultimately, the disappointment and emptiness return. Lord, You ever looked to Your Father, "I have meat that You know not of," You told Your disciples. And now that You are risen, we have that bread from heaven, that true manna, Yourself to feed upon from Your word and fellowship through the Holy Spirit. You valued fellowship with Your Father above all else, and Your soul was satisfied as with the choicest foods. The daily communion with Your Father was very life to You.

And if You, the perfect man upon earth, had this need and burning desire, then how much more should it be for me? When I lay down or awaken in the night, may I think on Your grace and meditate on Your mercy and love for me. When I awaken in the morning, let it be my first desire to meet with You, to hear from You. While my heart is still, before the pressures of the day beset me, have me set my compass to true North. As I go through my day, please teach me to follow and not to lead, to watch for Your guiding eye, to hunger and thirst after Your righteousness and be satisfied by Your hands.

Psalm 63
A Dry and Thirsty Land

Vs. 4—Thus will I bless thee while I live: I will lift up
my hands in thy name. (KJV)

Do I, do *you*, truly see the world, the world system for what it truly
is? God so loved the world, the natural world with all of its beauty,
diversity, wonder, grandeur, and order, that He wanted to see it
redeemed from the curse of sin and death and restored to its true
state. But man, in his sin, greed, and avarice, has superimposed
upon this world a system of government, morals, and economics
reflecting his fallen state so that everything is designed to oppose
God and the truth. Jesus, who is the truth, stood before Pilate
who would ask scornfully, "What is truth?" And such is the irony
of man, to reject the light of God's truth and remain in darkness.

We are told that love for the world, this Christ-rejecting world
system, is enmity with God. Enmity is an attitude of automatic
hostility, that there is in fact no common ground upon which
a compromise or reconciliation could be made. As believers, we
must never lose sight of the fact that this is a Christ-rejecting
world, that man killed Jesus once, and if he were given the chance,
he would do it again. The world has nothing to offer the Christian
soul; no level of culture, refinement, education, art, or science has
anything to feed its needs, that only Jesus, the living bread from
heaven, the true Manna, can feed and nourish the soul.

Psalm 64
Preservation from Fear

Vs. 1—Hear my voice, O God, in my prayer: preserve
my life from fear of the enemy. (KJV)

Lord, in the gospels You are always in such control, so calm amidst
the stormy circumstances. But this was not because You had divine
power, for You showed Satan in the wilderness that You would use
none of Your divine prerogatives without explicit direction from
Your Father. You were confident that God heard Your voice in
Your meditations. You knew You could present all to the Father,
knowing He had all power and love and not have to fear, for You
relied implicitly upon His love. Teach me that kind of repose. As
I read in this Psalm, You know all about their machinations, the
plots, plans, and schemes that are being prepared against You. You
hear their words, how they blaspheme You and try to ensnare You
or get You to incriminate Yourself. So, Your repose is neither born
of ignorance nor naiveté but of a settled confidence in the God of
heaven. You know that, in the end, they are the ones who shall be
in fear when all comes to failure, and You rise triumphant.

So, Lord, teach me to love God like that and be able to rest in His
love. Teach me the meaning of providence, not happenstance.
Teach me to gain strength from the work of Your hands in history and then in my story so that I trust, I have repose, and I learn
dependence to praise You for the marvelous things You have done.

Psalm 64
The Heart is Deep

Vs. 6—They search out iniquities; they accomplish a diligent search: both the inward *thought* of every one of *them*, and the heart, *is* deep. (KJV)

Paul writes, "No one knows a man except the spirit of man that is in him." Jeremiah asks, "The heart of man is deceitful above all things and desperately wicked. Who can know it?" Writing to the Hebrews, Paul tells us that the word of God "is a discerner of the thoughts and intents of the heart." Because of sin, the human heart is such a muddle of conflicting thoughts, attitudes, and motivations that we cannot always untangle the knot of our own confusion. In this Psalm, David is contemplating the depth of evil to which man can stoop and the designs and schemes for evil that he makes. He sees that they are glorying in the shrewdness of their plans, reveling in the certainty of their success. But God is deeper and more profound than all the plans of man and can overturn all of their designs.

For us as believers, we have been given the mind of Christ; we are called to bring every thought into captivity to Christ. Paul reminds us that "No one knows the things of God but the Spirit of God." God wants us to enter into His thoughts and see things His way. To do this, we must become simple. All the turbulent thoughts and mixed motivations that characterize our lives must be abandoned. We are to be children before God open to His every suggestion, putting aside reasonings and disputes, to accept what He has for us. Let us be wise as serpents but harmless as doves.

Psalm 65
May I Approach?

Vs. 4—Blessed *is the man whom* thou choosest, and causest to approach *unto thee, that* he may dwell in thy courts: we shall be satisfied with the goodness of thy house, *even* of thy holy temple. (KJV)

In the courts of royalty, it is an honor to be summoned to appear before the king or queen. Men and women of great accomplishment will give a command performance for them. They could never presume to request to perform; they must wait upon an invitation. What a privilege to be chosen by the God of the universe to appear before Him to give Him praise. As one who was so full of sin, so caught up in myself and having scant thought for You, my iniquities had prevailed over me, and You had to bring me low. But thanks be to God that You provided an atonement in Jesus, and not like those of old, but one which gives complete deliverance, total release.

What Jesus has done has fully satisfied Your righteous demands against my sin, and now I can approach You with praise. What holy boldness I can have now, Lord, not in temerity or fear of judgment, but in the assurance of Your love for me as Your child. May I never take You for granted or in arrogance come before You, but always in the consciousness of my standing solely by grace—no merit of mine. My praise awaits You, Lord God, my praise for who You are and what You have become for me. Every day, I see Your common grace extended to all creatures, Your providential grace in the ordering of my times, and Your sanctifying grace purifying me. How wonderful to begin each day in Your presence.

Psalm 65
To Approach Him

Vs. 4—Blessed *is the man* You choose. And cause to approach *You, That* he man dwell in Your courts. We shall be satisfied with the goodness of Your house, Of Your holy temple. (NKJV)

In America, we do not comprehend what it means to approach royalty, but this is the sense of what David is saying here. He knew from experience the privilege it was for one of the Israelites to approach him as their king, how difficult it was to gain audience before him as king, and how blessed one felt when they were chosen to be ushered into his presence. This is in his mind as he contemplates the blessedness he has that God has chosen him and caused him to approach His presence. For a subject it is presumption to attempt to come into the presence of royalty without being summoned.

Yet, we, as believers, can come boldly, and confidently into the very presence of God. Though we are subjects of the King we are His slaves and also sons of God. All these words, subjects, slaves, and sons, communicate something different about our relationship. However, it is as sons that we are chosen and caused to enter His presence. Paul writes that those who are led by the Spirit of God are the ones who are acting up to the level of sonship, whereas those who are under the law are not acting as sons but as immature children still under nannies and custodians. Let us enjoy and live up to our privilege of sonship by walking in the Spirit and coming boldly and confidently into His presence.

Psalm 66
Rich Fulfillment

Vs. 12—You made men ride over our heads; We went through fire and through water, Yet You brought us out into a *place of* abundance. (NASB 1995)

Truly, Father, all the earth shall worship You and the Son for His great work of redemption. All creation groans, awaiting the coming of Jesus Christ and the revealing of the sons of God. Until that day, Lord, You are working to purge, cleanse, and refine us. You know how much dross there is in my life; You know how prone I am to be weighed down and beset by sin. You know the power of indwelling sin, and You have broken its power and are delivering me every day. Eliminating dross from the silver requires so much heat, and if it were left up to me, I would shout, "Stop! Enough already!" Lord, don't let me interfere with your work; don't let it stop until it has done a complete work. You, Lord, are testing me, trying me, shaping me, and purifying me, and as that work is done, there is rich fulfillment.

In You, I am satisfied; in You alone, I am complete. Oh, that I may know You, and the power of Your resurrection, and the fellowship of Your suffering, as I am being conformed to Your death. To know You more, Jesus, to experience Your life-giving power over sin in my life, to suffer for You as You use me, to no longer have any will of my own, but only Your will. This I will declare, this I will boast in, this is my glory that I have diminished, and Your new life has increased in me.

Psalm 66
Come and See

Vs. 16—Come and hear, all you who fear God; let me tell you what he has done for me. (NIV)

It was with those same simple words spoken to John and Andrew on the shores of the Jordan that Jesus invited them to enter His life. God wants us to enter into His life, thoughts, and ways. Paul tells us that we have the mind of Christ. Just consider what a holy privilege it is to be brought into God's world! We are so used to this fallen world of sin and death that we believe that it is normal. In fact, sin and death is a deviation from what God's desire for our life was. We chose this path, not God. But now God beckons us by the gospel to come and see. Through Jesus, we are able to know and experience the Father. In this Psalm, David exhorts us to see the mighty works of God as He overthrows the rebellion of men, firstly at the Red Sea and then at the River Jordan (verse 6).

But we have greater things than those to contemplate. Jesus has vanquished a far greater enemy through the cross than Moses ever met in Egypt. And when Jesus, in weakness, defeated Satan at the cross He bought us through the waters with Him. This is what Paul means when he writes in I Corinthians 10 that we are all baptized into Jesus as they were all baptized into Moses. And then Jesus brings us into the promised land, our inheritance by faith. So, we see in the crossing of the Jordan coming out in resurrection to enjoy the spiritual blessings we have in heavenly places. Come and see what Christ has done, how He has defeated Satan and Death, and has brought us with Him as the spoils of victory.

MAY 29

Psalm 67
God's Face

Vs. 1—May God be gracious to us and bless us and make
his face to shine upon us, Selah (ESV).

"No man has seen God at any time. The only begotten, who is
in the bosom of the Father, He has declared Him" (John 1:18).
"Show me thy glory ... No man can see me and live" (Exodus 33:18,
20). "But we all, with unveiled face, beholding as in a mirror the
glory of the Lord, are being transformed" (II Corinthians 3:18).
What is it that brings joy to the face of God? Is it not only His Son
Jesus? He could speak from heaven and say, "This is my beloved
Son in whom I am well pleased."

Never before had God been so satisfied with a man upon earth.
And so it was that God's face was ever turned toward Him and
shone upon Him until that dark day of Calvary and those three
hours when He made His soul an offering for sin. Since I have life
in Christ and His Spirit dwells within me, God has caused His face
to shine upon me "to give the light of the knowledge of the glory
of God in the face of Jesus Christ" (II Corinthians 4:6, NASB).
Such is the wondrous place to which the love and grace of God
has brought me; to be in Christ, not in my own righteousness but
to have Him as my righteousness, to be accepted in the beloved,
made a member of the body of Christ, part of His glorious bride,
seated with Him in heavenly places, joint heirs with Him, and the
object of divine favor. Your face shines upon me because of Jesus.

Psalm 67
God's Way

Vs. 2—That thy way may be known upon earth, thy salvation among all nations. (KJV)

Isaiah was told, "Your thoughts are not My thoughts, nor are My ways your ways" says the Lord. God thinks from the perspective of eternity and with the knowledge of omniscience. He knows the ripple effect of every single decision as it rebounds through time, affecting other events. God has a divine purpose in view, and a perfect plan to bring about that purpose, which is why we know that all things work together for good; every possible contingency, all possible decisions, each exercise of man's will and God's interventions have all been incorporated into His divine unfolding of human history so that nothing happens outside of the scope of His will or randomly to catch Him by surprise.

God's way, known completely by Him, becomes known to us either by revelation (prophecy ahead of time) or by the gradual unfolding of the events displaying it (divine providence). God has revealed to us His way of salvation, and there is only one way. That way is through His Son Jesus. Jesus died on Calvary's cross for the sin of the world "according to the determined purpose and foreknowledge of God," was raised from the dead, gaining victory over sin and death, and has entered into heaven there to appear before God for us. This gospel, a stumbling stone to the Jew and foolishness to the Gentile nations, is the wisdom of God and the power of God. It is His only way to Himself.

Psalm 68
Arise

Vs. 1—Let God arise, let his enemies be scattered: let them also that hate him flee before him. (KJV)

Father, when You arise, who can hinder You? When You decree, who can stand against it? What You have established, who can resist? What You have decided who can confound? All powers, all enemies, and resistance must give way before the greatness of Your glory, majesty, and power. And as Your enemies would flee before You in fear, pleading for the mountains to cover them, we, Your children, rejoice. Your Spirit is stirred at the injustice of men, the abuse of power, the oppression that You behold every day. Yet in longsuffering, not willing that any should perish, but that all should come to repentance, You endure the contradiction of sinners. We pray, "thy will be done on earth as it is in heaven." And how is Your will done in heaven? Your will is executed immediately, unquestioningly by the myriads of angels about You faithfully and joyously, for Your angels' greatest desire is to please and serve You.

That is not how Your will is carried out on earth, for there is an adversary, Satan, and a world full of sinful men who love their evil. It is in my heart and life where Your will could be carried out as it is in heaven. Father, shake me to the very core, uproot from me anything that hinders or resists Your will, let nothing be left but what pleases You. You have redeemed me, You have bought me out of the slave market of sin, the ransom price has been paid—and what a terrible price it was, the wrath expended on Your beloved Son. May I be Your slave now whose thought is toward You continually.

Psalm 68
Arise

Vs. 4—Sing to God, sing praises to his name; lift up a song to him who rides through the deserts; his name is the LORD; exult before him! (ESV)

What a triumph, Lord Jesus, You did have. In triumph, You rose from the dead, giving proof of Your victory over Satan, Hades, and death during the 40 days before Your ascension. You condemned sin by nailing it to the cross and all the condemnation of the law that was against us. Now "You have ascended on high and led captivity captive." In Your resurrection and ascension, You emptied the domain of death of all those Old Testament saints and took them to heaven with You. You have risen and are seated on the right hand of the majesty on high.

I must ask myself, "Are You enthroned in my life? Have You, like a morning star, arisen in my heart, shedding its light to every corner of my life? Am I looking for and hastening the day of Your return by giving You the chief seat in my life and living to please You daily?" One day Your Father will tell You that the time has come to rise up and return to the earth, where man said "We will not have this man to reign over us," and establish Your throne and exercise Your rule over all creation. Righteousness will reign, for it will be You reigning with a rod of iron. There will be a great announcement, a glorious procession, singing of praises, hymns of adoration, and all creation will celebrate the revealing of the sons of God. All nations will submit to You. Let this be true of me now; that you rule and reign in my life.

Psalm 68
Daily Benefits

Vs. 19—Blessed be the Lord, who daily bears us up, God
is our salvation Selah (ESV).

In His model prayer, traditionally called the "Our Father" Jesus instructs us to be thankful for God's daily provision for us. He knows how prone we are to begin to take Him for granted, for us to believe that the level of health, wealth, and prosperity is our birthright, and to cease to express heartfelt thanksgiving and dependence upon God. It is a perverse aspect of our human nature that we are usually at our best spiritually when we are in the most dire of circumstances. Rather than prosperity increasing our thanks to Him and prompting even more praise, we begin to ascribe our success to our own efforts and despise the goodness of God.

David is so mindful of all that God has done and sees the intimate connection between His deeds and His character. God always acts consistently with His nature providing good things for all His creatures and defending the most vulnerable of society—the fatherless and the widows. He sees God at work providentially all around him, leading Him to extol God. The little Sunday school song "Count Your Blessings" is not only for the children but also for all of us. As jaded adults, we can become so dull of heart that it takes something extraordinary to capture our attention enough. Little do we realize that what we call common is extraordinary, that daily reminders of His benefits surround us, and it is befitting of us as His children to thank Him for ALL His benefits.

Psalm 69
My Prayer is to You

Vs. 6—Let not them that wait on thee, O Lord GOD
of hosts, be ashamed for my sake: let not those that seek
thee be confounded for my sake, O God of Israel. (KJV)

There is so much I can learn by watching how You responded to
trials and suffering. And what do I see? That Your prayer was continually to God. God, who has all love and all power, yet allowed
You to endure so much contradiction from sinners, could have
prevented You from ever enduring any suffering. You were perfect,
spotless, holy, and therefore deserving of none of it, but He did
not prevent it. And You were never questioning or accusatory. But
if God had kept You from suffering, then how were You to learn
lessons of obedience (Hebrews 5:8), or how were You to be fitted
to be our faithful high priest? (Hebrews 4:15)

Even Job, whose blamelessness God commends, fell into complaining and accusing through his suffering, but never You. Why?
Because You were so utterly convinced of the character of God
that there was no room for doubt. You would ask to be saved; You
would tell God of Your difficulties, You would remind Him of
how difficult suffering in this fallen world is, You would point out
those who hated You and sought Your destruction, and even bring
up Your commitment to God's interests and glory. Yet through it
all, You remain ever faithful. Let this be my disposition too. "But
as for me, my prayer is to You." Lord Jesus. May I let You have Your
way in my life. Keep my little hands from interfering, my little
thoughts from interjecting little ideas. Make me learn to submit
to Your will, trust in Your love, and wing my prayers to You.

Psalm 69
Failing Eyes in a Fainting Heart

Vs. 13—But as for me, my prayer *is* unto thee, O LORD, *in* an acceptable time: O God, in the multitude of thy mercy hear me, in the truth of thy salvation. (KJV)

What hath sin wrought? Was it not my own doing? Did I not choose that path that has led me to this point? I plead to You, O God, to save me. Partly, I need to be delivered from and through these circumstances; I also need You to plumb the depth of my heart and severely deal with my flesh. I sink in the mire of my own failure, but know it will not overwhelm me, for You are with me. For now, Lord, I accept Your hand upon me; I do not resist Your strokes, knowing they are motivated by love. But it hurts, and my eyes fail while I wait for You. Some wish to compound my grief, but I must leave that in Your hands.

Your hand has struck me and so I accept Your chastening; keep me from those who would add to my suffering. My prayer is to You, Lord, for with You is mercy, and mercy triumphs over judgment. Out of these deep waters I call unto You; hear me, Lord, and answer from the storehouse of Your loving kindness. I have brought shame to Your name and brought reproach upon You. For me, this is the worst part. To think that I have done this to the one who died for me! My heart fails me. I am poor in spirit and mournful over my sin, but Your salvation will come; deliverance and restoration are Your goal, and I can thank You now for what You are doing and praise You now for everything that is happening in my life.

Psalm 69
Praise the Name of God

Vs. 18—Draw nigh unto my soul, *and* redeem it: deliver me because of mine enemies. (KJV)

When I sit back and consider for a moment what You have wrought in my life, how can I do anything other than praise Your name? When I think of what sin had done to my heart, how I had allowed bitterness and anger to poison every spring, and from this, Your love has freed me; how can I do other than praise Your name? And when do I praise Him? I praise Him in want and in plenty. My praise may be about the circumstances in my life, but those circumstances do not dictate to me. I praise God in all things because He works all things to my good. It may look awful to me, and I may think that oppressors are having their way, but God only allows what His love can work for good.

And what do I praise Him about? I praise Him for all his dealings with me. I may not understand what He is up to (in fact, we usually don't even have an inkling of what He is after) but I know it is for my good. He wants to conform me to the image of His son Jesus. This means that we need to be softened through suffering so that when He presses us up against Christ, our lives are reshaped to take on His contours. The only thing that pleased the heart of God so much that He could say how much He was well pleased was Jesus Himself. Notice in this Psalm how the desire to praise comes at the end of much suffering, rejection and shame. Let us not only praise Him when we are satisfied with what He has allowed into our lives, but praise His name in all things.

Psalm 70
Seek and Be Glad

Vs. 4—Let all those that seek thee rejoice and be glad in
thee: and let such as love thy salvation say continually,
Let God be magnified. (KJV)

The Lord has guaranteed that those who ask receive, those who
seek find, and those who knock find it opened. The prophet also
was told that those who seek God first find Him when they have
searched for Him with all their heart. Many times, this is used,
appropriately so, in the gospel presentation, but this relationship
of seeking and finding God applies to everything in our lives. Paul
wrote that whether we eat, drink or whatever we do (the most
common, ordinary, mundane things of everyday life), we do it
unto the Lord. We are to seek to see God in every detail and circumstance of our lives. And those who exercise themselves in this
find a joy in life, a gladness of heart that other believers do not have.

This You have taught me, Lord, in these past several years. As I
see You in every detail of my life and accept that You are providentially orchestrating my times, my heart is free to rejoice. Do
I face a difficulty? You have already measured out the intensity
and have packaged it for my good. Do I experience pleasure? This,
too, is from Your hand, for You receive pleasure from seeing Your
child enjoying the life You gave me. Am I oppressed? You are my
strength, helper, and deliverer, and I know by faith that You will
not delay; You are not slack as men count slackness. In everything
I can be glad. You have taught me to be content in whatever circumstances I am in.

Psalm 70
Poor And Needy

Vs. 5—But I *am* poor and needy: make haste unto me,
O God: thou *art* my help and my deliverer; O LORD,
make no tarrying. (KJV)

Do we really have the right view of ourselves before God? The Laodiceans believed they were rich, had become wealthy, and needed nothing. Jesus revealed to them their true condition as being wretched, miserable, poor, blind, and naked. How could a group of believers be so woefully mistaken about their true spiritual condition? Paul refers to the church of the Laodiceans in Colossians 4:16, telling the Colossians to pass their letter on to them and to get a copy of the letter the Laodiceans have. Yet now, less than four decades later, Jesus scorches the Laodiceans with this indictment.

Jesus sees us as we really are and, through His Spirit, communicates that to us. In the Sermon on the Mount, He stated the beginning of all spiritual blessing—seeing ourselves as poor in spirit, spiritual paupers. In myself, I am always destitute with nothing to offer God but hands full of sin. But by faith in Christ, I have been made a new creature in Him and can walk in that new life in His power—the power of His resurrection, i.e. victory over sin in my life. The more I walk with Christ, the more I see my own emptiness and His all-sufficiency. In myself, I am nothing, but in Him, I am complete and have everything I need to live a life pleasing to Him. May I ever be emptied of self and full of Christ, poor and needy in myself but having the fullness of His Spirit.

Psalm 71
Upheld from Birth

Vs. 6—By thee have I been holden up from the womb:
thou art he that took me out of my mother's bowels: my
praise *shall* be continually of thee. (KJV)

This Psalm tells me so much of the character of Your life. Even from the early part of Your youth, You had learned to trust in God. You saw Your life under the providential care of God, that He was ordering Your life. God had knit You together, and He had His eye on You in the womb. And this was not solely because You were the Son of God, but this is true of all of God's elect. Luke writes that You grew in stature and favor with God and man. Those quiet, silent years that the gospels pass over so briefly were formative in Your character and manner of life. You lived Your life ever in the consciousness of being before God. From Your youth, You were in God's school and brought up by Him.

So when wicked men rose up against You to destroy You, You instinctively turned to God as Your refuge. You had the authority to call down legions of angels who would have happily come to Your deliverance, but what would that have shown? What we see, Lord, is Your tremendous strength of character coupled with Your supreme gentleness. So many men falsely interpreted Your gentleness as weakness, but how more mistaken could they be! Your hope was continually in God; even on the cross, when in agony of body and soul, You still called out to God. You knew You had been forsaken for our sins, but God would bring You up from death itself, from the depth of the earth, to exalt You at His right hand in glory.

Psalm 71
Continual Hope

Vs. 5—For thou *art* my hope, O Lord GOD: *thou art* my
trust from my youth. (KJV)

When life begins to unravel and things are not turning out how
you think they *ought* to, where do you turn for the strength to
carry on? And how do you find a reason to pick up and keep
going? Such is the role of hope in our spiritual lives. Hope takes
us beyond ourselves and our small, provincial outlook in our lives
and causes us to look outside of ourselves to God for the reason
for living and continuing. Hope is not a vague, wistful, pie-in-
the-sky power of positive thinking. Hope is grounded in the firm
expectation that God is true to His word and what He has promised shall come to pass. One thing He has promised, "I will never
leave you or forsake you." Jesus was forsaken on the cross by God
so that we may never be forsaken. His presence with us is assured,
which communicates that His power and resources are also with
us during the trial.

Another promise is that He makes all things work together for
good. Paul does not explain how God does that nor does he tell
us what the good thing specifically is that God will bring about,
but we are assured that He is doing exactly that. This communicates to the soul that the events of your life are not random, not at
the whim of forces outside of control acting in any fashion they
choose, but that everything is purposeful and completely under
God's sovereign control. No matter how illogical life appears
and pointless it seems, God has a meaning and purpose for all
events and all human suffering and shall reveal that purpose at the
coming of Jesus. Until then, we rest in His love, place our faith in
Him, and lay hold onto the hope He sets before us.

Psalm 72
He Shall Reign

Vs. 4—He shall judge the poor of the people, he shall
save the children of the needy, and shall break in pieces
the oppressor. (KJV)

What a glorious day it shall be when Jesus reigns supreme over
all the earth and subdues all powers and authorities. When He
reigns, righteousness will finally have full sway and expression in
this world. There will be justice, not corruption; peace, not conflict; righteousness, not oppression. Any human king or human
authority that would dare to oppress the poor or needy will be
broken in pieces. There shall be fear of God throughout the world,
respect for His authority and dread of his judgments. Because evil
is suppressed, righteous people flourish and experience joy in their
God. All the nations serve Him.

Isaiah tells us of how the nations bring their glory to King Jesus
in Jerusalem and if they do not, then rain is withheld and they
are afflicted with plagues. "He shall live." Jesus is the one who
died and is alive for evermore and so He tells John in Revelation.
Truly, Lord, the center of all the world's attention, all the world's
blessing, all the world's glory will be You personally. So, let it be
now in my life. May You reign supreme and uncontested in my
heart. May You ruthlessly uproot any sinful, wicked, selfish ten-
dency that would spring up within. Do not spare, dear Lord, for
it all must go. Let Your Spirit look into every nook and cranny and
remove any vestige of mere fleshly indulgence. Let me even now
be so captivated by Your glory that I can say, "Not I but Christ…"

Psalm 72
Daily Praise

Vs. 17—His name shall endure for ever: his name shall
be continued as long as the sun: and *men* shall be blessed
in him: all nations shall call him blessed. (KJV)

This Psalm, ascribed to Solomon by David or written by Solomon
himself, has a far greater fulfillment than any mere human poten-
tate (monarch) could accomplish. Only Jesus Himself reigning in
His splendor could ever accomplish all that this Psalm intends in
the future display of His glory on David's throne. But why should
we wait for some future day when we, who comprise subjects of
His Kingdom on earth, can now acknowledge His sovereignty
in our lives? When we look at our relationship with Christ, we
are both His body, members of Him who is the head in heaven,
and also, in relationship to this world, citizens of His Kingdom
in heaven exercised in our hearts and lives here on earth. Hence,
we are His ambassadors representing the King whose Kingdom
is not of this world (not of human origin or built upon human
principles), yet one day will come with Him to this world.

Until then, we can show Him our fidelity by praising Him daily.
Our daily praise will be a constant reminder to us that we live for
Him who gave Himself for us and that our lives only have meaning in relationship to Him. It will also be a constant reminder to
the world that the One they have rejected is seated at God's right
hand, is coming one day to this world, and with Him they must
give account. Let our praise daily rise to Him as a sweet savor.

Psalm 73
In the Sanctuary

Vs. 17—Until I went into the sanctuary of God; *then* understood I their end. (KJV)

In the sanctuary is where I need to be, Lord, so I can see things as they truly are. There, I can have Your perspective and be assured of Your sovereign care. When I'm out in this world, I see evil triumphing, wickedness having its own way. Here in the trenches, it can feel as if You are so remote, unaware, uncaring, and untouched by the affliction I experience. In the world, I get envious, my flesh is stirred up, and then I have to catch myself. Can I ever truly understand anything apart from Your perspective? Everything in life must be seen in its relationship to You, for You are the center of all of God's plans and counsels.

It is never to be about me, it is always about You, Your glory, Your interests, Your desires, and then about how my life can be an example, a testimony to them. Even my sin, as awful as it was, will still somehow be used to Your glory, though I can't conceive of how. Faith tells me it is so. When I consider life and all of its suffering and sorrow, it can be quite painful and, apart from You, unbearable. But now I see Your sovereignty, Your power to bring to pass what Your wisdom has conceived, and Your love formed in Your mind so that the vexation and agitation have been replaced by peace and rest. Whom have I but You to which to turn, from which to draw strength, to whom to draw near. I am learning what it means for You to be my all in all.

Psalm 73
Embittered

Vs. 21, 22—When my heart was embittered … Then I was senseless... (NASB 1995).

What a terrible trap bitterness truly was. It poisoned and distorted my every thought toward the object of my bitterness. And it didn't end there. It slowly began to seep into other areas of my life and affect them as well. Bitterness becomes an obsession. Each new instance of conflict reinforces the bitterness. As the mind mulls over it, it adds new layers of blaming, rationalization, and justification to whatever feeling one has. No longer can you look rationally at the person. They become the reason and cause of your problems, so you absolve yourself of any weakness or responsibility. You pour over every detail and new offense to strengthen the false logic you have used to harbor those feelings against them. You make yourself the victim rather than looking to the Lord for the deliverance you need.

Paul describes this root of bitterness that springs up, defiling many, but long before it springs up, it has been laying down its tentacles, securing it within. What you bury inwardly will eventually be expressed outwardly. What a hard thing God had to do to bring me to my senses. He knew my heart; He knew that I would never come clean with it on my own and that He would have to dynamite it all out. But thanks be to God that after the blast destroyed the tree with its roots, He was still there to put the pieces of my life back together again.

Psalm 73
God is Good

Vs. 28—But *it is* good for me to draw near to God: I
have put my trust in the Lord GOD, that I may declare
all thy works. (KJV)

And why is God good to Israel? Is it due to their righteousness,
their dedication to God's things, their own goodness or greatness?
The answer is a categorical "No!". God is good to Israel because
of His love for them, which originates solely within Himself and
not in response to anything on their part. And so it is for us who,
by faith, have become children of God, sons of Abraham spiritually. All that we have and all that we are, we owe to God's grace
ministered to us in Christ. God's goodness is the expression of His
love in practical ways. All the blessings and all the promises stem
from God's love made available to us through Christ. Let us never
try to earn God's goodness; let us never think that God is good to
us because of anything we have done, that in any way we deserve
God's goodness, that He is obligated to us in any way. All of it is
pure grace; all of it is because of what Christ has done.

Truly, God is good to us; He is a blessing God. He loves to give
good things and wants to bless us more than we could ever imagine. Ephesians tells us that we are blessed with all spiritual blessings
in heavenly places in Christ. Though eye has not seen nor ear heard
what God has prepared for us, He has already revealed that secret
to us through His Spirit if we would only see and hear. God is
good; may we never doubt His goodness.

Psalm 74
God's Turtledove

Vs. 19—O deliver not the soul of thy turtledove unto the multitude of *the wicked:* forget not the congregation of thy poor for ever. (KJV)

What a beautiful picture of the Lord Jesus—as a turtledove, innocent, gentle, harmless. In Leviticus, we read of how a burnt offering could be a turtledove. That tells me of how You were offered completely, totally to God as a sweet-smelling savor, as my acceptance! No acceptance have I in myself, only what I have in You. The turtledove could also be offered as a trespass offering. And is it not I who has trespassed, crossed the line and violated God's holy standard? Yet it was You who has suffered for my transgression and made restitution to restore what You did not take away. When the time came, You had to go all the way to death for me, to be delivered up to the wild beast, to death, so that I might not be.

When I read this Psalm, I see that You do not cast off forever; it only feels that way while undergoing Your chastening. Your anger does smoke, for although you hate my sin, you still love me. I see the havoc that sin has brought into my life, but know that in Your perfect will, You are cleaning out my life so that I can be a vessel, sanctified, and meet for Your use. When You withdrew Your hand, the hedge of protection, it was actually for my good so that You could deal with my flesh and I could learn to be cast upon You. And now I see You arising in my life, ascending the throne, taking Your rightful place. You have made me Your turtledove.

Psalm 74
Cast Off?

Vs. 7—They have cast fire into thy sanctuary, they have defiled *by casting down* the dwelling place of thy name to the ground. (KJV)

Sometimes, we, as believers, feel cast off by God. We pray, but heaven seems silent; we are in distress, but God seems to either not see or not care. At times like those, God is trying to tell you something. He is trying to speak to you, but He can't get through to you. If we think of our mind as a radio, then we have the notion that we can pick up signals from many different sources. However, unless we have set our radio to the proper station, then we either get static or pick up the wrong station and get the wrong message.

Jesus was forsaken by God for us so that we would never be forsaken. So, when we feel cast off and forsaken of God, it is only the way it feels experientially, but not the way it is objectively. So, as the Psalmist Asaph does, go to God with all of your feelings and tell Him what you are experiencing. He desires honesty in our inward being. Then, tune out the loud reasonings of your mind and the anxieties of your heart. Fear screams so loudly that it can drown out the still, small voice of God. Just stick with God, keep supplicating Him, bring your needs to Him, and let Him calm your fears. As your mind quiets and your heart settles, you will begin to hear faint sounds of His voice get through the noise. You will find that He has been there with you all the time.

Psalm 75
God My Judge

Vs. 7—But God *is* the judge: he putteth down one, and setteth up another. (KJV)

When David had sinned in the matter of numbering the people, he did not follow the law described in Exodus 30 and brought judgment upon himself and his people. When God gave him three choices, he said, "Let us fall into the hands of the Lord, for His mercies are great, but do not let me fall into the hands of men" (II Samuel 24:14, NIV). Lord, You have taught me the value of these words. It is to You that I am primarily responsible for all my evil, and from You as my Judge that You have dealt with me. And that has been in mercy, for You have not punished me after the manner that my sin deserved, but according to Your mercy. You knew how to deal with me. You bore with me in longsuffering and patience, and I frankly wonder how You could put up with me for so long. I acted so wickedly and with such callous disregard, but then You brought me before Your judgment seat and began that great work of sifting, refining, threshing and separating.

May I not interfere with Your great work. Man may punish me for what I have done, but their punishment will not accomplish Your ends. May Your Spirit have free access to every area of my life and purify my heart. I will have so much to declare of Your hand of restoration; may I praise You daily for what You are doing.

Psalm 75
The Proper Time

Vs. 1—Unto thee, O God, do we give thanks, *unto thee* do we give thanks: for *that* thy name is near thy wondrous works declare. (KJV)

As you read the gospel of John, note how often it is written that they couldn't take Him for it was not His time. God has His proper time when He, in His sovereignty, has decreed that such and such a thing shall take place. If God could not work something to the good to serve His purpose, then it just wouldn't happen. Our difficulty comes when we cannot accept a circumstance in our life and, like Job, challenge God to explain Himself. God rarely explains Himself but allows us to see the unfolding of His ways and be strengthened in our faith.

Another difficulty arises when we want God to be on our schedule, to execute His plan in our time frame. But God doesn't build an oak tree in a day; He not only has the end in view, but the when in view. We, by faith, must trust God for both the results and the timing for them. In this Psalm, Asaph is expecting the judgment of God to fall on His enemies. Now if you had asked the early church who was their biggest enemy they would have nominated Saul of Tarsus as their poster child. But God had other things in mind and, at the proper time, revealed it. When what God is doing makes no sense and His delay in providing deliverance is equally wrapped in mystery, trust in the character of God and look for Him to work all things to the good in His proper time.

Psalm 76
God Makes Himself Known

Vs. 8, 9—Thou didst cause judgment to be heard from
heaven; the earth feared, and was still, When God arose
to judgment, to save all the meek of the earth. Selah.
(KJV)

God shall be known, and He shall be owned. He shall either be
known personally or shall be experienced providentially. Lord,
You have taught me both ways. You taught me to know You
through Your love, energy, and forgiveness of my sins. Through
conversion and new birth, I was brought into Your family, made a
member of Your body, and became a living stone in Your temple.
You taught me how to honor and worship You, to pray and supplicate Your name, to rejoice in Your presence. I learned that You
dwelt within me, that I had new life, and was animated in that new
life by Your Holy Spirit who was shed abroad in my heart to cause
me to love and worship You. All the more does it show how terrible
my sin was—to have spurned Your face and ignored the conviction
of the Holy Spirit in order to continue in it. Your word teaches me
that even "the wrath of man shall praise You."

Your sovereignty is so absolute that everything that happens is part
of Your unfolding plan leading to Your glorification. Somehow,
You will work this sin to Your glory. It is inconceivable to my finite
mind how that could possibly be, but then again, if I could comprehend Your ways, that would make You pretty small. Since You
have dealt with me harshly, as I needed, You have made Yourself
known so much more clearly. As Paul said, "To know Him" is the
highest privilege, and I thank You for it.

Psalm 76
God is Known

Vs. 4—Thou *art* more glorious *and* excellent than the
mountains of prey. (KJV)

It is the great privilege of the believer to know God and to be
known by Him. Our knowledge of God is not that of the philosopher who, using his reason, thoughts, and experiences, creates
a God that appeals to him and his ideas, gratifying and excusing
himself. But we know that God is inscrutable, that it is only by
revealing Himself that we ever have a right knowledge of Him.
And God has fully revealed Himself in His Son, Jesus. When
Philip asked that Jesus show them the Father, Jesus replied, "If
you've seen Me you've seen the Father." All that can be known
and understood of God has been fully revealed and seen in Jesus,
His nature, and Godhead.

In the law, some aspects of the nature of God, such as His righteousness, holiness, and greatness, were on display. But there was
so much more that God wanted to reveal of Himself and a deeper
relationship into which he wanted to draw men to Himself than
the law could ever accomplish in that it was weak through the
flesh. So, "in the fullness of time God sent forth His Son." In Jesus,
God has fully made Himself known and invites us to enter into
a relationship with Him through Jesus. By faith in Him and His
sacrifice on the cross, we have been born of God by incorruptible seed and made partakers of the divine nature. We are now
complete in Christ and seated with Him in heavenly places. He
wants us far more than we could ever want Him and proved it at
the cross. Draw ever closer to Him, give your heart and life fully
to Him, and let Him make Himself ever more known to you daily.

Psalm 77
To Be Truly Comforted

Vs. 1—I cried unto God with my voice, *even* unto God
with my voice; and he gave ear unto me. (KJV)

What would it have taken to comfort Your soul while walking
here below? Was there anyone who could have? You were the perfect man living in this fallen world, seeing all of the sin, knowing
that we were destroying ourselves by it, and giving no thought
to You. What it must have been like, day in and day out, dealing
with our hardened hearts and the consequences of our sin and we
were giving so little concern to it at all. And then the time came,
Your hour when You would be made an offering for our sins. You
had to drink of the cup of God's wrath unmingled, and no one
could share that burden with You, no way that the load could be
lightened. You could not then be comforted.

Will the Lord cast off forever? No! Just look in the sanctuary, and
You shall see. Will He be favorable no more? No! For God is the
One who does wondrously. Has His mercy ceased, His promises
failed? No! For with His arm, He has shown His strength. Has
God forgotten to be gracious? No! For with His arm, He has
redeemed His people. Your time of comfort would come because
"You would look upon the travail of Your soul and be satisfied";
You had a joy set before You so You would endure. Your Father
would receive You back into glory.

Psalm 77
Songs in the Night

Vs. 6—I call to remembrance my song in the night: I commune with mine own heart: and my spirit made diligent search. (KJV)

Asaph is crying out to God amid his distress and need. He is beset by troubles way beyond his control. The difficulties are so great that he is unable to receive comfort. Evening, rather than being a time to rest and rejuvenate, becomes a long stretch of anxiety and supplication. He doesn't understand why he is so beset; he complains to God about his circumstances, he feels completely overwhelmed by his trials, and even thinking about God doesn't ease his sense of trouble. Have you ever been where Asaph has been? If not, then trust me, one day you shall. And what is one to do when in the midst of that? Keep coming to God; never give up on God; keep assailing the throne of grace.

As we are honest with God about our feelings, thoughts, and desires He can slowly begin the transformative work He has in mind. Our prayers begin to change from telling God what He "ought" to do to accept what He is doing. Our thoughts, running wildly in circles, begin to spiral in on His will to be done. Our feelings of anxiety and dread give way slowly to songs of praise. Asaph begins to call to mind all of God's former care and faithfulness toward him; he meditates upon them and composes songs in the night. We can anchor ourselves amid life's tempestuous seas upon one simple truth: "I am the same yesterday, today, and tomorrow." Compose your songs in the night and rejoice in the continuity of God's character, meditate within your heart and rest in His love.

Psalm 78
Our Hope Set in God

Vs. 7—That they might set their hope in God, and not forget the works of God, but keep his commandments...
(KJV).

What does it take for a man to set his hope in God? Unfortunately, for many of us, it comes only after all other resources have been expended, all our ideas have come to naught, and we are brought to our extremity. We read the stories in the bible as if they were mythological fairy tales, that they really didn't happen, rather than seeing them as history more certain than the morning paper. Or we read the stories in the bible, but conclude that God just wouldn't, couldn't, doesn't act that way anymore, as if we have a different God from them. But God has recorded these stories for us so that we would set our hope in Him. You have made known Your deeds to prior generations, and they have become our heritage of faith so that we would not repeat their foolishness and stubbornness but set our hope in God. But just as they sinned, so do we too. We don't sin the same specific way, but the end result is the same: we rebel against You and Your revealed will.

When You take us into the wilderness, it is not to starve us, to afflict us, but that we might learn that You are the only source of satisfaction and sustenance. You gave them manna so that they would learn that "man does not live by bread alone" (Deuteronomy 8:3). You test us in our hearts to reveal to us what is really there. You know what is there already and engineer the circumstance to expose it to the light of truth. May we learn, precious Father, to depend upon You having our hope, our hearts, set.

Psalm 78
Eating Angel's Food

Vs. 25—Man did eat angels' food: he sent them meat
to the full. (KJV)

When I am hungry, what do I desire? What do I look for to satisfy my needs? Do I really understand what my need truly is? The woman at the well came thinking she knew what she needed and how to satisfy it, but after a short conversation with Jesus, she discovered a deeper need and another supply. In the wilderness, the children of Israel hungered after meat. God gave them their desire but judged them for it, and they were sickened when their desire was fulfilled. Isn't that how we are? We desire after things and conceive of how God ought to meet our need (or is it just a desire, a want?) to show us that it cannot satisfy. He gave them the bread of heaven; they ate angels' food.

I must realize that I do not truly know what my needs are much less how they are to be met and satisfied. God always has a higher idea than us. We would be satisfied to settle for far less than what God has in mind for us. Did they not know that they fed upon what angels had been enjoying for their entire existence—the Son of God? (John 6:33) Even then, it was not enough, not to their liking; they would grow to loathe that light bread. Dear saint of God, examine your heart carefully; let the Holy Spirit search it out. Have you lost your first love and begun to hold to the head less and less? No one was more surprised to read that than the Ephesians. Keep feeding on Jesus, His body and blood, His person and life.

Psalm 78
Limiting God

Vs. 8—...a stubborn and rebellious generation, whose
hearts were not loyal to God, whose spirits were not
faithful to him. (NIV)

When He slew them, then they sought Him. Such is the perversity
of sin that we bring God to such an extremity before we seek Him.
We pray for things to go well, and when He blesses us, what do we
do? We go on as if we don't need Him; we are unthankful and soon
disregard Him. Have you been there? I have, and what a terrible
thing He had to do to get me to earnestly seek Him and return to
Him. When I had sinned so great, then He laid me low so He could
forgive me, lift me up, and restore me. He was so full of compassion that He did not deal with me after the manner of sin deserved
and forgave my iniquity. He knows that I am but flesh, but that
is no excuse. I had Christ living in me and all the resources of the
Holy Spirit at my disposal, but I indulged my flesh and yielded my
members as instruments of unrighteousness.

It is I who limited the effectiveness of God in my life. God did not
violate my will. I continued to grieve the Holy Spirit and, by my
actions, dared Him to act. Lord, you brought me to the point of
seeing my wretchedness for what it truly is, to see my flesh to be
as corrupt as You always knew it was. Lord, let there be no more
provoking, tempting, or grieving Your heart. I don't want to limit
You anymore. Teach me Lord to trust and depend on You, to worship and adore You, to love You fully and completely—without
limitation.

Psalm 78
Putting God to the Test

Vs. 18—And in their heart they put God to the test…
(NASB).

Lord, I know that You must test my faith. You teach me in Deuteronomy 8:2 that You test my faith to reveal what is in my heart. Peter states in his epistle that trials reveal the genuineness of our faith. When You put me through a trial, it is not that You need to find out anything, but that You need to reveal it to me. And as the assayer uses fire to separate and purge out the impurities, so You do for our faith. Why, then, do I put You to the test? What is there about me and my nature that I would presume to put you to the test? According to this Psalm, I do this in order to please my own fleshly desires. I see within me something that screams out , "I want it my way and I want it now!" My deceitful heart tells me that if You really loved me, then You would do this for me. And then when You don't dance to my tune, I complain against You and accuse You of a lack of love. Little wonder Jeremiah would proclaim the heart to be deceitful above all things and desperately wicked.

But there is another way that one can put You to the test – it is by persisting in sin. I look back now and see that by pursuing my sinful course, I was actually daring You to do something about it. Was I going to stop myself? Why should I? My flesh was enjoying itself. And as Your Holy Spirit sought to bring conviction to me, I persisted. And why was that? My life and circumstances made me so utterly miserable that my sin gave me the only pleasure to my life. What a miserable wretch I had become! It was Your love that would finally arrest me in this downward course. You saw all along where it was leading, and, in Your love, brought it to an end.

Psalm 78
Ready to Seek God?

Vs. 34—When He killed them, then they sought Him…
(NASB).

What is it about my human nature that required You to go to such an extent? What is it about sin that makes it so hard to relinquish it? It is not that the sin benefits me, that it will enhance my life or fulfill me. So, what is it? It is that I have indwelling sin—the sin that is in my flesh. And what I found is that being born again did not redeem my flesh. Yes, I was given a new nature and made a new creation. Yes, I had Your Holy Spirit dwelling in me. I was given spiritual life as well as a new heart sanctified by Your presence and Your word. Is that now what You meant when You told Nicodemus that he had to be born of the Water and the Spirit? But all that left my flesh unchanged, and though I have this treasure from You, it is in an earthen vessel.

Your word tells me of how You first tried to draw me back to You with kindness, but as that proved ineffective, then You must use strokes of chastisement. But even in those strokes, I can still see Your love and compassion. You didn't just level the boom all at once; rather, You gave me any number of opportunities for escape. Your word assures me that I will not be tempted over what I can bear but will, with the temptation, give me a way of escape. But I did not want to escape, did I? So I drove down the highway of my sin and ignored Your exit ramps. You saw that my mind was set upon satisfying my flesh to comfort myself in my misery. I forced You to slay me, to destroy my life, but You gloriously gave it back to me renewed and refreshed (albeit a little banged up for wear). Thank You, Jesus, for Your unspeakable grace.

Psalm 78
His restraint

Vs. 38—...And often He restrained His anger... (NASB).

Have you ever thought of how angry God is with sin? And that is not with sin in general or with sinfulness but with your sin and mine specifically. God hates all sin; all sin is an affront to His pure, holy nature. If God were not a God of absolute love, then His absolute holiness would have demanded the immediate judgment of Adam and Eve once they had sinned. Just consider how often He must restrain His anger. Every errant thought, word, and deed is copiously recorded in His books, and everyone who is not covered by the blood of Jesus will be brought up and dealt with at the Great White Throne. We who are mortal flesh and so accustomed to sin make light of much of our sins. We are so used to sin that we often do not even see it. And we spend much of our lives excusing, rationalizing, minimizing, and justifying our sin that we have fooled ourselves into believing that God sees our sin the same way we do. But He does not!

It is only because of Jesus' death on the cross that He restrains His anger at all. For any who have placed their faith in His finished work on the cross, rest assured that His blood fully pays for your sin, and you are completely justified and made right in your relationship to God. And once having been justified by His blood, let us not revert to those games we once played—for God does not play games with sin. If I do revert back to game-playing about my sin, then God will chasten me as His son, but I will never be an object of His wrath. Jesus bore God's wrath against my sin; He was forsaken so I would never be!

Psalm 79
Tender Mercies

Vs. 10—Why should the nations say, "Where is their God?" Before our eyes, make known among the nations that you avenge the outpoured blood of your servants. (NIV)

When we are going through difficulties, sorrows, or chastening, we are prone to ask God, "How long?" We know He is a God of love, but it doesn't feel very loving. We know He is a God of wisdom, but there doesn't appear to be much sense to it. We often forget to consider that, long before we ever asked that question of God, He asked it of us. How long, oh man? Will your lust burn forever? Will your desires burn like fire within your heart? Will you not stop yourself, responding to the prompting of My Spirit, or must I strike you?

Before Nebuchadnezzar's army would slay the multitudes in Jerusalem, Ezekiel saw the angel marking on the forehead those who God chose to survive (see Ezekiel 9). That is a terrible work, but it is what my sin compels God to do. He must decide the level and extent of the chastening necessary to accomplish His ends, which are perfect in love and wisdom. The fact that I am not consumed is a tender mercy. The fact that so much of my life has been swept away is a tender mercy, for He has left so much that remains. Lord, I need to begin seeing this all from Your perspective. Spare me from the torment of Job, who began on a high note of faith and was goaded by his three "miserable comforters" to question God's character. What You are doing in my life is for Your glory, to glorify Your name. And for this, I can give You thanks forever.

Psalm 79
Your Wrath

Vs. 2—They have left the dead bodies of your servants as food for the birds of the sky, the flesh of your own people for the animals of the wild. (NIV)

There are times when it seems like the world can't get any worse, yet it does. We wonder how God can put up with a world that is so depraved, far from God, uninterested in His interests, and hostile against His people. Then we start wondering, as Habakkuk did, asking how much longer He can put up with the evil He sees. Our Lord said, "I have not come to judge the world, but to save it." If Jesus had set Himself up as Judge, then where would it end? Who would have been left standing? But Jesus came to die on the cross, and it was upon Him that God was finally able to fully pour out His wrath against our sin.

Now, Jesus wants us to take His gospel of forgiveness to an unforgiving world; He wants us to take this glorious news to lost mankind so that they too can be under the blood and saved from the wrath that is surely coming. Now is the day of grace; now is the time for men and women to repent of their sins, for a day of wrath is coming, and who will be able to stand on that day? In the Revelation, we read of a day when the saints will once again be asking God, "How long?" They plead for God's vengeance and wrath to be poured out, which shall be appropriate. But for this day of grace, let us pray for men to repent and ask for forgiveness while there is still time.

Psalm 80
Between the Cherubim

Vs. 1, 2—Hear us, Shepherd of Israel, you who lead
Joseph like a flock. You who sit enthroned between
the cherubim, shine forth, before Ephraim, Benjamin
and Manasseh, Awaken your might; come and save us.
(NIV)

To any who reads Your description of Yourself as "dwelling
between the cherubim," he must sit bolt upright and take note.
These are not the cute, pudgy, baby-like beings falsely portrayed
in art but the awesome, wondrous guardians of Your honor. They
knelt over the ark of the covenant and overspread their wings.
Inside the ark were the (second) tablets of the law, Aaron's rod
that budded, and a container of manna. Upon the lid of the ark,
the mercy seat, was placed the blood of the goat from the Day of
Atonement. The cherubim looked down upon that blood, showing that only a sacrifice stood between God's wrath against sin
(embodied in the law) and us, his sin-cursed creatures. That blood
was the fulcrum upon which the fate of the entire world pivoted,
and only the death of Christ on Cavalry provided the perfect sacrifice, the perfect blood which alone could put away sin.

Isaiah, in his prophecy, describes a vision of seraphim, the guardians of Your holiness, flying and declaring "Holy, holy, holy." Glory
and holiness, glory and holiness. I must never let my thoughts
of God descend to a merely human understanding. This great,
mighty, majestic God condescends to let me call Him Father, and
He calls me His child—all because His Son Jesus perfectly upheld
God's glory and holiness in this sin-cursed place. Hallelujah.

Psalm 80
Making a Meal out of Tears

Vs. 5—You have fed them with the bread of tears; you
have made them drink tears by the bowlful. (NIV)

You, Lord, know the path of true restoration. How much I would
like to be spared that deep work in the soul required before real
restoration can occur. You must bring me to the point of true,
godly sorrow leading to repentance. I must see my sin for what it is,
taste the awfulness of Your sensibilities regarding it. If I stop at the
consequences of my sin in my life I remain selfish. If I stop at the
consequences of my sin in the lives of my family and my friends,
then I stop at human sorrow. I must go all the way to godly sorrow,
to see my sin in all of its awfulness and offense to you, to abhor
my flesh which craved it, to abhor myself in sackcloth and ashes
(Job 42). I must let You feed me with the bread made from my
own tears—to do as the priests did and eat the sin offering, and to
drink deeply of the sorrow Your Spirit brings; to do nothing that
would in any way try to soften the blow, to take no wine mingled
with gall to deaden the pain.

And when Your work is done (and only You can set the time for
that, for only You know the heart), the work of restoration has
begun. How long? You were only angry for awhile; it just seemed
like forever. You have restored me, Your face shines upon me, and
the joy has returned. It is like coming back from the dead, being
revived and having life back.

Psalm 81
Will I Listen?

Vs. 13, 14—If only My people would listen to Me, if Israel would follow My ways, how soon I would subdue their enemies and turn My hand against their foes! (BSB)

Just what does it take for God to get your attention? What does He need to do to get you to take notice? For Elijah, it was in the small, still voice. Are you only responsive to a shout, a yell, a thunderclap? God should not need to speak above a whisper. If He needs to, then what noise is over-shouting His voice? Have I allowed worldliness to creep in? Have I begun to indulge myself in *harmless* ways that crowd out time with the Lord and His interests? Has sin begun to gain ground? Am I even noticing? So what will You, Lord, do when my heart grows distant and cold? When I was in need and called out to You, You heard me. As troubles came upon me, often of my own design, You delivered me.

But a time comes when You must test me to expose whether I have grown. What is my Meribah going to be—the place where you will put me to the test? Whatever the specific will be, it will have this feature: Will I trust You to be true to Your word for my life? Oh how You must admonish and hem me in and frustrate my plans. Have I made an idol out of my lifestyle, my family, my job, or my possessions? Lord, I must confess how easy it is to forget about You, to have a day go by and give You so little thought, so little of me. Your Spirit is beckoning to me; I have come to desire You, desire time with You. Give me an attentive heart.

Psalm 81
Given Over

Vs. 11, 12—"But my people would not listen to me; Israel would not submit to me. So I gave them over to their stubborn hearts to follow their own devices." (NIV)

Lord, I must confess that I just would not listen to You. You tried to get through to me, but my heart was hardened. Your Spirit tried to convict me, but I would not respond. I persisted in what I desired, tried to manage it, and kept it under wraps. What I see now is that You gave me over to it. You could have struck me down, but You chose to give me over. Is this what Paul means when he writes, "To turn one over to Satan for the destruction of the flesh that his spirit may be saved in the day of the Lord Jesus"? It is a terrible thing to be given over to one's sin—to the stubborn heart that seeks to pursue its course. And why did You do this? So that I would listen. You knew that nothing less would finally get my attention, but You also knew just how severe it had to be to finally reach me.

You have my attention; I am listening. Teach me to walk in Your ways. I don't mean the do's and don'ts of what people commonly consider walking right. No, Father, I want to walk in Your **ways**, Your thoughts, Your feelings, Your attitudes. I want to begin seeing things Your way, no longer trying to get You to see it my way. At Meribah, You fed them with quail and water from the rock. You had wanted to feed them with honey from the rock. Dear Father, may that sweetness become part of my life; may I be given over to Your service.

Psalm 82
Ye are god's, but...

Vs. 6, 7—"I said, "You are "gods"; you are all sons of the Most High.' But you will die like mere mortals; you will fall like every other ruler." (NIV)

What does "Ye are gods" mean? In Exodus 4:16, God tells Moses that he shall be god to Pharaoh, that he shall stand in the place of God, not that Moses shall be a god. And so the principle is established that to those who represent God in this world, who stand in His place as visible representations of Him, He declares, "Ye are gods." And our Lord in John 10:34, 35 makes this same point, "If He called them gods by whom the word of God came..." To have the privilege to be God's representative in this world is a high and holy one, and along with it comes the commensurate responsibility to be holy as He is holy. But if not... then what?

The judgment God pronounces is to die like men. This Lord, You have executed in part upon me—to have preached Your word and taught Your people has brought upon me a severer judgment, and that is to be expected (James 3:1). I do not chaff at what You are doing, do not argue, plead, or fuss. Whatever goads You have used on me to move me in the way I need to go I will not kick against. Everything You do is good, all planned out by Your beneficent providence, measured out by Your love and grace, and will continue until Your wisdom sees the end accomplished. I did not die like a man. My old life is gone; a new life looms ahead. Your grace has triumphed over judgment, and I am glad.

Psalm 82
God in the Midst

Vs. 1—God presides in the great assembly; he renders judgment among the "gods" (NIV).

We know that, "where two or three are gathered unto my name, there am I in the midst of them." But is this only sentiment or living reality? Is it only a theological position, or is it truly my spiritual position? We have the awesome privilege of God in our midst, Him in the congregation of His saints. Since this is true, how does it affect my conduct, my demeanor, the solemnity and the respect I give to Him there, and do I prepare myself ahead of time to enjoy His presence? I must confess that there are times when I have been more preoccupied with worldly things and not the things of Christ. Let me never take the fact of His real presence casually. Let it never become a ritual or cold formality. It should be fresh.

We all know the difference between fresh fruit and stale fruit. Am I letting my life for Christ become stale and commonplace, or is there freshness to my spiritual life? When I open the word, do I expect the Holy Spirit to give me a precious thought of Jesus or a deeper, more genuine understanding of a truth? When I pray, do I do so knowing that God is listening, and do I then listen to "hear what the Spirit says to the churches?" Do I expect a blessing in the gatherings of the Lord's people as we meet together around Him? God is in the congregation; let us be mighty ones.

Psalm 83
Do not be Still

Vs. 1—O God, do not remain silent, do not turn a deaf
ear, do not stand aloof, O God. (NIV)

You told David that because of his sin, he gave occasion for those to
blaspheme Your name. For us who carry Your name and represent
You in this world, it is an awesome, humbling, and terrible responsibility. I knew that there would be many who would take occasion
by my sin to persecute and afflict. I expected it of the world, but
I have been startled by the measure that the Lord's people have
meted out recrimination and unforgiveness. Many see the suffering under Your hand of chastisement and in *righteous indignation*
seek to add to it and take advantage of it. I bear them no ill will, for
I know it is all in Your sovereign hands, and You will work even the
wrath of man to Your glory. All I can do is be faithful, to be true
to the restoration You have wrought in my life and soul. If that
cannot speak for itself, then no amount of words on my part shall.

Let the grace of the Lord Jesus be on display to vindicate and
let those who see it rejoice and give glory to You for what Your
Spirit has accomplished. Maybe they will examine their own lives
and reason that if one who fell so far can be delivered from the
power of indwelling sin, why not themselves? Let them seek Your
name, that they may know You as the great deliverer. May they be
brought to honor You in their bodies and in their spirits, which
are the Lord's.

Psalm 83
That They May Seek Your Name

Vs. 16—Cover their faces with shame, LORD, so that
they will seek your name. (NIV)

One of the great mysteries of God and life is the matter of suffering. How is it that a God who proclaims to be love allows so much suffering? His thoughts are not our thoughts, nor are our ways His ways. God told Job from the whirlwind in chapters 38–41 (and I paraphrase), "If I tried to explain it to you, you'd never understand it." Asaph is struggling with the ways of God, wondering why He is silent, delaying to bring deliverance rather than vindicating the cause of His people. God appears to be allowing the enemy's plans to progress, the conspiracy to form, and their goal to become achievable. But Asaph is caused to see that God does have it under control, and He will be using this circumstance to bring glory to Himself.

There are times when God, for a while, allows evil to prevail in order to expose the full purposes of those who are perpetrating it to bring down upon them the guilt and shame of their actions. And once the weight of that comes upon them, some will seek God's name in repentance, asking forgiveness. In the meantime, it is hard on the saint of God who is being unjustly afflicted, but this is how we can share in the sufferings of Christ. No greater injustices ever happened to a man upon earth than what happened to Jesus, the perfect man. Yet "He learned obedience through the things He suffered," and by His one act of obedience brought life and forgiveness to all men. Our lives are part of a vast, incomprehensible plan, and let us, by faith, rejoice in the role that God has assigned us.

Psalm 84
No Good Thing Withheld

Vs. 11—For the LORD God is a sun and shield; the LORD bestows favor and honor; no good thing does he withhold from those whose walk is blameless. (NIV)

This, Lord, is a wonderful truth, particularly when we can proclaim, "Every good gift and ever perfect gift is from above, and comes down from the Father of lights" (James 1:17, KJV). Do I lack anything? Let me ask of God, who gives liberally. The Lord is not miserly; He is neither stingy nor is He a reluctant giver. So, what good thing am I asking for? Do I desire His presence? Do I look forward every morning to another opportunity for communion with my God? Does my soul long for Him? Do I want to eat angel's food? Does looking into His word thrill my soul with expectancy?

Do I hunger and thirst for righteousness to be displayed in my life? If you are not there, then do you want to be? Then let me tell you the pathway. It is through the Valley of Tears. Once your heart has a clear understanding of the flesh and a vision of the holiness and sanctity of God, then you will have entered that valley. Your heart sees itself as a pilgrim in this world with no abiding city, moving toward the celestial one whose builder and maker is God. You will mourn over the wasted past, and the shame brought to your Lord, but you will go from strength to strength, for you will be letting go of your strength (which is really a hindrance) and moving on to His strength. Your strength will be revealed as the weakness it truly is, and His strength will be perfected in Your weakness.

Psalm 84
One Day

Vs. 10—Better is one day in your courts than a thousand elsewhere; I would rather be a doorkeeper in the house of my God than dwell in the tents of the wicked. (NIV)

What would you do differently if you knew that you only had one day? We commonly experience that with the last day of summer vacation before school begins, or the last day before we move to another city, or the last day on the job before taking another one or retiring. When it comes to our lives, we don't know when we awaken that day that this day may be the last one. But James reminds us that we should approach all of life each day by saying, "If the Lord wills..." The psalmist tells us here what one day means to him. To spend one day in God's courts is to be treasured more than a thousand lived for himself; that there is more value in one day living in the conscious knowledge and reality of being in God's presence than a thousand lived just any old way.

This is a huge statement of the value of quality over quantity. To be a doorkeeper in the house, a *menial* job of letting people in and out and ensuring that no one or anything defiling is entering the house of God is better than fine living and a good situation in the world. What do I value as important? In economics, there is this concept of opportunity cost—what I lose by foregoing option A to pursue option B. Which would Korah rather have: one thousand days living for himself or one day in God's courts? As far as the Psalm writer Korah is concerned, there is no opportunity cost because option A is of such insignificant value.

JULY 11

Psalm 85
Wrath removed

Vs. 3—You set aside all your wrath and turned from
your fierce anger. (NIV)

Have I truly apprehended the blessedness of having all of my sin covered and all of God's wrath taken away? I only have to look at Calvary to see what it took to accomplish those two wonderful blessings. Jesus had to become sin for me, all of the guilt of my sin had to be transferred to Him, and then He had to suffer the three dark hours while an eternity of separation and hatred for my sins was compressed together and its fury unleashed upon Jesus. Do I have any comprehension of suffering like that? No, I never could; but I can partially comprehend His physical sufferings and see in them a small glimpse of the moral, spiritual suffering He endured. It is only upon this great work of Calvary that forgiveness is made possible.

I am not able to be forgiven because God loves me and desires to have a relationship with me; rather, God sent Jesus to die for my sins because He loves me and desires to have a relationship with me. No wonder Jesus could pray in John 17 that the Father loved Him—Jesus made all of God's desires possible. So, now God can in righteousness forgive, revive, and restore. Jesus said that he who is forgiven much loves much. Which one of us hasn't been forgiven much! May the Holy Spirit fill me more and more with love for the Lord for His great love for me.

Psalm 85
Met and Kissed

Vs. 10—Love and faithfulness meet together; righteousness and peace kiss each other. (NIV)

Mercy and truth have met together. What a wonderful reality. I
know how much I needed mercy. God's Spirit had awakened my
sleeping heart to its lost condition, that in my sin, I was under the
condemnation and wrath of God. The Spirit also showed me my
powerlessness to help myself. How did He awaken this realization
in me who was dead in trespasses and sins? I do not comprehend,
but He did, and I cried out for mercy, and He answered. The truth
of the holiness of God and the truth of the sinfulness of man made
it look like an impossibility for there to ever be reconciliation ...
until Jesus came. Righteousness demanded a perfection that I
could never deliver, a level of perfection that Jesus alone could
provide. Because He in righteousness met all of God's righteous
demands, there is nothing I can add to it, nor is anything lacking
that needs to be added.

So now, peace can be made with God, I can and have been reconciled to God by virtue of the work of Calvary appropriated to me
by faith. Lord, You have done that which for me was impossible.
How could I ever thank You enough, love You enough, obey You
enough, worship You enough? It could never be done! It will take
all the endless ages of eternity, and still, the treasures of Your grace
will not be fully revealed. And surely I shall treasure You and love
You more and more each day.

Psalm 86
You Will Answer

Vs. 1—Hear me, LORD, and answer me, for I am poor
and needy. (NIV)

Of whom could it be said, "for I am holy?" Or of whom could it
be said, "You have delivered my soul from the depths of Sheol?"
Who else could be designated "Your servant" as completely as the
very Son of God Jesus? This Psalm is about Jesus and I sit back
in awe and wonder at this conversation between Father and Son.
Jesus had such total, absolute confidence in God's character that
He could go all the way to Calvary, all the way to death, even to go
to Sheol—the place of death—for He had complete, unwavering
confidence in His Father. And in that very thralldom of death
where Satan's power of death was seen to its fullest extent, Jesus
would go to "destroy him who had the power of death, that is the
devil" (Hebrews 2:14, KJV) and rise victorious. How can I ever
doubt?

Why do anxious thoughts arise? Is it because I feel powerless in the
face of my circumstances? Then, I can call out to God, who has all
power, and He will answer. Perhaps I am anxious because I believe
taking care of it is up to me. What a deception. Jesus has already
told me, "Apart from Me, you can do nothing." Why doubts and
fears? Because I am not praying! How can God answer if I do not
call out? "Be anxious for nothing, but in prayer..." Anxieties flee in
the face of prayer. Because Jesus has so pleased the Father, there is
nothing He will not do for His Son; no request can ever be denied.
Spirit, give me strength to pray as I ought; take that groan of mine
and present it to my Savior. Jesus, intercede for me in the presence
of Your Father. I, too, will be answered.

JULY 14

Psalm 86
For You are Great

Vs. 10—For you are great and do marvelous deeds; you
alone are God. (NIV)

God is great. Let that sink deeply into your soul and your spirit.
When your soul fully accepts this simple truth, what a difference
it will make in your life. Am I facing a difficult decision? God is
great and has my life in His hands; He has a plan for my life, and
I can trust Him with my future. Am I anxious or worried? God
is great. He is above and over all things. He is the God of my circumstances and has ordered all things. Nothing can happen to me
apart from the explicit will of God. I may not like it and certainly
don't understand it, but nothing can happen unless He can work
it for good and His glory. Is my life going well, my job successful,
and my family healthy and well provided for? God is great. Give
Him the glory and thanks, for it is not due to your great merit, but
His great grace.

When your spirit has fully accepted this simple truth what a difference it will make in your worship and relationship with God.
You shall be awed by the prospect of being in the presence of God.
You will rejoice in His presence and look forward to worship as a
thirsty man longs for water. You will consider time in God's word
as your necessary food and will happily make it a priority. You
will look forward to times of prayer. Rather than seeming to be
tedious, they will be invigorating; rather than being rushed, they
will be longed for and savored. You will enjoy coming boldly, confidently to the throne of grace because you know the One who is
seated there to be your Father and your beautiful Savior is at His
right-hand. Great is the Lord and greatly to be praised.

Psalm 86
You Will Answer Me

Vs. 17—Give me a sign of your goodness, that my enemies may see it and be put to shame, for you, LORD, have helped me and comforted me. (NIV)

God always answers. The bigger question is, "Are you listening?" How often would we have to admit that many of our prayers are little more than our attempts at having God rubber-stamp our plans? Have you ever prayed a prayer that amounted to telling God rather than asking God? Maybe you were more intent on seeking an answer from God than seeking God Himself. Appending a little catchphrase such as "in Your name" or "Lord willing" will not energize a wrong-spirited prayer. Read this beautiful psalm of David's; breathe in the atmosphere of dependency and submission mingled with sublime expectancy. See how he presents himself before his God; consider the relationship he knows he enjoys in God's sight, the confidence he feels in God's presence. He knows that in the day of trouble when he calls upon God, He will answer.

Many of us neglect our times of prayer with God; we are not used to the sound of His voice or the manner of His answers, and wonder why He's not answering. Perhaps we haven't yet learned to listen. Through the crucible of experience, David had learned to listen and honed his conversation skills with God. Having presented the little "things of life and lived a life of open dependence before Him" prepares us for the large struggles that come. God will answer. Let us follow our Lord's example when, as a man upon earth, He lived in dependency and put everything before His Father. And when the struggle reached its climax He could say, "Not my will, but thine be done."

Psalm 87
Where are my Springs?

Vs. 1, 2—He has founded his city on the holy mountain. The LORD loves the gates of Zion more than all the other dwellings of Jacob. (NIV)

Where are my springs? Do I know in a conscious, experiential way where they are? As I meditate upon this question, the Spirit asks another one: What are your springs? Springs of water, as opposed to a pool of water, remind us that the source is ever being renewed. As water, it reminds us of its life-giving and life-sustaining power. Little wonder the Lord said "The water that I shall give him will become a fountain of water spring up into everlasting life." Your springs were all in God because He alone was the source of life, the sustainer of life, the One in whom You had placed all of Your hope and joy. As You walked through this world, Lord, You found nothing here for Your soul to draw from for strength and encouragement. It was only in God and His word.

This Psalm directs me to the City of God, the same city Abraham longed for, the same "place" You have gone to prepare places for us in that holy city New Jerusalem. For a tired, thirsty soul, the smell of the water begins the revival, and then to drink deeply of the water is sheer ecstasy. Do I see Your word that way? In this world, there is nothing to sustain, comfort, or refresh my spirit; it is all in You. Anything I set in my life as having primacy over You and Your interests is idolatry. Lord, I direct my heart to have all of its desire and satisfaction in You.

Psalm 87
His Foundation

Vs. 7—As they make music they will sing, "All my fountains are in you." (NIV)

For the Jew, they had Jerusalem and the fortress of Mt. Zion. To them, it represented their special place as God's people and His dwelling in their midst. But in their fleshly zeal, they looked upon the physical Jerusalem almost like a good luck charm; that God would never allow His city to be violated. But He did, and in Ezekiel, we read of how the glory of God lifted up and departed from the city and the temple. Paul writes of Abraham, who looked for a city whose builder and maker is God. In John 14, Jesus tells His disciples of His soon departure back to the Father to prepare a place for them, for us—the heavenly Jerusalem of which we read in Revelation 21–22 which descends out of heaven as a bride adorned for her husband. But until that day, we now also have a foundation for our lives, "For no other foundation can any man lay than that which is laid which is Christ Jesus" (I Corinthians 3:11, NKJV). We have an unmovable foundation that will never be taken away from us; we have an unshakable foundation that can withstand all the assaults of the evil one.

Our foundation is Jesus Himself and His work on Calvary's cross, which has secured our salvation for time and all eternity. What security we have in Him! It is not the strength of our convictions or the depth of our faith that forms the basis of our security but the all-sufficiency of Christ. What calm assurance we can have knowing that as a child of God, we are an object of His love and divine favor.

Psalm 88
Your Wrath Lies Heavy

Vs. 7—Your wrath lies heavily on me; you have overwhelmed me with all your waves. (NIV)

What a terrible thing to hear You say, Lord, that God's wrath lies
heavy upon You. I would understand God's wrath laying heavy
upon me, for I am a sinner; sin dwells in me. It is I who fails God;
it is I who stumbles and falls; I am the one who hardens the heart
against the Spirit's conviction. I have often grieved and quenched
the Holy Spirit in my life. But You have done none of those things.
You are sinless, spotless, unblemished. Satan, the prince of this
world, came at You and found nothing in You (John 14:30); he
found no chink in Your armor, no entry point where he could
hook You and reel You in. So, God transferred all of His wrath
from me to You on Calvary. What a terrible experience You went
through for me, not only all the trouble and affliction from man,
"the contradiction of sinners against You" (Hebrews 12:3, KJV),
but that God would take You not just to the brink of death, the
pit, and the grave, but all the way there for me.

But God, Your God, would not, could not leave You there, in that
place of destruction where there is no declaration of God's loving
kindness and faithfulness! He would raise You up, out of death,
Sheol, and the grave to show His pleasure in You and Your victory. No wrath, no condemnation for me in Christ Jesus. You have
done it all. Hallelujah.

Psalm 88
God of My Salvation

Vs. 1—LORD, you are the God who saves me; day and
night I cry out to you. (NIV)

My salvation is God's work and will brought about in my life. He
is not willing that any man should perish. And even though we
know that men do, it is not because it was what God willed for
them, but yet their condemnation was within the will of God.
God wanted me saved long before I felt any conviction or desire
in my soul for Him. In fact, He desired my salvation before I was
ever born, foreknew it, and chose me in Christ from before the
foundation of the world. God, desiring to save man and knowing
beforehand that man would fall and be brought into the bondage
and condemnation of sin, conceived of the great plan of salvation
whereby His Son would become a man, take on flesh, and for sin
die to deliver us from sin.

Salvation was God-planned, God-purposed, God-initiated, an
accomplishment from eternity to eternity. I, by faith, have become
the blessed recipient of this grace. He has become the God of my
salvation, Jesus is the author and finisher of my faith, and the Holy
Spirit has begotten me of incorruptible seed. He now wants me to
work out my salvation, to conform my outward life to the inner
life He has given me in His Son. He has good works for me to do,
and I have been created to walk in them. May our lives be glorify-
ing to the God of our Salvation.

Psalm 89
Incomparable

Vs. 6—For who in the skies above can compare with the LORD? Who is like the LORD among the heavenly beings? (NIV)

There is nothing, no one, that can be compared to the Lord. To put anything else side by side with God would only be an insult to His majesty. Your mercies are so great that they looked down the portals of eternity and chose me to be in Christ before the world began. You, Lord, knew all along that the creation of man meant Your Son's crucifixion and death. Could any love compare to that? No. And then You desired to enter into covenant with us. Such love is beyond our comprehension, but it is true and more certain than the world itself.

You are the sovereign God over all created things both in heaven, on earth, and infernal beings as well. No power can stand against Your will; no plan can prosper apart from Your assent. You are awesome and to be held in highest regard so that nothing would distract my heart from You. You are mighty; Your will and power are irresistible, and all of Your plans and counsels shall come to pass. Heaven is Yours, the habitation of the angels, and it cannot contain You. The world is Yours and all of its fullness, and I rejoice at the beauty, grandeur, and breathtaking wonder of Your creation as it reflects the invisible attributes of Your diving nature and eternal godhead. May You fill me ever more with the glorious sense of Your wonder, greatness, majesty, and love.

Psalm 89
Your Holy One

Vs. 7—In the council of the holy ones God is greatly feared; he is more awesome than all who surround him.
(NIV)

As I read Your vision addressed to Your holy one, who else could it be but Jesus Himself? In Your word, there are others, like David here, who were privileged to be types of the Lord Jesus, but they all fail ultimately compared to Your Son Jesus. He is truly the Holy One of Israel, the only true Servant of God who fully, perfectly satisfied Your heart, O God. He came lowly as a babe, born into humble circumstances, just waiting to be found and exalted. He was anointed by the Holy Spirit, and all of Your plans are made possible by Him. How wicked men did hate Him and try to outwit Him; even Satan tried to go toe-to-toe with Jesus, but was forced to depart, unable to achieve his goal.

Throughout Jesus' life, Your faithfulness and mercy watched over Him, and He always acknowledged You in all of His ways. He reveled in calling You Father and rejoiced at being Your Son, the firstborn of all creation—having that preeminent place, a name above every name. In His death, He established Your covenant, for He shed that perfect blood that confirmed greater promises eclipsing all others. So, Your new covenant is eternal. When we read the Lord's prayer in John 17 and come to understand in a small way the eternal nature of this wonderful plan of salvation, the depth of the love between Father and Son, and the great love of Jesus for His own how our hearts bow in awe and worship and the overflow of divine love that embraced us and took us in.

Psalm 89
My Time is Short

Vs. 45—You have cut short the days of his youth; you
have covered him with a mantle of shame. (NIV)

Life is brief, and I have been like a child playing with sea shells
while an unexplored ocean of love lies before me. How foolish
it is to forsake Your commandments by which You said I could
prove my love to You through obedience. Your burden is not like
the demands of man or even like those of the law, for Your yoke is
easy and Your burden light. But I do break Your commandments;
do not love my enemies, do not bear others' burdens, and do get
angry and sin, so You have to come in with chastisement.

How comforting to know that You chasten a son You love and
do not withdraw Your loving kindness from him. I am learning,
Lord, just how short my time really is. May I recognize the futility
of all merely human endeavors, no matter how well-intentioned.
Everything I do merely for myself shall be swept away into the
dustbin of history one day, but what is done for You shall endure
for eternity. Help me to have the eternal perspective in mind so
that if You have to smash my plans and overturn my schedules; I
will freely let them go so that You can bring in something greater.
Better, Lord, to have suffered the loss of so much, yet I wonder if
there will be time enough to work for You left. But then I remember that though the quantity of time may be short, the quality of
that time and doing for Jesus makes all the difference.

Psalm 90
My Iniquities Before You

Vs. 8—You have set our iniquities before you, our secret sins in the light of your presence. (NIV)

Before the world had been formed, You were always there. Before I ever was conceived, had done or said anything, You knew all about it. For You, a thousand years is like a blink of the eye; for me, a thousand years is 14 lifetimes. How could I even begin to understand as You do? So why set my iniquity before You? If you have separated me from my sin as far as the east is from the west, if You are of purer eyes than to behold evil and cannot look on wickedness (Habakkuk 1:13), how can this be? It is because I need to face it in the light of Your truth and see it as You see it. Jesus has borne the wrath for me so there is no question about judgment and condemnation. But God cannot pass my sin by. These secret sins, these hidden lusts and desires nursed and cultivated in the dark, must be brought into the light of Your countenance.

How I need to see the horror of it as You do so I can fully repudiate it and never again desire these things. This is mercy in action, not wanting me to settle for anything other than Your holiness (a hatred for sin) and righteousness in my life. You have satisfied my heart with Your mercy; I have felt the strength of Your love. At first, I trembled in Your presence, but now I see the beauty of Your holiness; it rests upon me and has settled me.

Psalm 90
Satisfy Us

Vs. 14—Satisfy us in the morning with your unfailing love, that we may sing for joy and be glad all our days.
(NIV)

What does it take to satisfy you? What do you look for to satisfy you? "The eye is not filled with seeing or the ear with hearing." The physical part of us can never be satisfied but for a time after which it will desire more. When Jesus addressed the Samaritan woman, He drew upon her evident need for water to lead her to identify and satisfy a deeper need. Jesus could give her living water whereby she would never thirst again. Still perceiving Jesus' words purely naturally, she expressed her desire for that kind of water which would relieve her of her daily chore. So, Jesus made her see deeper by bringing her sin to her attention.

Jesus alone has what can satisfy the thirsty soul—it is none other than Himself as the life-giving truth. Later in the gospel, Jesus goes further to explain how the Holy Spirit would then become a well of water springing up to everlasting life, and the believer would be a conduit of that living water going out to others—a more than adequate supply for the believer with a plenteous overflow to others. Has Jesus fully satisfied your heart, or are you seeking supplemental sources of satisfaction? There are no others; Jesus is the only one who can satisfy the soul's deep need and bring us to God. Let us be satisfied early; then, we can rejoice and be glad for all He has richly bestowed upon us.

Psalm 91
The Secret Place

Vs. 1—Whoever dwells in the shelter of the Most High
will rest in the shadow of the Almighty. (NIV)

You, Lord Jesus, knew that secret place as well. You were "in the bosom of the Father." He delighted in You from eternity past, and when You came as a babe and grew into manhood, You were ever the Father's delight, always in the bosom of His love. No wonder You evidenced such calm, even amid Your most severe trials, for You never questioned the Father's love, never chaffed at doing His will. Your supreme confidence in Your Father's sovereign, providential care kept You calm, settled, and secure even while everyone around You was falling apart.

Satan even tried to use this Psalm against You, for You to put the Father to the test to see if He really did have His angels watching over You. You knew where Your security lay: in the bosom of the Father's love, in the center of His Will. Such is the protection, "the shadow of the Almighty." This place is my place by birthright, too. I am in Christ, in You, seated with You in heavenly places, the object of the Father's love. I must learn to dwell, to rest, to abide in Your love. As I abide in You and my heart finds its rest there, I dwell where You dwell. Let me learn to trust in Your love, to never question what or why You are doing what You're doing and look to see You work all for good.

Psalm 91
I Will Deliver Him

Vs. 14—"Because he loves me," says the LORD, "I will rescue him; I will protect him, for he acknowledges my name." (NIV)

As you read this Psalm, note the blessings that come upon the one whose trust is in the Lord. It all begins with where you live. Where are you abiding? Are you enjoying His secret places, the times of private prayer and fellowship with the Father? Is your mind on things above or on the things of the earth? It is a sad truth that most of us are so earthly minded that we are of no heavenly good.

To abide in Christ is to be dwelling in the secret place of the Most High. To abide in Christ is to be intimately connected to Him, to be vitally connected to Him and to be drawing our life sustenance from Him. That places us in a position of protection. This protection is not necessarily an earthly one for "all who live godly in Christ shall suffer persecution." We need protection from the demonic forces which propel the natural forces. What follows in the Psalm is all the ways this protection, shelter, is realized: God our refuge, our fortress, our covering, our shield and buckler, He sends His angels to protect us. After the psalmist has delivered all these blessings (verses 1–13), God comes on the scene and speaks. He says, "Because He has set his love upon Me..." Isn't this what God is always looking for. He desires a response of love from us for all the love he has showered upon us. And when we do, He responds with even a greater overflow of blessing. "I will deliver him and honor him."

Psalm 92
Made me glad

Vs. 4—For you make me glad by your deeds, LORD; I
sing for joy at what your hands have done. (NIV)

You, Lord Jesus, have made me glad through Your work on
Calvary's cross and then through the work You have done in my
heart. Without the cross nothing of blessing would be possible
for me; condemnation and wrath would stand against me. But
you did the work none other could do, paid the debt You did not
owe that others could not pay, and set me in a place I could never
have imagined. You have brought me into the bosom of Your love
triangle: Father—Son—Holy Spirit.

My heart exults in You and gives You thanks and praise. You have
brought me into the wide expanse of Your love, and I exult in the
relationship into which I stand. Your thoughts are so deep. Who
would have imagined that You could take poor, sin-cursed, fallen
creatures and raise them up to such a place of nearness; yet this is
what Your love does. I had bemoaned a wasted life and wallowed in
self-pity when all along the grandeur of Your love was beckoning
to me. Now, You assure me that I can and shall bear fruit in old age;
that though the outward man is perishing, the inward man is being
renewed day by day. Oh, to grow like a cedar tall and majestic, to
flourish like a palm tree planted by an oasis of living water!

Psalm 92
You Are on High

Vs. 1, 2—It is good to praise the LORD and make music to your name, O Most High, proclaiming your love in the morning and your faithfulness at night... (NIV).

It is a wondrous truth that You, Lord Jesus, are on high, that You have Your glorified body and are seated at the right hand of the Father. One day You will be sent by the Father to visibly take the reins of world government to judge and reign from David's throne. All power and authority has been placed into Your hands by the Father in gratitude for bringing Him such glory. And how wonderful that through You I have access into the very presence of God. You are not at such a distance that You are unapproachable nor have You forgotten what life in this flesh is like.

Though exalted, You remain sympathetic toward all of our infirmities and weaknesses and are able to comfort us in all of our sorrow and tribulation. How important it is to me to know that even while being on high You are also nigh unto me. Your Holy Spirit indwells me and keeps You ever personal. I can go to You with all my need, all my care, in prayerful dependence knowing that the Holy Spirit will make intercession for me. When You prayed to Your Father that great high priestly prayer in John 17, You spoke of Your undying love for your disciple and for all of those, me, who would believe in Your name. You wanted them with You one day to behold Your glory that You had from eternity with the Father. Now You share that glory and one day we will behold it.

Psalm 93
Holiness Adorns Your House

Vs. 5—Your statues, LORD, stand firm; holiness adorns
your house for endless days. (NIV)

Your house is Your abode, Your dwelling place, where You have designed to set Your name. We are Your house, both individually as a temple of the Holy Spirit, but more so as "a holy temple in the Lord, in whom you also are being built together for a dwelling place of God in the Spirit" (Ephesians 2: 21–22, NKJV). Your house is to reflect Your character and desires. Your will and preferences. We "as living stones are being built up a spiritual house" (I Peter 2:5, NKJV). And holiness adorns Your house. An adornment adds to and enhances the beauty that is already there; it brings out the beauty, it doesn't create it. Your work of redemption and imparting Your life to us in regeneration is the beauty, the substance, the reality.

Now as I exhibit Your life, Your mind, Your thoughts and attitudes, my life can be used to hang an adornment in Your house. Holiness is what You want for You said "Be ye holy for I am holy saith the Lord." Holiness is what You desire; that hatred and abhorrence of sin that characterized You is to characterize me. This is Your life coming out through me. When we read of the New Jerusalem and its splendor and magnificence in Revelation 21 and 22, it is so magnificent because everything about it radiates Your glories.

Psalm 93
The Lord Reigns

Vs. 1—The LORD reigns, he is robed in majesty; the LORD is robed in majesty and armed with strength; indeed, the world is established, firm and secure. (NIV)

That is a fact; the Lord does indeed reign. His power and might are infinite, His presence ubiquitous, His will irresistible. As we often pray, "Thy will be done on earth as it is in heaven." And how is God's will done in heaven? He has multitudes of angels at His disposal whose greatest joy is to carry out some facet of God's will. God's will is carried out in heaven completely, irresistibly, immediately, unopposed. But what does His will face on earth? It faces opposition; it contends with a creature who is living in rebellion and sin and has no thought for or pleasure in God. And that is not necessarily just from the unregenerate.

As His people, we must confess that often times we do not want God to have His way in our lives because it infringes upon our plans. So, we resist, complain, moan and groan, and pray that He will let us have it our way. When we pray, "thy will be done on earth..." we are firstly praying that He have His way in our heart and life. Does He reign in my heart? Is He enthroned there presiding over all of my affairs? Or do I have Him seated beside me as an adviser rather than a sovereign? May I give Him the preeminence in my life, may I see myself as His slave, His bondservant! Do I really understand what it means, "You are not your own, you are bought with a price?" Let Him reign in your heart by faith.

Psalm 94
The Lord Knows all Thoughts of Men

Vs. 11—The LORD knows all human plans; he knows
that they are futile. (NIV)

It's not only my thoughts You know, but the thoughts of all men
at all times. You are fully acquainted with all of their intentions
and plans. And what do You tell us of them? That they are futile.
All of our plans made apart from You are pointless and futile. The
wickedness of the human heart is directed toward its own ends,
pursuing those ends by its own means, deceiving itself that either
You don't see or You don't care. But You do see and understand
all the motivations. And Lord, You saw mine too.

I now wonder how You could have let my sin go for so long. It is so
easy to harbor bitternesses and resentments, to allow the thoughts
to fester and eat like a canker, until they have erupted and defiled
many. I do not understand Your ways, but I have felt Your hand of
judgment and justice. Even in Your chastening of me, I acknowledge Your mercy. Oh, that men might see Your mercy and grace
and repent of their evil ways before it is too late. Oh, that men
might see that Your longsuffering with them, with me, is neither
a license to keep sinning nor an indication of Your indifference,
but Your grace to lead them to repentance. You had to teach me
the hard way, to let me go all the way down before I would listen.
Thank You for bringing me back up on the other side.

Psalm 94
The Lord Knows the Thoughts of Man

Vs. 18—When I said, "My foot is slipping," your unfailing love, LORD, supported me. (NIV)

Nothing ever takes God by surprise. Everything that has happened and has yet to happen has already been foreseen and known by the omniscient God. He knows every thought you will ever have, yet they are still your thoughts for which you are responsible. (God's foreknowledge is not deterministic.) God has already incorporated every thought, option, contingency, and intervention into His infinitely vast and comprehensive plan so that everything goes exactly according to His purpose. God knows the thoughts of man, and they are futile. Man thinks that in his puniness, he can upset the outworking of God's divine plan. But even man's sin is incorporated and within the scope of His will. Man exercises his will and thinks that his will is autonomous and supreme, even thinking that by exercising his will, he can overturn or frustrate the plans of God. But that is futile.

Blessing does not come to the believer through the exercising of his will, but through the *yielding* of his will. By submitting our thoughts to God, by bringing them all into the captivity of Christ, we have liberty. When we strive to exercise our wills then we are constrained by the narrowness of our limited, feeble minds and become slaves to our flesh. When we submit to God, He opens up to us vistas of possibilities that, up until then, we had never foreseen. Slavery is the path to freedom, yielding the path to liberty. Submit your thoughts to God, and have your options expanded.

Psalm 94
The Multitude of Anxieties

Vs. 19—When anxiety was great within me, your consolation brought me joy. (NIV)

What do anxieties communicate? For one, they indicate that it is something that you consider important. If I am anxious about this *thing,* I should ask myself if its importance in my imagination is out of proportion with its real importance. Consider the possibility that you are building things up in your mind to have an unjustifiable significance. Perhaps you can prune out some of those anxieties by having a clearer perspective. Another reason we have anxiety is due to our sense of powerlessness. We are facing a situation whose outcome is important to us, yet we have no direct power to effect a change in or direct the outcome of the situation. So, we find ourselves fretting over the situation, hoping for the best, fearing the worst, and imagining all sorts of scenarios one way and the other.

The Psalmist reminds us that God's comfort delights his soul. How can we receive God's comfort amid this multitude of anxieties? Pray. If it's worth worrying about, pray. If it's important enough to fret over, pray. Are you powerless to do anything about it? Pray to the One who does have all power. If, after praying, you are still anxious, then pray some more. Pray until you have peace. That is what the comfort of God will bring: peace, the peace of God which guards your heart and mind. Only then will you be able to delight in the Lord. If the outcome is to your liking, then you will delight in the outcome. But delight in the Lord precedes the outcome, and the delight remains even if the outcome is not to your liking because you will know it is of the Lord.

Psalm 95
The People of the Pasture

Vs. 6, 7—Come, let us bow down in worship, let us kneel before the LORD our Make; for he is our God and we are the people of his pasture, the flock under his care. (NIV)

What an immense privilege we have to come together in assembly and to sing His praises. What an object of worship and what a theme of praise we have. We can extol Him in His creation glory, adore Him in His sovereignty over all the created universe, and praise Him for His marvelous providential care for us. We can render thanksgiving and praise for the great salvation that has been purchased for us at the price of His Son's shed blood. What a contemplation of the love of God that would act in such a way toward us while we were yet sinners, rebellious, with no thoughts for Him ourselves, and nothing to commend us to the love of God; yet He commended His love to us.

What a joyful relationship into which we have been brought through redemption and faith in His work on the cross. We are the people of His pasture, the ones over whom He lavishes such care. How could we ever take our union with Christ for granted? How could we ever treat it as commonplace? And yet we do—*I* do. At times I want to selfishly live my life my way and for myself. It is as if we are telling God to stay out of it. Oh, God would tell me, do not harden your heart, do not grieve my Holy Spirit, do not quench the fire of His activity in your soul. He doesn't want to chasten but to bless. By chasten He will bring out even more from me, us, of the excellency of the life of Jesus.

Psalm 95
Your Comforts Delight My Soul

Vs. 2—Let us come before him with thanksgiving and
extol him with music and song. (NIV)

"Blessed is the man whom You instruct..." You have been so gracious in dealing with a hard-hearted man like me and persisting with me until I have learned. It is only in the learning that the value of the instruction takes root; it is only in the doing that the value of the instruction bears fruit. As You instruct me from Your word, my heart receives the truth contained therein, and I gain peace. It is not that the circumstances immediately resolve, but I see the God of the circumstances, Your divine providence, and I am at rest. Why should anxieties arise? Because I want to feel that I am in control and can handle it. Then Your Spirit reminds me that You are in control and are handling it and anxiety ceases.

Why was Elisha at rest and his servant anxious? Because the servant did not perceive God as clearly as Elisha did (II Kings 6:16). Unless You had been my help, my mainstay, my support, I would have been lost, set adrift on an ocean of uncertainty. If I begin to fear that my foot will slip, I am reminded that You could not only walk upon the waters but lift Peter up as he began to sink. If I look within and see anxieties, I look up and receive comfort, and Your comfort quiets and delights my soul. You ever prove Yourself faithful; I need to give You the time to demonstrate it and not presume upon You to meet my expectations.

Psalm 96
For He is Coming

Vs. 13—Let all creation rejoice before the LORD, for he comes, he comes to judge the earth. He will judge the world in righteousness and the people in his faithfulness. (NIV)

The Lord is coming. He is not slack as men consider slackness; God does not miss an appointment. Rather, He is not willing that any should perish, but that all would come to life. So, what appears like a delay to us is really His longsuffering and mercy. He waited for me to accept His salvation; how can I presume to be impatient for Him to come now to set things right just because it is convenient to me? So what should be my occupation now? To pray for God's judgment? No. I have a new song to sing, a song of redemption. God has placed into my heart a love for Him, a song of praise, a message of deliverance, and a proclamation of salvation for all men. Let God set the times and the seasons for His work of judgment; let me be about praise and proclaiming now.

God has given to us who believe in Jesus the unique opportunity to display the glory of Christ in our lives, to show forth the power of His risen life over sin in our mortal bodies, and to witness to the power of the Holy Spirit in our daily lives. So, let us display that glory and testify to Jesus through the offerings of thanksgiving, praise, and of ourselves. Holiness becomes Your house, and we are Your house, Your dwelling, Your temple, both individually and corporately. Let us worship You in the beauty of holiness; let our every thought, word, and deed be an expression of Christ in us that all may see not I, but Christ.

Psalm 96
The Lord Reigns

Vs. 10—Say among the nations, "The LORD reigns."
The world is firmly established, it cannot be moved; he
will judge the peoples with equity. (NIV)

Yes, the Lord reigns. He is sovereign over all the affairs of men and of nations. Nothing happens on this earth without His express permission. We may not understand it; we may not appreciate it, but by faith, we acknowledge it. All is ordered according to His will and inexorably is moving toward fulfilling His purpose. And where else should this be more visible than in His church and the lives of His own? We often pray, "Thy will be done on earth as it is in heaven." And how is His will done in heaven? It is immediately acknowledged, joyfully executed, and gloriously displayed without resistance or hesitation. The angels' greatest joy is in the execution of His expressed desires.

Is this my attitude? Do I pray that God's will be done in my life that same way? Do I read His word and then joyously submit to everything it says? Do I hesitate over its *difficult demands?* Jesus said that His yoke was easy and His burden light. Do I see it as such, or do I resent His intrusion into *my* plans? We say we look forward to the day Jesus returns, establishes His throne, and is universally acknowledged, but do we *really* mean it? If I do not accept now the reign of Christ in my life, if I do not acknowledge now that I am not my own, but His, if I do not joyfully submit to Him now, then I cannot honestly claim that I want His will done "on earth as it is in Heaven." Reign in me now, Lord.

Psalm 97
To Love the Lord

Vs. 10—Let those who love the LORD hate evil, for he guards the lives of his faithful ones and delivers them from the hand of the wicked. (NIV)

How do I know that I love the Lord? It is quite simple: if I love what He loves and hate what He hates, my spirit is in tune with His Spirit. Jesus asked Peter if he loved Him, and the proof was that he cared for His sheep. In I John, what is the proof of love? It is to obey His commandments and to love one another. To love the Lord is not about warm and fuzzy feelings. It is about the deliberate response of my whole being (will, thoughts, and emotions) to the love He displayed toward me in laying down His life for me (I John 3:16). I must personalize it as it is to be an active force in my life, for the life of Christ is to be displayed in me now, not my "old man" life.

If I love what Jesus loves, then it will sanctify me to hate what Jesus hates. What He hates above all else is sin. Do I tolerate sin in my life? I know that sin dwells in me through the flesh (Romans 7:17, 18), but I am not to yield my members to sin. Jesus calls me to judge every single piece of evidence of the motions of sin in my members, to recognize any time the flesh is seeking satisfaction, any means by which my will is seeking to assert itself against God's sovereign Spirit within me, and to put it in a place of death so that it has no power over me. Jesus hates all things that exalt themselves against God; so, too, must I as I seek to draw closer to Him.

Psalm 97
The Foundation of His Throne

Vs. 2—Clouds and thick darkness surround him; righteousness and justice are the foundation of his throne.
(NIV)

What a contrast we have between the foundation of God's throne and that of man's. Those men whose ambition and lust for power propels them in their quest for dominion and control are generally of a mind to suppress most impulses of conscience and to utilize any means or tactics necessary to achieve their ends. As a result, the foundation of their power is laid in murder, treachery, deceit, intrigue, scheming, and any other artifice at hand. Once their power is achieved, they rule ruthlessly and suspiciously, knowing that they have made many enemies on their rise to power and those same enemies would relish the opportunity to bring them down. In our Lord's day, King Herod the Great was such a man. But look at God's throne. It is established in righteousness and justice.

Righteousness emphasizes to us that everything God does is right, is consistent with His perfect character, so that He does not stoop to expedients or half-measures. As Abraham acknowledged when he contemplated what God had just told him of His plans for Sodom, "Shall not the Judge of all the earth do right?" (Genesis 18:25) Justice emphasizes that all of His thoughts and determinations are completely accurate and truthful. They have as their goal to execute a true judgment in every affair. There will be no respecter of persons, no perversion of justice, no hypocrisy in anything He does. This is the God with whom we have to do. This is the God whose wrath was fully expended on Jesus as he hung upon the cross. And now righteousness and peace have kissed each other.

Psalm 98
Sing a New Song

Vs. 1—Sing to the LORD a new song, for he has done
marvelous things; his right hand and his holy arm have
worked salvation for him. (NIV)

This is a new song for a new man. As the Lord clears away the
clutter and filth of my former ways, the anger and the bitterness
that poisoned my mind and soul, He has been making me a new
man. Gone are the reasonings and rationalizations I had used to
justify sin to myself or at least try to remove some of its sting. No
longer do I resist the Holy Spirit's promptings and convictions,
for they are part of His protection of me to keep me and guard me.
There is a song of praise. He has done marvelously. In His mercy,
He has delivered me out of my sin and into the glorious liberty of
the sons of God. He did not deal with me in the manner that my
sins deserved, but according to His grace. There is a song of joy.
He has given back to me the joy of my salvation.

No longer is there the misery of sin and the hidden shame that has
now come to light. I am starting to understand Proverbs 20:30 to
see how the blows from God and His stripes cleanse away evil and
purify the heart. There is a song of deliverance. He has set me free
from the bondage of sin, and I am now able to become the man I
was always intended to be. I see things His way, feel things as He
does, and no longer fear the emotional hurt. Is this the new song
the Psalmist writes about? I do not know, but this is the new song
the Lord has given me; it is new to me.

Psalm 98
He Is Coming To Judge

Vs. 9—let them sing before the LORD, for he comes to judge the earth. He will judge the world in righteousness and the peoples with equity. (NIV)

We are taught that, "Knowing therefore the terror of the Lord we persuade men" (II Corinthians 5:11, NKJV). When Jesus came the first time as a babe, He grew up among us, shared our life and plight, experienced the typical vicissitudes of life, and was tempted as we were yet without sin. He said that He had not come to judge the world but that the world by Him might be saved. What would have happened if He had come to judge the world then? That is what the Pharisees wanted Him to do in John 8 to the woman caught in adultery! Once He began to judge, He would not have been able to stop until He had judged everyone. And upon what basis would that judgment be made? Pure law, our works.

Before the cross, there would have been no other basis upon which to judge. All of mankind would have stood before Him condemned. But now, since the cross, righteousness has been reckoned to us by faith. There is no condemnation for He has borne the judgment of our sin. Jesus came the first time and made provision for the salvation of mankind. Now, when He comes again, He shall come as judge, for the Father has committed all judgment into His hands. For those of us who are saved, we shall all appear before the judgment seat of Christ to have our service judged by Him. For those on the earth at His coming, He shall separate them as a shepherd separates the sheep from the goats regarding what they did concerning Him and His people. Then He shall reign as King and Judge.

Psalm 99
The People Tremble

Vs. 1—The LORD reigns, let the nations tremble; he sits enthroned between the cherubim, let the earth shake.
(NIV)

Since the Lord is reigning, why should the people tremble? Because You reign in righteousness and holiness and cannot tolerate evil; it must be judged. You cannot ignore sin, but we like our sin; our flesh desires the satisfaction and pleasures of sin. We wouldn't engage in sin so freely if we didn't love sin so much. As I let sin reign in my mortal body, I trembled at the thought of You coming to reign in me. What You would have to do to clean up the debris of my life! But You did come and though it has been painful to deal with my sin, my past, my life, I am better for it. I wanted You to pass by my sin; You could not ignore it. I wanted to hold onto the bitterness and anger so I could excuse my spiritual failures; You had better things in store.

Now I no longer tremble at the thought of Your reigning; I welcome Your sovereignty. I have learned the hard way the consequences of Self reigning, and it isn't pretty. Having made me face it all in its ugliness and horror, I am free of it. "You were to them God ...Who ...forgives" (verse 8). Thank you for being such a God. Though You took vengeance on my deeds You have preserved me. Now it is a joy to have You reign, preside over my thoughts and desires, and bring everything into the captivity of Christ of whom I have been made captive.

Psalm 99
He Dwells

Vs. 5—Exalt the LORD our God and worship at his footstool; he is holy. (NIV)

The Lord reigns in heaven over the earth. He is sovereign over all the works of man and nature, making all to fulfill His purpose. But look where He dwells. Under the old economy, we see Him between the cherubim in the Holiest of Holies. How can a holy God dwell amid sinful men? It is because of the blood. Those cherubim gazed down upon the blood of the atonement, signifying that God's wrath had been appeased, man's sin covered for another year, so that God could come out in blessing rather than judgment. And where does He dwell now in the new covenant economy? By His Spirit, He dwells within His people—and that means me. I am blood-bought; my sins have been washed away; I am justified by Jesus' blood and justified through faith in His completed work on the cross.

Lord, be at home in my heart; be comfortable with what You see and freely arrange and rearrange anything You find that needs adjustment or correction. Proverbs 23:26, KJV says, "My son, give me thine heart." My soul replies, *All that I am is Yours.* Be at home in my heart and life and order my life any way You wish. I shall worship You and exalt You, Lord Jesus, for You have done wondrously and gloriously to forgive and to restore. You display Your greatness in judgment, but You display even more of Your character in mercy, compassion, and love. Oh, make me more like You.

Psalm 100
He Has Made Me

Vs. 3—Know that the LORD is God. It is he who made us, and we are his; we are his people, the sheep of his pasture. (NIV)

This is a wonderful truth and a source of great comfort as well. God has gone to the trouble of making us each individually. Science wants to rob God of His creation glory, His glory as the creator, and have us believe that everything is due to random, chance, impersonal forces. But God's word tells me that creation is intentional, purposeful, and personal. I know and believe that God has ordered my life and despite how I mess it up, or maybe even though I did, He is determined to bring out the excellencies of His Son through me by His Spirit. He has made me the way I am. Though sin has distorted and perverted His original design, His Spirit is still working to bring my life into conformity to the image of Christ—from glory to glory (II Corinthians 3:18).

What a blessing and a comfort to be a sheep under the care of the good shepherd, who laid down His life for the sheep, and the Great Shepherd, who can bring us all and lead us all to glory. Being redeemed, He invites us into His presence to worship before Him with thanksgiving and praise. And what a theme I have, for Jesus has given Himself for me, the just for the unjust, to bring many sons to glory. I thank Him for sacrificing Himself on Calvary's cross and praise Him for His wondrous love that motivated Him. Truly, God is good; everything He does is good, and Jesus has done all things well.

Psalm 100
Serving With Gladness

Vs. 2—Worship the LORD with gladness; come before
him with joyful songs. (NIV)

Our attitude toward service reveals much about our spirituality and relationship with the Lord. Jesus is our example of godly service. In Philippians 2:5–8, we read of the mind of our Lord, who was willing to undergo the greatest condescension in leaving the glory of heaven for the humiliation of earth. In doing this, He did not grudgingly lay aside His glory to take on human flesh but did so willingly for love and obedience to His Father. And when He came, it was not in pomp or splendor, but in lowliness to poverty and obscurity. Growing up, His sole motivation was to please His Father in heaven and to finish His work. No person was too insignificant, no task too lowly. to keep Him from His service. Notoriety did not attract Him; wealth or ambition did not distract Him from His purpose; this is our Lord, our pattern, our fulfillment.

Ours is not to decide where to go; it is the Master who tells the slave where he serves. Ours is not to decide what we do. The slave stands only to do his Master's bidding. Ours is not to decide to whom we minister, for we are bondslaves of Christ. Do I find this threatening to my freedom, contrary to my self-image, opposed to my culture? Or do I find this prospect exciting, exhilarating, and captivating? To be in the service of the God of the universe, to be at his disposal, like Philip, to not be attached to a work, but to a Master. What greater privilege is there than to "spend and be utterly spent for your sakes." I am fully His, bought with a price, to glorify God in and through my service.

AUGUST 15

Psalm 101
When Will You Come To Me?

Vs. 2—I will be careful to lead a blameless life—when will you come to me? I will conduct the affairs of my house with a blameless heart. (NIV)

Father, I have such a song of Your mercy and justice to sing, for I have seen both sides, know just how far my punishment is from what it deserved, and tasted mercy triumph over judgment. You know what You are about, the work You do in my heart to change me. The fears that assail me will not always be there, but You are always there. Sometimes You seem distant and far away, but that is really due to the agitation of my heart. As I learn to be quiet in Your presence, I hear Your still, small voice. I desire to have a perfect heart, one that is directed toward You and stayed upon You; so I must guard my heart and set no wicked thing before my eyes. My deceitful heart can turn anything, no matter how innocuous, into an idol.

So, who is to judge what is wicked? You do for only You know me thoroughly and completely, having fashioned me by Your grace. If You see me gazing upon any idol, no matter how innocent the thing may appear, bring conviction so that I can see it the way You do and judge it in my life. Let there be no resistance, no hesitation to Your prompting, neither reasoning nor rationalizations. The perversity and wickedness that had crept into my life is gone; may it never return! Lord, may Your eyes be upon me as one of the faithful; may I learn to walk as Jesus walked in that perfect way, desiring to please the Father.

Psalm 101
Behave Wisely

Vs. 5—...whoever has haughty eyes and a proud heart,
I will not tolerate. (NIV)

Jesus behaved wisely. Behaving wisely is not a matter of sinning versus not sinning; rather, it is a matter of using sound judgment in each situation and responding in each one to display God's character in your life and bring Him glory. We see it in the wedding feast of Cana: He meets the need and glorifies God without upstaging the feast or making a spectacle of Himself. For the woman at the well, He sends His disciples off so He can quietly talk with her and open up herself and her people to the gospel. He doesn't allow Himself to be drawn into the lynching of the woman caught in adultery in John 8, neither does He let her off the hook but confronts her regarding her sin.

He knows how to deflect and disarm the Pharisees trying to trap Him into a discussion about paying taxes. However, he can discuss with Nicodemus the truth he really needs to hear—a conversation that he never gets over and eventually leads him to faith. He can weave a scourge to drive out the thieves and robbers from the temple area and invite everyone to hear His wonderful words of grace. When the people wanted to make Him King by force, He dismissed both the crowd and His disciples so He could confer all night with His Father. If we say that Jesus could do all this because He was the divine Son of God, we say that only to absolve ourselves. When we look at His life of prayer and His intensely close relationship with His Father, we see the source of His acting wisely. May we seek God in prayer daily, intensely, taking nothing for granted so that we, too, can act wisely.

Psalm 102
Answer Me

Vs. 2—Do not hide your face from me when I am in distress. Turn your ear to me; when I call, answer me quickly. (NIV)

The Father always heard Your prayers; He was always attentive to Your every cry. But when You cried out, and nothing seemed to get better, when You poured out Your heart to God, and circumstances remained unchanged, You felt the isolation. Lord Jesus, You described Your loneliness like that of a pelican in the wilderness, an owl in the desert—so unnatural, out of place, and far from home. You experienced the difficulties of life in the flesh, and the feelings of horror isolation brings. And what added to Your difficulty was that those disciples closest to You, the ones You may have looked to for some solace or comfort, did not enter into Your sorrows. And even while heaven seemed silent, the clamor of man's hatred against You rose. Though man would reproach You and deride You for Your faith in God's deliverance (Matthew 27:43), You never swerved from Your devotion to doing God's will.

What man could not see was that You were to bear God's indignation and wrath against our sin, that You had to be lifted up, to suffer, bleed, and die for our sins, and then to be cast away to the belly of the earth for three days and three nights. What man took for silence and indifference became a loud proclamation when heaven answered Sunday morning with an earthquake, an angel's descent to earth, and Your glorious resurrection.

Psalm 102
The Set Time Has Come

Vs.13—You will arise and have compassion on Zion,
for it is time to show favor to her; the appointed time
has come. (NIV)

Yes, Lord God, Your time is always perfect. I have learned not to complain about Your hand in my life. Though I do not understand what You are doing, I have learned that love governs it, and faith rises up to accept what is from Your hand. As surely as times of chastening come, so also come the times of blessing and favor. Though it may look as if the wrath of man has prevailed, even that You turn to Your purpose. It is not Your will that Your people be overcome in their suffering and grief, but that they would look to You to take pleasure in, build up, and restore. You hear our groanings and shall deliver so that we, Your people, would praise You freely.

Lord, You know that I am but dust, weak and feeble, and need Your strengthening to endure; strengthen me in the midst of my years. Though the outward man is perishing, the inward man is renewed day by day. One day, my flesh shall waste away. One day even the whole creation shall pass away and be rolled up as a used garment to give way to the new heaven and new earth. But You are the same yesterday, today, and forever, and I can rest in the certainty of Your sovereign timing.

Psalm 103
Bless the Lord

Vs. 2—Praise the LORD, my soul, and forget not all his benefits... (NIV).

What a theme of praise You are and what a privilege You have given me that I can bless You. That You would even desire me to bless You is astounding for You are God, omnipotent, omniscient, omnipresent, thoroughly sufficient within Yourself. You need nothing, yet You desire praise. It's not my mouth that is to bless You; my soul, my life, and my entire being is to be an instrument of blessing to You. No longer is my body, my mind to be subject to the motions of sin which dwells within me, but all is to be subject to You. You have redeemed my soul from death; You have bought me out of the slave market of sin. You have paid the ransom price—Your own precious blood on Calvary's cross—to purchase me for Yourself. Now I am Yours, my life, my all is Yours, no longer live I for myself, but for You who bought me out and brought me up. No longer a slave to sin, I am now a slave to righteousness, Your slave to live for You and not for myself.

It is only in this way that my life can bless You and be a blessing to God's heart—that the life that is displayed is the very life of Christ showing through me: "yet not I but Christ lives in me" (Galatians 2:20), "Christ in you the hope of glory" (Colossians 1:27), "Christ who is our life" (Colossians 3:4). It was Jesus alone who pleased the Father; may He see the life of His son reflected in me.

Psalm 103
His Ways ... His Acts

Vs. 7—He made known his ways to Moses, his deeds to
the people of Israel... (NIV).

Ask yourself how much you want to know of God. How close,
how intimate do you want to be? The limitation is all on our side.
It is, firstly, God's desire to reveal Himself long before we desire to
know Him. If we are going to know God, it must be done on His
terms, not our own; otherwise, all we are doing is trying to remake
God in our image, to make Him more comprehensible. God first
reveals Himself in His acts. In creation, we begin to see the nature
and character of God—beauty, order, variety, grandeur, glory—
the invisible attributes of God displayed in His creation. But it is in
the ways of God that we begin to understand God, for in His ways,
we see His design, purpose, meaning, and end. His actions are the
means of achieving His ends, but *seeing* His ends, His goals, is
most important. Moses had drawn close enough to God for Him
to reveal His ways to Moses. He saw God's ways of righteousness
and justice, but also His ways of mercy and compassion.

Moses knew firsthand of God's anger at sin and His wrath against
it, but also how God forgave and how to make intercession. Moses
was brought to see God's glory. And why did he see God's glory?
Because he asked to, and God wanted to reveal Himself. Lord, that
I would want more and more to know You and Your ways of love.

Psalm 103
His Dealings in Grace

Vs. 13—As a father has compassion on his children, so the LORD has compassion on those who fear him... (NIV).

Your dealings with me, Lord, tell me so much about You. Over everything You do, I could ascribe the words "merciful and gracious." And how have You expressed this? You were slow to anger. If someone had done to me what I have done, I would have wanted to kill him. There would not have been slowness, mercy, or grace; I would have been screaming for justice. But I am the sinner, and You have been merciful. Whereas I could have only seen the sin, You see the sinner and look deeper for a different end.

You did not always strive with me, but that means You were willing to strive for a while. Eventually the time came when You knew that my heart was set and would not let go of its sin on its own, so You had to bring in judgment and justice. However, even in that You did not give me what I deserved; You did not deal with me according to my sin, and that has angered many people. It would be safe to say that had positions been reversed, I would be angry that he didn't get what he deserved. There is no explaining it except that it is Your sovereign grace. "I will have mercy on whom I will have mercy," And that is all there is to it. *Undeserved?* Most definitely. *Explicable?* No. Only God knows what He knows and how mercy fits His purpose of grace.

Psalm 103
His Dealings in Grace (cont'd)

Vs. 17—But from everlasting to everlasting the LORD's
love is with those who fear him... (NIV).

Just how high above the earth are the heavens? The atmosphere extends for maybe 20 miles, space for billions of light years, and the angelic heavens beyond that. Our little earth is entirely encompassed by layers of heavens: just so has God encompassed me with layers of mercy. As I delve into Your word and Your Spirit reveals more of Your character, I come to another layer of understanding of grace. So, just how far is the east from the west? As far as they need to be to remove the transgression from me so that I can never get to it and it will never rebound on me. Lord, You promise complete deliverance, and it is only available as I follow the path You have laid out in Your word to crucify the flesh, hold it in the place of death, walk solely in the Spirit, and offer my body (that old instrument of sin) as a living sacrifice and instrument of righteousness.

Lord Jesus, You can pity me, have sorrow with me over my suffering, for You know what it is like to live in this flesh. And though You were without sin in Your spotless nature, You were assailed by all the same temptations that beset me, felt them even more keenly because of Your holiness, and can sympathize for You have experienced the consequences of being a creature of the dust. You know the forces that rage within, the life that yearns for satisfaction and fulfillment in all the wrong places, understand our struggles with the futility of life and can point us to the place of true happiness (blessing) and joy—the Sovereignty, the Kingdom of God, in my heart and life.

Psalm 104
My Meditation

Vs. 34—May my meditation be pleasing to him, as I
rejoice in the LORD. (NIV)

As I contemplate the wonder, the vastness, the beauty of Your
creation, it all speaks to me of Your wonder, Your vastness, Your
beauty. You are great, splendid, magnificent, and Your creation
reflects that. You have clothed the heavens with splendor and
majesty as You are clothed in light, You "who dwells in light unapproachable" (I Timothy 6:16). Your sovereignty over the universe
is indisputable as You rule and overrule in all the affairs of men.
You demonstrated that so dramatically when You destroyed the
world that then was with a flood and washed from the face of it
the vileness of wicked men.

How beneficently You provide for Your every creature. You provide food and water, a place for them to dwell, and a sphere within
which each lives. And You provide us food in its season, even wine
to gladden our hearts. We behold the rhythmic movement of the
seasons, the sun and moon in their regularity, reflecting Your order
and design. You rejoice over the works of Your hands. May You
be able to rejoice over my life, may You see the reflection of Your
Son in me, and may I gladden Your heart as I seek to live like He
did through the power of Your Spirit. As I behold all Your works,
may my faith be strengthened to trust in You more. It will only be
as I look unto Jesus and am changed from glory to glory by Your
Spirit. Bless the Lord, O my soul.

Psalm 104
Clothed With Honor and Majesty

Vs. 1—Praise the LORD my soul. LORD my God, you are very great; you are clothed with splendor and majesty. (NIV)

Before the Fall, Adam and Eve were naked and unashamed. They were perfect before God in the pristine glory of their nature. As Moses' face shone from being in the presence of God, a glow of which he was unaware, so the man and his wife shone as those having the image and likeness of God stamped upon them. But sin came, and man was no longer clothed in that same glory, and God had to provide skins, the result of death, to cover man's shame until the seed of the woman would come. And after 40 centuries, God's promised Man had come. In what was he clothed? He made Himself of no reputation; He took the form of a bondservant; He humbled Himself. The Lord of Glory clothed Himself in humiliation to feel the hunger, thirst, hatred, rejection, suffering, pain, and injustice of this life to lift us above it and set us with Him.

Now we, who by faith have been given life in Christ, have put on Christ. We have put off the old man, that old sin nature we all receive as our common inheritance from Adam, and have put on the new man, which is renewed by the regeneration of the Holy Spirit. We who are Christ's have crucified the flesh with its lusts and are clothed with Christ, who is our righteousness. He who came to die now lives at God's right hand, clothed in glory and majesty, and we are seated with Him. To be like Him and live His life in these mortal bodies brings glory to Christ and fulfills the destiny to which He has called us.

Psalm 104
How Manifold Are Your Works

Vs. 24—How many are your works, LORD! In wisdom
you made them all; the earth is full of your creatures.
(NIV)

God is the ultimate naturalist. In the all-encompassing vastness
of His design of the natural world, He demonstrated His love for
beauty, color, simplicity, variety, complexity, grandeur, wonder,
and life. Even after the Fall, and in spite of it, the natural world
still bears the stamp of the original design, although it is marred.
In this Psalm, we see a God who is involved in every detail of this
world's functioning; it is under His scrutiny to declare His wonder
and greatness. And after recounting the many ways God demonstrates His beneficent care, the Psalmist makes this declaration.
Jesus would try to teach us this same simplicity and apply it to our
lives. "Look at the lilies," He declared, "they neither toil nor spin,
yet…" Isn't that "yet" glorious, or do you dismiss it? He asserts
that we can look at them and learn not to worry. Do I believe it
or discount it as merely a fanciful rhetorical device? Jesus took it
seriously, so much so that He lived and died it. He spells it out
quite clearly and leaves us no wiggle room, and He leaves us the
challenge of believing it and acting upon it.

God takes His word very seriously and never speaks idly. The
question is never whether He means it, but whether we believe it
enough to act on it. From the vastness of the universe to the minu-
tiae of microscopic life God has stamped it all with His imprint.
Only faith can embrace who God is and respond to what He has
said. Let His work in your life be manifest.

Psalm 104
While I have my being

Vs. 33—I will sing to the LORD as long as I live: I will sing praise to my God while I have my being. (KJV)

This is to be the attitude of the believer's life. We cannot allow our praise to be driven by circumstances. Is it only when life is going well that I praise Him? Do I praise Him only when He does what I want Him to do? Is my praise to the Father transactional—that He gets some from me when I get something from Him? Have I ever given to the Lord thinking that my giving has now obligated Him to be a certain way toward me, to prosper me somehow? I wonder how often and easily I have fallen into this thinking! Have I ever said, "Why are you allowing this to happen to me?" Surely I have, and just like Job, I begin to question His wisdom, His love for me, and His good intentions (grace) toward me. And just like with Job, He patiently waits me out, bears with me in all of my venting, and then quietly reminds me that He is still God, still in control, and intends to bless.

So, what am I to do when life gets hard, when things are making no sense, and when I am overwhelmed by my circumstances? Faith must arise. Jesus did tell me that He would never leave me nor forsake me. God did assure me that nothing can separate me from His love. My spirit must lay hold of God's promises in His word. If I cannot praise God in the hard, difficult, confusing times, then what is my praise worth that I give Him in the good, easy, understandable times? While I have being, I *WILL* praise the Lord.

Psalm 105
The Testing of the Word

Vs. 16, 17—He called down famine on the land and
destroyed all their supplies of food; and he sent a man
before them—Joseph, sold as a slave. (NIV)

God is always testing us. Does He test us to find out something
about us? No, for He already knows everything about us and
the outcome. He tests us to reveal our true selves and character
to ourselves (and at times to others). And how do we see Joseph
tested? He was given a revelation about himself and his future
(and a pretty heady revelation for one so young). Now what did
he do with it? He gloried in it. Big mistake! Pride is never the right
response; it should always be humility at the thought that God
would be pleased to honor him. He suffers rejection, hardship,
and then an elevation in Potiphar's house. When tested he didn't
respond in vanity and pride at the wife's attention; he responded
in horror. He suffered betrayal, slander, and false imprisonment.

Now where are his dreams and the God of that revelation? Would
he abandon it, turn from God in disappointment and disgust? He
does not! Can a man who is destined to wield as much power as
will be placed in Joseph's hands, who will literally have the power
of life and death over people, wield that power if he is petty, vindic-
tive, or vengeful? Can he be entrusted with that kind of power if
he is vain, proud, or corruptible? Will he stay true to the heavenly
vision in the face of all outward circumstances? With God, the test
is not Pass/Fail. He is an assayer who removes the dross and tests
the purity to prepare one for His service.

Psalm 105
Brought Out With Joy and Gladness

Vs. 43—He brought out his people with rejoicing, his
chosen ones with shouts of joy... (NIV).

This is almost too incredible to believe. Can it truly be that after
so many years of slavery, hardship, toil, and suffering it can all be
replaced with joy and gladness? Yes. It was almost too much for
my heart to accept. My mind told me *yes*, but my heart told me
impossible and condemned me; but God was greater than my heart
(I John 3:20); His grace and Jesus' blood was more than sufficient.
I knew the terrible "Egypt" I had been in, the awful bondage to the
lusts and strongholds Satan had erected (and I had assisted in con-
structing) as brick-by-brick, I closed myself in and shut God out.

And as I looked out from behind my bunker and dared God to
get through to me, I was cutting myself off from my only deliverance. Those walls have come toppling down, the foundation of
that stronghold broken. You have brought me out of my Egypt
but at such a terrible price of sin and shame, sorrow, and pain. I
gave You no choice; You could not draw me out, so You had to lay
siege and break through forcibly. Now I am Your captive, Lord,
captive of and captivated by Your love. It was such a relief when
You finally broke in, and I found that along with the sorrow and
shame over what I had done came the joy and gladness over what
You had accomplished. There has been much rubble to clear away,
but let it be gone!

Psalm 106
Standing in the breach

Vs. 23—... he said that he would destroy them, had not
Moses ...stood before him in the breach... (KJV).

Did the Israelites realize what they had done? Did they have the
slightest inkling that they were on the precipice of annihilation?
Moses had just been receiving the law from the hand of God. He
had spent 40 days reviewing and discussing it in intimate detail.
Moses, who had experienced God so intimately and had such a
glimpse into God's glory and absolute holiness as revealed in His
law, was appalled when told that the people had built a golden calf
to worship (Exodus 32:8). Moses knew what was at stake. When
he descends the mountain, Joshua is confused, but Moses knows
(Exodus 32:17–18). What is God going to do? What is Moses to
do? He smashes the two tables of the law and intercedes for the
people. Is it not just this that Jesus has done?

Long before the horror of sin finally touches our souls, long before
we realize just how serious a judgment is upon us, Jesus interceded
for us. And what did He say? "Father, forgive him." I didn't even
know I needed such intervention, but He did. But, unlike Moses,
who had to smash the tablets of the law lest they enter the camp
and destroy the people, Jesus fulfilled all of the righteous claims
of the law. And having fulfilled all and been found spotless (nothing externally that would disqualify Him) and without blemish
(nothing internally that revealed an inner, evil nature) He was able
to bear the wrath of God against my sin by being made sin for
me—by becoming my sin on the cross. I know what I deserved for
my sin, but my Moses stood in the breach, interceded for me, and
separated me from my sin.

Psalm 106
Leanness

Vs. 15—And he gave them their request; but sent leanness into their soul. (KJV)

Oftentimes, the worst thing we can get is what we ask for. As petu-
lant children, we ask amiss and then complain to You that You
have not answered our prayers. So, we blame You when we should
blame ourselves. Lord, when this happens, let me always recall that
You are good, that there is no good thing that You will withhold
from those who love You, and that Your withholding of something
from me is an indication of Your mercy. For what happens when
I ask amiss? (James 4:3) It is actually not a prayer to You, but an
expression of my lusts. And what would happen if You fulfilled
it? I would feed those lusts. And then what? Those lusts are never
satisfied but grow stronger, louder, and more insistent.

But I won't let up; I pout, throw tantrums, accuse You of not
loving me, and withhold myself from You to *punish* You. Since I
will have it no other way, since I am given over to this desire, You
allow it—but at a price. The price is leanness unto my soul. God's
desire for me is fatness, for fatness represents and indicates health,
vigor, and vitality; fullness in Christ and of His Spirit. But all my
energy and thought have been directed to this other thing—i.e.,
self-directed thought. The only way for God to get it out of me
is to give it to me and let it sicken me, so I reject it for myself and
return to God in repentance. Such, at times, is His severe mercy.

Psalm 106
Cast down by God

Vs. 26—Therefore He swore to them That He would have them fall in the wilderness... (NASB).

Have I ever despised the pleasant land? Have I ever looked upon what God wanted to give to me as a blessing and spurned it? Every time I sin and act in my flesh, that is what I am doing. I may have plenty of reasons; I may have even rationalized it in my own mind and justified it to myself, but in the end, it is all lies. In Christ, God has laid before me so much that is good. He has blessed me with all spiritual blessings in heavenly places. He has raised me up and made me to sit in Christ in heavenly places. So, how could I turn away from such a bounty and return to the beggarly things of this world? It is because my flesh still desires the things of this world. The devil is not my problem; he merely seizes the opportunities my flesh offers him. The world is not my problem; it merely provides the sources of those opportunities. The flesh is my problem. And it is in my flesh that no good thing dwells. So, when I reach for one of those dainties, I despise the things He has for me.

There is no way to get from Egypt (slavery to sin) to the promised land (freedom in Christ) without going through the wilderness. And when you get to the promised land, what do you find? Spiritual warfare, principalities and powers in high places. Moses said that it was only an 11-day journey from Mt. Sinai to Kadesh-Barnea, yet it took them 38 ½ years. And why? Because of their stubbornness. Lord Jesus, deliver me from this bondage of wanting my own way, free me from the tyranny of my own will, and lead me into Your liberty where I only want what You want for me.

Psalm 106
Sacrificed to sin

Vs. 37—They even sacrificed their sons and their
daughters to the demons... (ESV).

What a terrible thing the children of Israel did by getting so
enmeshed with the nations around them that they began to adopt
their practices. Little did they know that, as the years rolled on and
successive generations were born, the degree of sin would escalate
to the point of human sacrifice. We look back upon them and
wonder, "How could they have ever let things go so far?" But does
any of us ever anticipate the end from the beginning? Does the
alcoholic see in that first drink his future dissipation? Or does the
drug addict see his future overdose death while enjoying his first
high? Or does that man see the ultimate separation from his family
in that little fling he's having? No, and neither did I.

Satan always seeks to blind us to the ultimate end of sin—which is
death. Long before physical death comes, there are many casualties
along the way. Yes, the children of Israel literally sacrificed their
children to demons, but we, through our stubborn persistence
in sin, sacrifice much. We sacrifice our health, our time, our energies, our devotion, our spouses, our children, our families all on
altars of money, power, pleasure, fame, glory, success, comfort,
or any number of other things. And perhaps you will pull back
from the precipice before you have lost it all, but some damage to
relationships has already been done. Once confronted by my sin, I
thank You, Lord, for accepting my confession and repentance and
leading me into restoration.

Psalm 106
They Changed Their Glory

Vs. 39—They defiled themselves by what they did; by
their deeds they prostituted themselves. (NIV)

Sin is inherently self-destructive; it always tends to death rather
than life, sorrow not joy, bondage not liberty. So, why do I work
so hard to get something that truly cannot satisfy? Through
redemption, God has brought me out of bondage to freedom,
yet I yearn for the leeks, onions, and garlic of Egypt and come to
"loathe this light bread" (Numbers 21:5, KJV). How it is that sin
debases us and brings us to be lower than the animals, than the
brute beasts! But what is man? He is in the image and likeness of
God. We are described as being the glory of God (I Corinthians
11:7). Whenever I debase God, I reduce Him to a lower level than
He truly occupies (and this is the principle of idolatry). I have
also reduced myself in whose image and after whose glory I have
been made.

The idolatry at Mt. Horeb with the golden calves began a chain of
events—ignoring God's works, despising God's promises, mur-
muring and complaining, intermarriage, and human sacrifice. Just
as Israel of old, so have I followed a downward spiral and have
been brought low for my iniquity. But thanks be to God, that
is not the end of the matter, for Your mercy is great. Your Spirit
has worked. He has brought conviction, confession, repentance,
and restoration. Whereas through my sin I had changed glory for
shame, God, through His Spirit, is transforming me from glory to
glory, to remake me after the image of His Son.

Psalm 106
Objects of Compassion

Vs. 46—He also made them *objects* of compassion in the
presence of all their captors. (NASB)

After all that Israel had done, after following their sin and idolatry
so far as to even sacrifice their children to demons by passing them
through the fire, God had finally been forced to bring judgment
down upon them and carry them off into exile. But even there,
amid their captors, the Babylonians , God still had His hand of
favor upon them. He had placed Daniel as prophet in the very
courts of power and Ezekiel as prophet amid the captives. In a
situation where they had no power over themselves, their lives, and
their destiny, they had God's watchful eye upon them. Lord, how
I thank You that You do not think like I do, that Your ways are not
like my ways. If it were up to us, we would take that person who
had sinned against us, throw them in some prison of misery and
throw away the key. But You didn't do that to me. Where I had
sinned grievously against You, You still had Your hand of forgiveness stretched out to me so that I would repent and be restored in
my relationship to You.

After having such compassion on Your part shown to me, how is
it possible that I would not respond in that same manner toward
those who have hurt me? Lord, teach me the depth of Your love
and grace so that I can express through You that same love and
grace toward others. As You said in Luke 7:47, (KJV) "...her sins,
which are many, are forgiven for she loved much But to whom
little is forgiven, the same loves little." This causes me to see how
much I have been forgiven so that I can love others as You do.

SEPTEMBER 4

Psalm 107
The Giving of Thanks

Vs. 1—Give thanks to the LORD, for he is good, his
love endures forever. (NIV)

Four times in this Psalm, we are implored to give thanks to the Lord for His goodness (verses 8, 15, 21, 31). Why so many times? Because my heart is prone to taking God for granted, to receiving blessings from God as a matter of course as if that is all God is for, and neither recognizing nor acknowledging His beneficent hand. I must get firmly in my mind and deeply in my heart that God doesn't owe me anything and that anything good that comes from God's hand comes out of the bounties of His grace, the overflow of His love.

No wonder I am spiritually flat sometimes—it is because I have neglected thankfulness. What does thankfulness accomplish in me? For one, it causes me to live in the constant reminder of the true nature of God, which is love. It takes the focus off of me and places it upon God. For another, it keeps me cognizant of the fact that all I have, all I am, I owe to God. There is nothing I have that has not been given to me. Then, I am kept constantly aware of His grace. God is never obligated to me. Now the Father is obligated to the Son and we are let in on this divine secret as we listen in on Jesus' prayer to His Father in John 17; but God is never obligated to me. So, it is all of grace. Is it possible to thank God enough? If all the skies were parchment and all the oceans ink, would that be enough to express fully the love of God?

Psalm 107
Satisfying the Longing Heart

Vs. 8, 9—Let them give thanks to the LORD for his unfailing love and his wonderful deeds for mankind, for he satisfies the thirsty and fills the hungry with good things. (NIV)

What am I longing for? What does my heart really want? Is it merely an easing of my circumstances so that life isn't so hard? God knows that to rearrange the deck chairs of my life will not prevent me from colliding with the icebergs of life. Lord, I mistook externals for internals way too long. For too long, I tried to manage the problems within by controlling my outward life, but that did not satisfy. So, You had to let my carefully constructed life collapse before I would get serious with You. In my brokenness and emptiness, I called out to You, and You answered.

You have always been there. You gave me to drink of Your water, caused me to eat of Your bread, fed my soul with mercy, grace, and forgiveness, and satisfied the deepest longings of my soul. Now, I cannot help but give You thanks every day; each day is a fresh reminder of Your grace. I have walked in darkness and have hid myself from Your searching light, but no more. I give thanks that You persisted, have exposed all the evil, and have cleaned out all the filth of my life. Your word has brought healing. Whereas before I made bitterness my drink, resentment my food, and my soul abhorred what You tried to set before it, now I can feast on Your Son and drink deeply of the Holy Spirit. Lord, You have done marvelously, and I give You thanks.

Psalm 108
A Steadfast Heart

Vs. 1—My heart, O God, is steadfast; I will sing and make music with all my soul. (NIV)

Lord, when I look within, I see a heart that is so easily distracted, so readily turned aside to its own way, so prone to be attracted by the things of this world. But when I read the gospels, I see that You were the man with the steadfast heart. Never distracted, never deterred, always desirous of pleasing the Father. How often do I read of you praying until late into the night or rising a great way before morning to meet with Your Father in prayer? Herein lies the secret of the steadfast heart—the heart so set upon pleasing the Father that it becomes thoroughly dependent and submissive to His will. So, for the man Christ Jesus, inwardly there was joy, though outwardly He was a man of sorrows and acquainted with grief; inwardly there was praise and rejoicing, though outwardly He pleaded with men to be reconciled to God; inwardly there was great contentment, though outwardly He was under unrelenting stress.

As You made Your way to Jerusalem, to suffer the death of the cross, Your heart was still steadfast, knowing that You were doing the will of the Father and bringing glory to Him. Rather than seeking deliverance for Yourself, You delivered Yourself up, awaiting the full deliverance of God through death and resurrection. Such is Your glory, blest Savior, and such is the exaltation You have received, for You were steadfast.

Psalm 108
God Speaks In Holiness

Vs. 5—Be exalted, O God, above the heavens; let your glory be over all the earth. (NIV)

When God speaks it behooves us to listen; He does not like to repeat Himself. And when God speaks what He has to say is important; He does not speak casually. God's voice and His words have creative power to speak into the darkness and bring new things into existence. When God speaks, everything He says is truth; God is not a man that He should lie. When God speaks, His word stands; no one can add to it, and no one can take away from it. When God speaks, His pronouncements are just; in Him there is neither partiality nor respect of persons. When God speaks, He does so in holiness; all of God's thoughts, words, and deeds are in perfect harmony with His character. God is absolutely pure in His nature, being, and essence, and everything He is about reflects that reality. We deal with a holy God, one who hates sin, whose constant disposition toward sin is wrath. Does this thought scare you?

The measure of God's holiness and the extent of God's wrath are both seen at the cross. Jesus, the only righteous man, bore our sins on His own body on the tree fully absorbing and extinguishing God's wrath against our sin. Now in Christ, we are made holy and made partakers of His divine nature. So, when God speaks to us, it is "like speaking to like" in that God is holiness speaking to our new nature made after the image of His Son. He is speaking to the new man. The flesh has no place or standing before God; it is to be reckoned as dead, crucified with Christ. Have ears to hear, let the new man be built up in love as God speaks to you His wonderful words of grace.

Psalm 109
Given to Prayer

Vs. 4—In return for my friendship they accuse me, but
I am a man of prayer. (NIV)

What is a man to do when heaven seems silent? What is he to do when all around him are those who seek his harm, who open their mouths in slander, deceit, and lies against him? What is a man to do when people hate him, though there is no cause for that hatred, that he has done no harm but only good to them? Do what Jesus did; give yourself to prayer. Jesus' heart was steadfastly set upon His Father. He knew that everything happening in His life was under the sovereign control of God, that all events were directed by God's love to accomplish His ends, and that God would work all things to His purposes for good.

I am not called to understand the ways of God but to trust in God. I am not brought in on God's counsel but to have confidence in the God of His counsels. I am to give myself over to prayer, cast myself upon His grace, draw from Him His strength, rejoice in His presence, be content in my circumstances, trust in His love, and be willing to be broken and poured out for His pleasure. All these things Jesus was and all was made possible because He was given to prayer. Prayer is dependence; prayer is confidence; prayer is the living connection to the living God. It is the respiration of our spirit, giving out praise and drawing in His love.

SEPTEMBER 9

Psalm 109
For Your Name's Sake

Vs. 21—But you, Sovereign LORD, help me for your name's sake; out of the goodness of your love, deliver me. (NIV)

Lord may it always be about You and not about me. Keep me from selfish preoccupation that brings me to esteem myself as being something in myself when I am nothing, yet everything in Christ. As I look at Your life, Jesus, I see the perfect man, the divine man, with all the fullness of the Godhead dwelling in bodily form. Yet You were the dependent, praying man who did nothing apart from the Father's will and mind. Your whole life was all about Your Father's name—to reveal Him to us. So, You could accept from Your Father whatever He gave.

You were born into a life of poverty and obscurity, did not have the advantages of society and education, poor and needy all of Your life, afflicted, pursued, hated, despised, and misunderstood by those who should have known You best. But You could say, "Let them curse, but You bless." Such holy submission, such divine compassion—submission to God, compassion for sinners! Deal with me, Lord, for Your name's sake. Crush me any way You need to draw out the wine which would rejoice Your heart. Let my life, Lord, be a trophy of Your grace. Give me that mind of Christ to be submitted to You and compassionate to the lost and hurting.

Psalm 110
The Right Hand of God

Vs. 1—The LORD says to my lord: "Sit at my right hand until I make your enemies a footstool for your feet." (NIV)

That is where You are, Lord Jesus: exalted to the right hand of God the Father. You are enthroned in heaven, seated beside Him on His throne awaiting the time when He shall send You forth to subdue and rule the earth. Into Your hands has been given all power and authority in heaven and on earth (Matthew 28:18). And why have You been enthroned in glory and made to sit with the Father on His throne? Because You have by Yourself purged our sins (Hebrews 1:3). The Father was so pleased with the work of the cross, His heart so joyful at the life You had lived in total submission to His will, God's righteousness so vindicated by being able to finally expend all of His pent-up wrath against man's sins upon You that He now shares His throne and His glory with You as a man upon His throne.

As the apostle Paul writes in Philippians 2:9, KJV "Wherefore, God has highly exalted Him, and given Him a name which is above every name." And Peter also pronounces in Acts 4:12, KJV "For there is none other name under heaven given among men, whereby we must be saved." You, Lord Jesus, have the name above all others; You have the place of dignity where no other could sit. You have the full approbation of the Father, and I am seated with You in those heavenly places by virtue of your blood. Thank You, Jesus, for bringing me into a place of blessing.

Psalm 110
Rule in the Midst

Vs. 2—The LORD will extend your mighty scepter
from Zion, saying, "Rule in the midst of your enemies!"
(NIV)

How much do all Your people really want You to rule in the midst
of Your enemies, to put down all that opposes Your sovereignty
and Lordship? Then let us prove it by giving You that preeminent
place even now in our hearts! We see all the evil, violence, sin, and
degradation in this world and ask, "How long?" Then why don't
we look within our own hearts at the same time and welcome Him
to clean it all up? Lord, before You will ever set foot in this world
again You challenge me to submit all I am to You and have You
rule in my heart where the flesh and indwelling sin still wage war
and are at enmity with You (Galatians 5:17). At Your trial You told
them exactly who You were: the Christ, the son of God (Matthew
27:63), the Son of Man (Matthew 27:64, Daniel 7:13), the son of
the Blessed (Mark 14:61), the son of God (Luke 22:70), the King
of the Jews (John 18:33). But they did not understand that You
were also the Lamb of God (John 1:29) and the suffering servant
(Isaiah 52:13–53:12). They had rejected this key of knowledge
(Luke 11:52) that the suffering must precede the glory (Luke
24:26), and they had rejected the will of God (Luke 7:30), thus
the kingdom would be taken away from them (Matthew 21:24).

Lord now is the time for Your rule to be expressed in my heart and
life and Your sovereignty acknowledged in the Church as we await
Your coming when You shall rule in the midst of Your enemies.

Psalm 110
Priest Forever

Vs. 4—The LORD has sworn and will not change his mind: "You are a priest forever, in the order of Melchizedek." (NIV)

When Abraham met Melchizedek that day, he met a man who preserved in his life and actions the knowledge of the true God that Noah brought with him through the Flood. In the brief encounter, Melchizedek would make a huge impression and would form the basis for this great type of Your perpetual priesthood. And now You are my high priest; You have entered into Your service upon completion of redemption and Your being installed in heaven. You are the high priest of the heavenly tabernacle (Hebrews 8:2, 5; 9:11; 10:23–24), the mediator of a better covenant (Hebrews 7:22, 8:6, 9:15), bringing a better law (Hebrews 7:12, 16; 8:7, 13; 10:1, 9), instituted on better sacrifices (Hebrews 7:27, 9:12, 14, 26; 10:12, 14).

By Your Spirit, teach me more of what it means that You are no longer standing and ministering (as the high priest of old did), but seated at God's right hand forever making intercession. Such a blessing, having my conscience purged from sin, to know that I am accepted in Your presence by virtue of Your precious blood, that I am a member of Your body, a child in Your family, and seated with You. My heart fills with adoration and praise at the wonder of Your person, the greatness of Your offering, the terror and victory of the cross. And then to know that the Father doesn't see me in my sin and vileness, but in Your righteousness and perfection. Oh, that the Father would see His Son in me, that as He would gaze, it would not be I but Christ!

Psalm 110
Gracious and Full of compassion

Vs. 5, 6—The Lord is at your right hand; he will crush
kings on the day of his wrath, He will judge the nations,
heaping up the dead and crushing rulers of the whole
earth. (NIV)

One of the cruelest deceptions to which a Christian succumbs is
to believe that he alone is responsible for the progress and prosperity in his life. What a terrible darkness into which one falls who
discounts the activity of God's grace and compassion in his life and
fashions himself a "self-made man." How dare the clay boast of
itself to the potter as if he has turned the wheel himself. Paul would
say, "By the grace of God I am what I am" (I Corinthians 15:10,
KJV). This is where the realization must begin. Everything I am,
everything I have, all of my innate talents and acquired abilities I
have as a result of God's grace. And our God is not an Aristotelian
"Prime Mover" or "First Cause," an impersonal, uninvolved God
who plops the clay down upon the wheel, spins it, and says, "Form
thyself!" No, our God places the clay upon His wheel and lovingly,
carefully, jealously fashions the vessel of His choosing.

And what happens if the vessel is marred in the Potter's hands?
Oh, dear clay, do not complain or resist against the pressure of
those gentle hands. Though your sin has marred you, the Master
Potter can reform and reshape you to be a vessel of honor meet for
His use. Notice the compassion He has showered upon you that
you as clay did not end up on a refuse heap, nor did He settle for
a marred, misshapen vessel. God wants more out of His creation
than we, as His creatures, can imagine. Glory in His grace and
compassion; let that be your boast all the days of your life.

SEPTEMBER 14

Psalm 111
Food from God

Vs. 5—He provides food for those who fear him; he remembers his covenant forever. (NIV)

It is You, Lord Jesus, who is the food for my soul. You gave them manna in the wilderness in order to teach them that man does not live by bread alone, but by every word that proceeds from the mouth of the Lord. That manna could only satisfy for a day, but You, Lord, satisfy for all eternity. For my spirit, You are all I need for all that I can know of God is revealed fully in You. All that I can experience of God is because of Your life in me, and Your Spirit causes me to feed upon You.

Do I need to learn of love? Then I hear Your prayer to the Father. Do I need to learn of compassion? Then I hear of the good Samaritan. Do I need to learn of self-sacrifice? Then I hear of the good shepherd. Do I need to learn of strength? Then I see You fasting forty days in the wilderness. Do I need to learn of courage? Then I see You unshaken before Your accusers. Do I need to learn of service? Then I see You with the woman at Sychar's well. Do I need to learn of bravery? Then I hear You defy and denounce the scribes and Pharisees on their own turf. Do I need to learn of compassion? Then I see You touched by our infirmities and healing. Do I need to learn of honor? Then I see You uphold God's honor and the sanctity of His house. Do I need to learn of pity? I only need to hear You weeping over Jerusalem. Do I need to learn of forgiveness? I hear Your voice plead for forgiveness from the cross. Anything and everything I need for life, I see, hear, and learn from You.

Psalm 111
He has sent Redemption

Vs. 9—He provided redemption for his people; he ordained his covenant forever—holy and awesome is his name. (NIV)

When God sent redemption to this world, in what form did it come? It came in the form of a baby. The omnipotent God came packaged in the weakness of a baby to fight the battle of the ages. Do not despise the manner in which God will send you deliverance. Samuel had to learn this lesson too. God had to tell him that God does not look at outward appearances as man does. The angels announced Jesus' birth, for they knew exactly who He was and what He had come to do, but there was barely a ripple of notice on the part of men. Did not Jesus thank the Father for having hidden these things from the wise to reveal them unto babes? Did not Paul write of how God has chosen the weak things, the simple ones, to confound the high and mighty?

When Jesus expired on the cross, He said, "It is finished." To man's ears, it might have sounded like the final resignation of a beaten, defeated man. But the centurion knew otherwise. Men did not expire on the cross with a triumphal shout. When he heard Jesus' cry, he pronounced that "Surely, this was the son of God." Jesus had triumphed, and He let all creation know. God's power is made perfect in weakness. It was that way with Jesus, and it is that way with me now. As I yield to You and give You free access to my life, I see your power come into and through me. No longer do I react in my flesh from my own nature, but now I can respond in the power of Your Spirit. I can now be triumphant over indwelling sin in my life and experience the power of His resurrection life in me.

Psalm 112
The Steadfast Heart

Vs. 7—They will have no fear of bad news; their hearts
are steadfast, trusting in the LORD. (NIV)

A heart that is steadfast and immovable is one that is sunk deeply
into the soil of God's love. Just look at the Lord Jesus. Whose
heart was more steadfast than His? How could He be so fearless
in the face of Herod's threats, the Pharisees' traps, the Sadducees'
schemes, or the might of Rome were it not His great, awesome fear
of the Lord? His view of the Father was so great that it thoroughly
eclipsed all others. He was so grounded in the word of God, had
so completely given Himself over to it, and fulfilled all of it that
He could not be diverted from His purpose. Truly, Lord, You are
this man, and in all the varied circumstances, You displayed the
calmness that could only come from a relationship of dependence
upon God. Your confidence was always in Your Father, not even
relying upon Your own divine power as the source of Your stability.

When You wanted to return to Judea to raise Lazarus, You were
warned that they sought Your life; but it was day, Your time to
work. Thomas said, "Let us go and die with him" (John 11:16,
KJV). When one trusts in God rather than circumstances, then the
commonsense no longer makes any sense, only trusting the Lord
makes sense, and the heart is established. Lord, You know what
life is like; You understand and have felt the rise of fear. You know
how uncertainties can plague and You saw beyond. So, I have to
choose between two paths: fear or faith. I choose You.

Psalm 112
Blessed Is the Man

Vs. 1—Praise the LORD, Blessed are those who fear the LORD, who find great delight in his commands. (NIV)

What does it take for one to be a blessed man? Before you can answer that question for yourself, another question must be posed: is your measure of blessing internal or external? For most believers, sad to say, the measure is externals, borne by circumstances. They will look to their health, consider their wealth, tally their educational degrees, the number of possessions, or their physical beauty and assess God's level of blessing in their life. If your measure of blessing is in the externals, then what is your view of God, the blesser? If your measure of blessing is in the externals, then how much loss could you suffer before you abandoned the blesser?

Paul said he could suffer the loss of all things to obtain Christ; if anything hindered his pursuit of Christ, he would gladly endure the loss. The externals may be evidence of the blessing of God, but they are never the measure of it, and they are very imperfect evidence of that (see Psalm 73). But what of the one who fears the Lord, who holds his relationship with God as such a treasure that he holds other things in relative contempt? He is blessed! He will have the proper balance of the externals and the internals. He will know how both to mind the earthly things, for he knows that he must fulfill his earthly responsibilities, and the spiritual things. As we are faithful to God in whatever commonplace way He has set before us He will bless, for our God is a God who loves to bless. Let us rejoice in His blessing and not presume on how He shall bless.

Psalm 113
He Humbles Himself

Vs. 4—The LORD is exalted over all the nations, his glory above the heavens. (NIV)

Do I have a vision of how highly exalted You are, Lord? Have I entered into even a small understanding of Your greatness and glory? I think not. For if I did have an appreciation of how You are high and exalted over all things, then I would treat You with the honor You are due: I would pledge my life, my being, to Your service. You were exalted as Son from all eternity past and ever the delight of the Father (Proverbs 8:30), yet You humbled Yourself just in becoming a man and then humbled Yourself even further in death. This Psalm tells me that for You to even look upon this earth, much less to come here, is a humble act to You, a holy condescension on Your part.

When I contemplate You, now highly exalted above all creation, and see Your splendor and majesty, my soul bows in worship to consider Your humility in incarnation. Yet You came to raise the poor in spirit out of the dust, to lift us who were in such need and poverty from the ashes after all of our own hopes and dreams had gone up in smoke and been consumed. You became a man to enter into the circumstances of our life, so You could get underneath us and lift us out of our lost condition. Give me a vision of Yourself, Lord Jesus, that I may see all of You, the agony and the ecstasy, the humility and the glory.

Psalm 113
From the Rising to the Setting

Vs. 3—From the rising of the sun to the place where it sets, the name of the LORD is to be praised. (NIV)

This expression: "from the rising of the sun to its going down," teaches us that our entire day, all of our thoughts and activities are to be done with an awareness of God's place in our lives. God is never so silly to think that we are to suspend all life activities to praise Him; rather, He wants us to incorporate Him into even the most mundane activities of life. This is how God can imbue all of life with purpose and meaning. Whether cutting the lawn, painting the house, fixing the meal, or running the family taxi service, God is in it when we serve others cheerfully as unto the Lord out of a loving heart. This is how God Himself acts as he blesses all of His creation, providing for each what is needful. When we serve like Him, we bring Him praise. When we love like Him, we glorify His name.

To glorify a name is to act in accordance with the owner of that name, to exemplify the characteristics and qualities of the one who holds that name. To do every action in this awareness, to speak our words with grace seasoned with salt, to have in our minds thoughts of Christ to govern our hearts and minds will result in a day of praise to God the Father. The Father said of Jesus at the Jordan, "I am well pleased." Jesus hadn't done miracles, signs, wonders, or preaching but had merely been a faithful son, a caring brother, a hard worker in the carpentry business, had supported the family upon Joseph's death, and lived an ordinary life so that folks wondered whence came His brilliance. God treasures the ordinary and draws praise from it.

Psalm 114
Tremble in His Presence

Vs. 7, 8—Tremble, earth, at the presence of Lord, at the presence of the God of Jacob, who turned the rock into a pool, the hard rock into springs of water. (NIV)

Of old, You made Your people Your dwelling place. The tabernacle and sanctuary provided a means by which You, the holy God, could dwell amid sinful men without consuming them. A thin red line of sacrificial blood is all that stood between them and utter judgment. All creation responded to the awesomeness of Your presence and the greatness of Your glory and trembled before You. So, how could it be that my sin didn't cause me to tremble? If the earth is shaken to its very foundation, then how come my being was not shaken to its very core? Oh, the flesh is a terrible thing! It cannot submit nor shall it ever submit to the sovereignty of God. It is unredeemed and nonredeemable and must be put to death, ultimately shall die, so that the life of Christ can be displayed.

So I went to church, taught Sunday School, and was all along living in hypocrisy. Since I did not tremble before him with my sin, He had to bring me down. In my depth of despair I cried out to Him and He was there. It was prayer that I had lacked, prayer that would have brought me before Him so that I might not fall into sin. But I avoided prayer for it would have placed me too uncomfortably in the light of His presence. Lord, keep my heart tender now, and make me sensitive to anything that would divide my heart from Yours.

Psalm 114
Judah His Sanctuary

Vs. 2—Judah became God's sanctuary, Israel his dominion. (NIV)

God created us for fellowship and that fellowship is not only
social with others but also with Himself. Though God Himself
has no needs of His own and is perfectly content with that fellowship within the Godhead as Father, Son, and Holy Spirit, yet He
desired to share His eternal joy and love with creatures. We were
made for His pleasure, for the joy He would receive from having
us with Him sharing in His love. And even though sin has come in,
God's love has super-abounded in grace to overcome that sin. This
world is His world, yet man in his sin and rebellion has rejected
God and will not have His Son to reign over him.

So during this time of His rejection, He has sought out for Himself
a sanctuary, a dwelling place. And just as it was for Israel of old that
it was built upon the foundation of redemption, so it is now. We,
who by faith, have accepted the substitutionary death of Jesus on
the cross of Calvary, have been redeemed out of the slavery of sin
and brought into the family of God by adoption. What a privilege!
We are the body of Christ, the household of faith, the habitation
of God by the Spirit, being built up as a holy temple in the Lord,
espoused to Him as His bride, one day to be wed to Him and
have all the host of heaven rejoicing at what God has wrought for
Himself in Jesus. May the joy of Jesus be made complete in us!

Psalm 115
As He Pleases

Vs. 3—Our God is in heaven; he does whatever pleases him. (NIV)

The desire of every sinful heart is to be able to do exactly what pleases it. Sinful, fallen man defines freedom as the ability to do as one pleases, to be able to make that choice and carry it out. Free will is even defined as the absence of constraint to be able to choose the course that pleases one. But we know what happened in the garden, that Adam saw it this way and our sad human history is a testimony to the fallacy of such thinking. Only God can do as He pleases, absolutely and without constraint. Sinful man bristles at this thought and would dare to accuse God of being arbitrary, capricious, whimsical. But, as Abraham said, "Shall not the judge of all the earth do right?" (Genesis 18:25, KJV)

I did what I pleased, followed my lusts, sinned grievously against God, and caused much harm. God has done what He pleased. He sent His Son Jesus into this world to live perfectly before Him as a man, to testify to the love and mercy of God, and to die on Calvary's cross to redeem mankind. We were pleased with our sin, though we didn't enjoy its consequences; we were pleased with our idols and pleased with ourselves. It was God who was not pleased with our lost condition. How wondrous is the pleasure of God now that He can see in me the image of Him who gave to His Father's heart such pleasure: Jesus Christ.

Psalm 115
The Lord is Mindful

Vs. 11—You who fear him, trust in the LORD—he is
their help and shield. (NIV)

What a wonder it is to contemplate that the Lord is mindful of us.
"For what is man that You are mindful of him?" (Psalm 8:4) We
exchange the knowledge of God for a lie and the glory of God for
an idol. We make idols of so many things—possessions, ambitions,
achievements, notoriety—but these can never deliver to us what
they purport to be able to provide. They are no different than the
idols of old which, having hands, feet, eyes, ears, and mouth, have
only an appearance of power. God looks upon all of our futile
struggles and has subjected all of it to vanity to turn us to Himself.
And once "we turn to God from idols," we find One who is mindful of us and desirous to bless. And bless me You have done!

To have followed my sin for so long, to have grieved the Holy Spirit
so often, to have quenched Your activity in my life so consistently
and then to find You still mindful of me, is more than my soul
could have hoped for. It is one thing to know in general that You
bless Your people, but it is an entirely different thing to experience the blessing of the Lord personally. And bless You do. Each
morning I feel Your blessing of health and strength, even as the
outward man perishes. In my soul I experience the joy, wonder,
and expectation of a new day, the child-like freshness of a new
thing of possibilities and experiences of You. In my spirit, there is
Your abiding presence, the fresh communion, the rejoicing in the
life of Christ within.

Psalm 116
Trouble and Sorrow

Vs. 3, 4—The cords of death entangled me, the anguish
of the grave came over me; I was overcome by distress
and sorrow. Then I called on the name of the LORD:
"LORD save me!" (NIV)

Why does trouble and sorrow so distress us? Do we think we
should be immunized from the trials of a fallen world? Do we
believe that God is too good to allow distress to come? Just what
is our expectation? Jesus said, "In this world you shall have tribulation." Since it is assured to us, let us not be overthrown by it, but
overcome. You, Lord, knew distress, trouble, and sorrow throughout Your life, which intensified the closer You came to the cross.
And what was Your resource but Your Father to whom You could
call out and were confident that He heard and answered.

If, in even the smallest extent, I look solely within for the resources
I need to face my trials and difficulties, then that will be the extent
to which I am inviting failure into my life. You would call upon
Him as long as You lived. Even at the point of death, after having
borne man's hatred and God's wrath, You committed Your Spirit
to the Father. How beautiful to see Your utter confidence in Your
loving Father to trust Him all the way to death (verse 3) and from
death (verse 8) by going through death. After having gone through
the deep waters of sorrow and coming up on the other side, we are
full of praise and thanksgiving to Him who delivers. And whatever
commitments we have made to God, whatever pledges of fidelity,
let us pay them for, He has done gloriously toward us.

Psalm 116
The Lord Preserves the Simple

Vs. 5–6—The LORD is gracious and righteous; our God is full of compassion. The LORD protects the unwary; when I was brought low, he saved me. (NIV)

Mostly, the term "simple" is associated with ideas such as simpleton, simplistic, simpleminded, or naïve. It is considered a derogatory term denoting one who is immature or of limited intelligence. In the eyes of the world, we should be sophisticated, nuanced, not given to black and white thinking, but always seeing all the shades of gray. But what of spiritual things? Are we to have the same attitude toward the things of God as we do toward the world's things, or is God due a deference and a reverence the world could never command? God desires our spiritual simplicity, not pitting our intelligence, wisdom, or experience against His omniscience and omnipotence, but bowing ourselves to Him.

In comparison to God, we are mere children; in the light of His omniscience, our knowledge is less than minuscule. Do you wish to be truly wise? Then learn at His feet, for the fear of the Lord is the beginning of wisdom. Put aside all of your reasonings, all of your ideas, and any preconceived notions you have and own your simplicity in the presence of God. As you begin to see things from His perspective, to see as He sees, then you shall be wise for you will have an understanding the world can never provide. When you find yourself in a tight spot, seek to receive His divine perspective. Allow His truth and insight to simplify the labyrinthine confusion; be simple in His sight. Then obey Him, and He shall preserve you.

Psalm 116
The Soul's Restoration

Vs. 7—Return to your rest, O my soul... (BSB).

Lord, how you have taught me that sin disturbs the rest You want to give me. In Hebrews, Paul wrote of how the Old Testament Jews did not enter into the rest after the exodus from Egypt because of their unbelief. But I had trusted in Jesus as my savior and had confessed Him as my Lord, so why was my soul so restless? But I was not able to experience the rest You had promised to me in this life. Sin had disturbed my rest; self-willed living had come in so that Self was the governing force in my life and not Jesus. I know You were still my Lord, but I did not give You that place. What a bitter lesson You had to teach me. I had to finally bow to Your conviction through the Holy Spirit. No longer could I ignore, blame, or deflect. I had to accept Your sentence of guilt upon me. Then I had to confess it all to You. I found that to be extremely hard. There was so much that I didn't want to own up to, so much that I didn't want to have your searching uncovered. My flesh always wanted to spare itself the knife of Your circumcision of my heart, but You were both gentle and firm.

Thank You, Lord, for being patient with me, giving me the time to face it and admit it—to you and to myself and to others. What freedom comes from finally having repented—no longer making halfhearted commitments to being *different,* but to fully abhor and repudiate all of it. Unless I hate my sin more than the plucking of my eye out, then my flesh will return to its sin. Now I have returned to Your rest. No more guilt, no more fear of being found out, no more of the yo-yoing. Now there is freedom. Sin persisted in is like a living death. Thank You, Lord, for delivering my soul from death.

Psalm 117
Merciful Kindness

Vs. 2—For great is his love toward us, and the faithfulness of the LORD endures forever. (NIV)

Where would I be were it not for Your merciful kindness? You
are more than a God of pity. Pity would be seeing one in suffering
and agony and seeking to alleviate it, to ease it, but not necessarily doing anything about the cause of the suffering. But You are
more than merely a subscriber of pain killers. In Your great mercy,
You saw me in my self-willed, sinful path, and tried to arrest me
in my course, but I would not have it. You have not dealt with me
according to the full measure of my sin but have dealt with me in
mercy. The worst thing that can happen to a man is to get exactly
what he deserves, and I am thankful that I did not fully reap what
I had sown. Not only did I experience Your mercy, but You have
also poured out kindness.

Now, how can that be? It could only be by Your heart of love.
I could never deserve mercy—it wouldn't be mercy, but justice.
So, also, I could never deserve kindness or it would not be kindness, but debt. Your merciful kindness is great because Your love
is so deep. And now I see Your merciful kindness everywhere. I see
it in nature where despite the Fall, there is still beauty, splendor,
and majesty. I see it in people's lives where there is love, grace, and
compassion shown. Though we did not want You to reign over us,
You never abandoned us nor left us to our own devices but showed
Yourself daily mercifully kind.

Psalm 117
His Truth Endures

Vs. 2—...and the faithfulness of the LORD endures forever. (NIV)

Dear Jesus, You are the living truth. When you tell me that you are "the way, the truth, and the life," You are not merely spouting polemics or lofty thoughts but speaking to my soul's deepest needs. I need to know that You are *THE* truth; I need that assurance that all that You speak and all that You are is truth. I have fed myself on lies and deception for so long. Is not that really what is at the heart of sin? I first deceive myself and then attempt to deceive others? Satan is a liar and the father of lies. He has deceived me long enough. May I ever live in the light of your truth. Your truth endures because You are the truth.

You fully embodied all that there was of God for me to know and displayed it perfectly in this imperfect world. You endured all the slings and arrows of man and came through in resurrection glory. Your truth endures because you endure. You have promised never to leave me or forsake me, so I know that I can endure as well. You are now risen, ascended, and seated at the Father's right hand where man can no longer touch You or reproach You. You have sent the Holy Spirit to dwell within me and testify to me of that truth. Knowing that I am now seated in You in heavenly places right now is enough for me to be assured that I shall endure in the life with You. Now I see that truth is not a set of propositions or principles, but is a person—Jesus.

Psalm 118
What Can Man Do?

Vs. 6—The LORD is with me; I will not be afraid. What can mere mortals do to me? (NIV)

Lord, You said, "Fear not those who kill the body but cannot kill the soul" (Matthew 10:28, NKJV). And that is the extent of the evil that man can do. So, why do I fear man so much? Because I do not trust You more. And why do I not trust You more? Because I do not have complete confidence in Your goodness. It is only to the extent that I fully accept Your goodness and loving care that I can trust You and act in faith. As soon as I begin to doubt Your care, reasoning begins and I fall back upon myself and my own resources. But what do I see in Your life as a man here on earth? I see a man fully persuaded of the sovereignty, love, and goodness of God to be unshakable in the face of human opposition. For truly, as compared to God, what can man really do? If I accept God's sovereignty, then man can only do what God allows him to do. If I accept God's love, then I believe He will always act from a heart of love. If I accept God's goodness, then I believe He will only allow what adheres to His loving plan, His providence.

It is, in fact, better to trust in the Lord than to put confidence in man, and that especially includes putting confidence in myself. God will bring down every human support system that does not have Him as its foundation. Lord Jesus, may I gain faith in You from Your example of dependence upon Your Father.

Psalm 118
The Lord's Chastening

Vs. 18—The LORD has chastened me severely, but he
has not given me over to death. (NIV)

You have chastened me severely, and because of my sin and self-willed disobedience, I needed it; but You have not given me over to death. Even in Your chastening, I see Your mercy. What a delicate work it is for You to know just the right amount of stress and strain to place upon me to break me yet not destroy me. What a promise that You would not give me over to death but use Your chastening to give me back life.

But no matter how much I see in this Psalm an echo of my situation and how You have dealt with me, what I see the most is the Lord Jesus Himself. He was sorely tried and afflicted like no other man. He endured hatred, taunts, derision, and threats from all directions: governmental, religious, social, and familial. He was pressured like no other and none of it was due to any fault or sin on His part, but only due to His perfect testimony to the truth. Even facing His passion and death, He could say, "What can man do?" His confidence was fully in God, His Father. As all the might and power of religion and Rome united to surround Him and destroy Him, He remained steadfast in God. He even acknowledged to Pilate that He was a king, has a Kingdom that is not of this world, and one day it will be here to rule this world. After chastening comes restoration and after suffering comes the glory.

Psalm 118
This Is The Day

Vs. 24—The LORD has done it this very day; let us
rejoice today and be glad. (NIV)

I know how we use this verse and apply it to each and every day as
it arrives. However, this Psalm speaks of a very unique day. And
what was that unique day? It was the day when, after Your rejection, crucifixion, and death (after You, the stone, was rejected by
the religious rulers, the builders), You were exalted by God and
made the chief cornerstone. It is always the suffering, then the
glory; it is always the natural before the spiritual. And so it was
for You, precious Savior. This was the key of knowledge that the
Pharisees took away (Luke 11:52) that was needed to unlock the
truth contained in Old Testament prophesy. Just who is "My
Servant" in Isaiah? Who is it that suffers in Isaiah 53? Are there
two messiahs? How can David's son also be David's lord? Who is
this Melchizedek priest, and why is he sitting at God's right hand?

And on and on it goes, the enigmas, the paradoxes from the Old
Testament made clear by one question of Yours, "Ought not the
Christ to suffer and then to enter into His glory" (Luke 24:26,
NKJV). Truly, Lord, that day was the glorious day of all human
and eternal history—that God Himself would submit to death
out of love for His creature to redeem him and then to be exalted
as man above all things physical and spiritual. All the world groans
until it can say, "Blessed is He who comes in the name of the Lord"
(Psalm 118:26, NKJV; Matthew 23:39).

Psalm 119
Blessed are those (Aleph)

Vs. 1—Blessed are those whose ways are blameless, who walk according to the law of the LORD. (NIV)

Just as the entire psaltery begins with a declaration of the blessed man, Christ Jesus, who delights in the law of the Lord and meditates upon it continually, so this great Psalm of the inner life of Jesus begins with a declaration of blessedness. Is it then expected that Your great sermon on the mount, the declaration of the law of the new covenant, should begin with blessings? This could only be You, Lord. And we see the inner spring from which it is drawn: You sought God wholeheartedly. It is the inner life seen only by God, which produced the outer life seen by man. You were undefiled, walking in the law of the Lord, yet Pharisees would dare to accuse You of eating with defiled hands. You could touch the leper, and he would be clean because no defilement could come upon You.

Your great desire was that You would please the Father, walk in all of His ways, keep all of His statutes and precepts, and not be ashamed when You looked into His word, for there would be no conviction of sin. Therein lay Your secret, not the use of self-will to hold the trials and temptations at bay, but to have a heart sanctified to the pleasure of God that would have a holy horror of anything that would divert You away from Him and His will. So, You could praise the Father from a heart that was in a right standing before God dedicated to His pleasure. That is a blessed life.

Psalm 119
With the Whole Heart (Beth)

Vs. 10—I seek you with all my heart; do not let me stray
from your commands. (NIV)

Here, we see the answer to what is laid before us in Aleph—the heart fully set on seeking God. And when does that begin? As a young man. It begins in the youth as the child expresses his own will and asserts himself on the world around him. We read in Luke's gospel how Jesus "became strong in spirit, filled with wisdom" as a child (Luke 2:40, NKJV). As He grew older, He was found in the temple surrounded by teachers. It is written that "He increased in wisdom and stature, and favor with God and men" (Luke 2:52, NKJV). This progression began with "taking heed," just simply paying attention to the word of God as it was spoken at home and in the synagogue.

From this simple beginning comes the hiding of the word in Jesus' heart, storing it up. How often had He organized and put away Joseph's tools? Now we see Him finding just those right spots for God's word so He can retrieve it when needed and feed on it. We also see Him *meditate* on God's precepts, "to consider a truth closely, carefully, from many different angles" to extract from it all the nourishment He could. Jesus *contemplated* God's ways, not just His deeds, in order to gain an understanding and appreciation of what motivates God. God's word was a delight to Him, bringing joy, peace, and satisfaction as nothing else on earth could.

Psalm 119
Open eyes (Gimel)

Vs. 18—Open my eyes that I may see wonderful things
in your law. (NIV)

As Jesus grew, His life became characterized by holiness, not just
righteousness. Righteousness is that outward display of what can
be seen and possibly faked. But holiness, that horror and abhorrence of all that offends the nature of God, is solely an inward
thing. As the Father opened His eyes to see more and more of
God's truth, He was in wonder and awe of God's word. Every day
was a new opportunity to experience more of God; each time,
gazing into His word gave a fresh insight into and connection
with the God of heaven and earth. He never grew weary. Though
the divine Son, He was a man upon earth going through all of the
same stages of growth and maturity, experiencing what we do—
the wonder of fresh discovery and gained insight.

The soul has two reactions to this growing realization within
Him. He became a stranger in this world, and this world became
a strange place to Him. And that produced even more longing
in His soul. When all around He sees man going on in his own
way with scarcely a thought for God (and even those who profess
religiosity pursuing after self-righteousness and not god-likeness),
Jesus longs even more for the fellowship of the Father. Is it His
place and time to set everything straight and everyone right? Not
yet. So, He meditates upon God, upon His word, filling Himself
with God's truth and delighting Himself while meditating on His
testimonies.

Psalm 119
Revive me (Daleth)

Vs. 28—My soul is weary with sorrow; strengthen me
according to your word. (NIV)

Jesus knows what it is like to live in this world of sin and despair.
He knows what it feels like to have life weigh one down, how the
burdens and cares of life cling to us like dust. He watched as men
tried to find their fulfillment in this world and saw its futility. At
the end of a sweaty, hard day of carpentry, He felt that need to be
revived, to be brought into the freshness and clean air of God's
word and be invigorated by it. He demonstrated that true revival,
the restoring of spiritual energy, does not come from positive
thinking, but from God's word, from meditation on His wondrous works. He would see all around Him the indifference of
men living their lives unto themselves and His soul was grieved.
But rather than being discouraged, He strengthened Himself in
God.

The way is always clearly laid out before us: *Will I follow the way
of indulgence and do what pleases me or follow the way of truth and
do what pleases God?* The folks around Him probably thought He
was crazy, probably thought He was taking it a bit too seriously
for one who is still a young man. Certainly His brothers thought
He was a little odd. But none of this shamed Him into diverting
Him from God's path. And rather than produce in Him a sense
of superiority or self-righteousness, it enlarged His heart to see the
needs of others even when they themselves didn't realize it.

Psalm 119
Incline My Heart (He)

Vs. 36, 37—Turn my heart toward your statutes and not toward selfish gain. Turn my eyes away from worthless things; preserve my life according to your word. (NIV)

Lord, teach me how to incline my heart to Your truth. When we are inclined, we are "tipped" in a certain direction; the flow of things in life will naturally follow that inclination of the heart. If I wonder what my heart is inclined to, all I need to do is look at how I use my two main resources: discretionary time and money. Do I incline toward worthless things that merely tease and satisfy the flesh? Then turn me away and revive me in Your things. For You, Lord, time with the Father and with His word was paramount, and so You persevered and pursued it to the end. Rather than looking at fellowship as a snack, it was the meal (John 4:32, 34).

You delighted in the things of God. They were not a drudgery to You, not some obligation that pulled You away from the real work of life, but the true source of real joy. You were devoted, given fully, freely over to the use of God. Your desire and delight were to please the Father, thus so little did this world's things attract. You would seek God daily, to be revived and breathe in the freshness of God daily, to display His righteousness through Your life. May this be my inclination as well!

Psalm 119
Walk in Liberty (Waw)

Vs. 45—I will walk about in freedom, for I have sought
out your precepts. (NIV)

The flesh always sees the law in terms of restriction, what it tells
me I cannot do. The law stirs up the flesh to commit evil, as
Paul writes, "the sinful passions which were aroused by the law"
(Romans 7:5). It is not that the law is evil, but evil is at work in me
and the law stirs it up. However, the spiritual man sees the law as
guarding and protecting him, creating a perimeter about him, and
he is thus at liberty to live his life within that protective hedge. This
is how Jesus lived in freedom before God: He was free to act, serve,
and love, for He knew the heart and the mind of God.

Pharisees and teachers of the law, knowing neither God's heart nor
His mind would reproach Him and accuse Him of all manner of
evil—violating Sabbath laws, purification laws, and even accusing Him of being a ringleader of demons; but He always had an
answer for their accusations to show who they really were. There
was nothing of which He had to be ashamed; no charge of sin
could they lay against Him. When there is delight in the commands of the Lord, they're not burdensome. Jesus told us that His
yoke was easy, His burden light; He didn't say we'd have neither
burden nor yoke. I am to take His yoke upon me, learn of Him,
and love His commandments of the new covenant and walk in
them.

Psalm 119
Hope, Life, Comfort (Zavin)

Vs. 49, 50—Remember your word to your servant, for
you have given me hope. My comfort in my suffering
is this: Your promise preserves my life. (NIV)

God's word spoke intimately to Jesus. He saw it as His Father's
personal message to Him. True, He was prophesied about in it,
but that was not what made it so special. In it, He made a close
emotional connection with God and knew that all the circumstances of His life would always be governed by the Father's loving
hand. And so He always had hope. To only look at what man did
to Jesus would be to conclude that life was capricious, just up
to chance, and would tend toward pointlessness. But He always
knew the Father's hand was in everything, so he had hope. Because
He saw God's hand at work in all things, He knew experientally
that God was sovereign over all the affairs of life. Since God was in
control and all ultimately came from God, Jesus was comforted.

Such comfort there is in feeling, knowing that God is right there
with us in all our affliction, that we have not been abandoned to
the cruelty of men nor the meaninglessness of fate. Jesus received
tremendous comfort from the word and the God who always
backs up His word. He could comfort Himself. I have marveled
at how difficult it must have been to carry on for God when no one
understood Him and most completely *misunderstood* Him. God's
word gave Him life, gave Him the strength to carry on faithfully
even though surrounded by unfaithfulness, assured Him of God's
sovereign care and undying love, and sustained Him through His
entire pilgrimage in this world. This comfort is there for us too.

Psalm 119
Consider My Ways (Heth)

Vs. 59—I have considered my ways and have turned my
steps to your statutes. (NIV)

In the book of Haggai, the Lord asks twice for the people to
consider their ways. It is not enough to examine our deeds; we
must also examine our ways, the underlying, hidden motivations
behind those deeds. Here, we see that Jesus laid His life open to the
examination of God and gave thought to His ways so as to keep
His heart and life pure. To do this takes supreme confidence in the
love of God, to be assured that He always is acting for our good
and that all the providential circumstances of life are working out
for good. With God as His portion, His word served up as a daily
meal, Jesus was continually sanctified by God's truth and blessed
with divine favor. Because His ways were continually before God,
His heart was ever attuned to God's desires, making Him eager to
do the Father's will. Even when afflicted by the evil, ignorance, and
selfish pride of men, He never deviated from God's way, for "He
learned obedience through the things HE suffered."

Early on, He would desire to have fellowship with His Father,
giving Him glory, thanks, and praise. What an example Jesus has
given to us. But we have more than a model to follow. We have His
very life within us by new birth, which has this same aspiration,
and we have the indwelling Holy Spirit that gives power to that
new life within. May I be found in the company of those of similar
aspiration to display the life of Christ and be changed from glory
to glory by His Spirit.

Psalm 119
The God of All Goodness (Teth)

Vs. 68—You are good, and what you do is good; teach
me your decrees. (NIV)

It is easy to believe in the goodness of God when circumstances are pleasant and are going my way. The true test of my conviction comes in the crucible of affliction. But before Jesus addresses the matter of His affliction, He professes His confidence that the Father has dealt well with Him, His Servant. But Lord, Isaiah 52–53 tells me graphically what You, as God's servant endured. How can that be good? Oh, the wonder of the cross that even in the greatest trial of man the world has ever seen, that You can say, "It is well." For the joy set before You, You endured the cross despising the shame.

As for me, I need affliction in my life to help me see the flesh for what it is and to help keep me from going astray. You, Lord, were afflicted though You never went astray. Perhaps this helps me to understand the words, "He learned obedience through the things He suffered." Such is the perverseness of the sinful heart that it needs affliction to help keep it dependent upon God, whereas You didn't need them. Yet You could say that it was good to be afflicted, for through it, You learned God's statutes. What was the secret of Your submission to this discipline from God? You delighted in God's truth; You wanted to keep it with His whole heart. Lord, by His Spirit, make this the desire of my heart, the direction of my life, so that I may be drawn closer and closer to You.

Psalm 119
Seeing Jesus (Yod)

Vs. 74—May those who fear you rejoice when they see me, for I have put my hope in your word. (NIV)

When I look unto You, Jesus, the author and finisher of my faith, I see a man for whom suffering came before the exaltation. But the suffering You bore was not due to anything deficient on Your part, but on mine. You bore it all for me to the satisfaction of God, and now I have hope. All the wrath, anger, judgment, and condemnation that was due me was placed on You. I see You fully accepted by God, and I am accepted in You, for I had no acceptance of my own. When I see what You have gone through for me, I know that all of Your dealings with me will be in love. In all of Your afflictions, You saw the faithfulness of God; You could look upon all the opposition, hatred, contradiction of sinners, misunderstandings, and rejection and still rest in the sovereign, providential love of God.

How much more do I need this attitude day by day, to be full of the mind of Christ, to have Your joy set before me? Even in Your chastening of me, I feel Your loving kindness, Your mercies by which You measure out Your love. Yes, it is good that I have been afflicted, for I have been brought closer to You. As I have learned more of the fear of the Lord, adopted more of God's hatred for sin and been drawn in reverence to Him, I have turned to You, Lord. I am complete in You, accepted in You, and beloved because of You.

Psalm 119
The Fainting Soul (Kaph)

Vs. 81—My soul faints with longing for your salvation,
but I have put my hope in your word. (NIV)

We see here the increasing intensity of the hatred and opposition of man's heart against the Lord. As the persecutions increased, so did the intensity of His pleading. He who had all the prerogatives of divinity and the resources of heaven at His disposal, yet He would use none of it to ease His burden. His human suffering was immense, yet His hope was in God's word, for in it, He found meaning, received comfort, and saw the sovereign hand of God. He saw that all of God's truth is faithful, that God personally upheld and fulfills it.

Yet man persecuted Him wrongfully. Do we hear Him whine? Is there a word of complaint? No! There is only the plea for God's help and the complete reliance upon God. Until God would allow it, until the hour had come, no one could touch Him. And so He would go to the Father to be revived, to be renewed in His spirit, to continue on in the work of God. He went often into a mountain to pray, sometimes praying all night, often being apart on His own, and one time ascending the mount to be transfigured by His communion with God. But each time, He would come down that mountain, for life is lived in the valley, to face the opposition as that faithful witness.

Psalm 119
Have I Seen It? (Lamed)

Vs. 93—I will never forget your precepts, for by them
you have preserved my life. (NIV)

Though Jesus was the divine Son of God, He was fully man. He was not aloof, unaffected by the trials and difficulties of life, but felt them all. In fact, He felt them even more acutely than we do because we harden ourselves against the pain and suffering of life, but He never did. His heart was always open to suffering mankind and the price of that openness was to be even more sensitized to His own sufferings. Had not the word of God been so firmly rooted in His soul, had not the fellowship of the Father been His delight, He would have drowned in the vast ocean of human suffering. He looked around Himself and saw men pursuing sin to their own self-destruction and enjoying every step of it, yet He had compassion on the sinner even as the sinner resented God's words of conviction.

God's word was such a part of Jesus' life that He could offer that living water to us for He had it in abundance. How would I sum up His life here on earth? "I am Yours" (verse 94). What more is there than for me to answer, "I am Yours. Save me." Teach me, Lord, to see my life in You, lived for You. "Yet not I, but Christ lives in me," or "When Christ who is your life," or "a living sacrifice holy, acceptable to God." "I have seen the consummation of all perfection," and it is You, Lord.

Psalm 119
Sweeter than Honey (Mem)

Vs. 103—How sweet are your words to my taste,
sweeter than honey to my mouth! (NIV)

How was it, Lord, that You had such understanding and insight, so much so that at the age of twelve, the doctors of the law were amazed at Your wisdom and knowledge? Was it because You were the divine Son of God? No, that is too simple an answer. The word tells us that You grew in wisdom, stature, and favor, that You experienced our same life of growth and maturity. This section tells me that You loved God's word, as one would love their necessary food, and that You meditated upon it; Your mind and heart were set upon it to consider it. Now, that would give one familiarity, but not true understanding.

And then I see it: Your understanding was anchored in obedience. Did You not say, "If you know these things, blessed are you if you do them"? Knowledge, unless put into practice, yields no understanding. It is through this daily proving of God's word, not putting God to the test, but me being put to the test, that growth occurs. "My God shall supply all Your need." I know this cognitively, but how can it be understood unless I am in that place of need and cry out for God's supply? When God has taught one the word of God in the schoolroom of life's experience and has been experienced in His faithfulness, then blessing come. When I have obeyed and all of my commonsense schemes are to no avail, God's words become sweeter to me than anything else.

Psalm 119
Forever, to the End (Nun)

Vs. 111—Your statutes are my heritage forever; they are
the joy of my heart. (NIV)

God's word was a lamp to Your feet, a light to Your path. A lamp
holds the light source, so God's word is that truth and light we
need. But a lamp only illuminates a small area right around me,
just enough to penetrate the darkness and allow me to place my
foot securely for the next step. Only as I step forward in faith does
the light illuminate the next step, then the next, and so on. Only
the obedience of faith moves the lamp forward to see the next step.
We want a flashlight to illuminate the next ten or 15 steps, but such
is not God's way.

Thus, Lord, You have shown us how to live in this fallen world
where enemies and dangers, both physical and spiritual, beset us
daily. You followed God's word and let Him be responsible for
the consequences and results. As You walked in faith, obedient to
God's word, Your praise went up to the Father as a sweet-smelling
savor. Your life was in God's hands; it was always as a responsible
man that You acted. You would never have made an excuse for
anything You did; such was Your reliance upon God's word. You
inclined Your heart, and the disposition of Your life was set to
obey, perform, and carry out the Father's will. And that You did
to the end, to completion, to fulfillment, to the greatest possible
extent. Having loved Your own, You loved them to the end (John
13:1), the uttermost.

Psalm 119
My Hiding Place (Samek)

Vs. 114—You are my refuge and my shield; I have put
my hope in your word. (NIV)

Where did Jesus go when the pressures and storms of life grew
to nearly intolerable proportions? He went to God. Whether the
outward response was to contend for the truth, defy the authorities, assert the Father's claims, establish His own claims, raise
the religious hackles of the leaders, go to Judea, leave Jerusalem,
climb into the mountain, or return to the valley, it was always in
dependence upon God. He had to face the hypocrites, the double-
minded, the evildoers, those who ignore the truth and wander off,
those who reject the truth and willfully oppose it, the deceitful,
the wicked, all those who love their sin and hate God's word; He
stood for God amidst a maelstrom of opposition.

So, where amid all of that did He find His refuge, His place to
rejuvenate, to be encouraged and strengthened, to be comforted
and borne? His Father God was that place. Occasionally, someone
around Him would sympathize with Him and enter into His feelings with Him as Mary did when she broke the box of spikenard
and filled the house with the fragrance of her worship. Few and far
between were such times of human comfort, but many were they
of divine solace. Teach me to make God my hiding place.

Psalm 119
Time for God to Act (AYIN)

Vs. 126—It is time for you to act, LORD; your law is being broken. (NIV)

What is left for God to do when man's heart has closed itself off and made null and void His word in its life? How many more healings will it take? If He raised a few more from the dead, would that be enough? I suppose not, since they had considered killing Lazarus rather than acknowledge Him (John 12:10–11). Maybe if He had fed them a few more times? That was Rome's solution: bread and circus, feed and entertain them to make them docile and distract them from their lives. He was not after a short-term gain, or else He would have followed Satan's advice, for after all, he had thousands of years of practice manipulating people. He was God's servant, not man's, and He brought God's word and salvation to us.

So what was left? He acted in justice and righteousness. However, rather than God's stroke of justice and righteous wrath falling on the deserving object, it fell on Jesus, the innocent one. In love, He interposed Himself between judge and judged and took the judgment for us. He allowed God to act toward Him on the cross the way He needed to act toward me so that He, in grace, could act toward me according to my need. A day will come when He will act in righteous judgment; He will return to earth and execute justice here and set up His righteous Kingdom, but thanks be to God that first He acted in love, mercy, and grace; otherwise, where would I be? Great is Your salvation.

Psalm 119
Your Word Gives Light (PE)

Vs. 130—The unfolding of your words gives light; it gives understanding to the simple. (NIV)

For You, Lord, God's word was ever Your delight. You didn't obey God's law from a sense of drudgery or duty, but from delight. The more God's word filled Your soul, the more wonderful You saw it, the more enlightened You became. When I let Your word into my soul, when I act upon it in the obedience of faith, I am enlightened and have light in my inward being. My soul pants with excitement at each opportunity to enjoy Your word, to look into it, and learn thereby. In it, I read Your commandments, which tell me of the divine mind and what You think. I see what You would have for my life, and I am instructed regarding Your mercy and love.

Slowly, I am coming to understand what You meant when You said to "hunger and thirst after righteousness." And what is the effect that You are looking for in my life? Simply that sin would no longer have dominion over me. Sin ruled in my flesh, resulting in unrighteousness while I was an unregenerate sinner. But now that I have become begotten of God by the living word, now that I have the life of Christ within me, the Spirit is to reign with righteousness. That is only possible as my life is transformed through the renewing of my mind by the living word abiding in me.

Psalm 119
All consuming Zeal (TZADDE)

Vs. 139—My zeal wears me out, for my enemies ignore your words. (NIV)

What is to be the all-consuming passion of a man's life? What object is worthy of his heart and soul's full, complete dedication? To what does the heart incline? If it is anything other than God, it is idolatry. But for most of us, what do we spend most of our discretionary time, energy, and money upon? It is Self, the pursuit of self-aggrandizement, self-fulfillment, and self-realization. This makes a god of our Self. Is not this the lie of Satan, that we will be like gods?

But what do we see in Jesus? We see a man who *actually was* God, laying aside all of His prerogatives as God and being fully given over to the will and work of God. Truly, it could be said of Him like no one else that His zeal for God, His dedication to God's work, and His commitment to fulfilling His Word was the total summation of His life. Jesus, You risked it all, gave it all to the Father, poured Yourself out as a drink offering upon the ground to please the heart of Your Father. You were poor, despised, and rejected by men but approved by God. Your life was sanctified and set apart to God, and the truth of God's word sanctified Your walk. You were never distracted, deterred, nor deviated from the divinely ordained path. Yours was a life fully consumed upon the altar of Your zeal for God. What about your life, dear reader? What about mine?

Psalm 119
When I Rise (QOPH)

Vs. 147—I rise before dawn and cry for help; I have put
my hope in your word. (NIV)

What a blessed privilege it would have been to rise with You early
in the morning and hear Your cry for help. Would it shock me to
hear Your total honesty before Your Father as You poured out the
cares, concerns, and burdens of Your heart? Would I be confused
as I heard You ask Your Father for the strength, determination,
and courage to face another day? Would I wonder as You spoke
to the Father of the pain, sorrow, and loneliness of Your soul? Is
it possible that I would be woefully unprepared to meet with You
in the realness of Your humanity?

As the cross loomed before You, as each day was as it were, another
turn of the screw increasing the pressure and danger of life, how
much You cried out to God early, often, and plaintively. But in
those night watches of fellowship, You were drawn to the word
and heard the voice of the Father speak in assuring tones, and You
were revived. The wicked ones drew near; they wove their scheme
of destruction, and they arrayed all their powers and forces against
You, but You had the Father. He was near, ever-present, and the
plan of salvation was proceeding perfectly according to the divine
script. All the players are in place, and You are resolved to glorify
Your Father at the cost of Your precious life. Bring me, Lord, to the
place where I can enter into Your honesty with the Father.

Psalm 119
The Entirety of God's Word (RESH)

Vs. 160—All your words are true; all your righteous
laws are eternal. (NIV)

Three times in these eight short verses You plead to be revived. I
cannot even begin to fathom the depths of suffering that called
this forth. Three times You prayed in Gethsemane, and three times
You asked if the cup would pass by You. Once, God even sent an
angel to strengthen You, the eternal Son of God, God in the flesh.
The perfect Man needed the strengthening of an angel because His
disciples slept and were not there to strengthen Him. I need reviv-
ing because I allow coldness, hardness, bitterness, and resentment
to enter into my heart and life, bringing deadness to my soul. Your
need for revival was from the relentless wear and tear of affliction,
opposition, and hatred of sinful men and from living in this fallen
world.

What a resource You had in the tender mercies of the Father, the
same mercies of David, the resurrection from the dead. Where is
one to turn in the most trying times? To the sovereign power and
providential love of God, who always works all things for good.
Always in Your life, Lord, do we see that movement toward God,
never away. We use our pain and suffering as justification for our
rejection of God; You used Your pain and suffering as reason to
move even closer to God. You gazed into God's word, You the
living word, the Word made flesh, and saw that it was truth in its
entirety, and it constantly drew You back to Your God.

Psalm 119
Standing in Awe (SHEN)

Vs. 167, 168—I obey your statutes, for I love them greatly. I obey your precepts and your statutes, for all my ways are known to you. (NIV)

In Eastern philosophy and mysticism, they hold forth as the highest ideal to disassociate from the world around us as if it weren't really there and didn't matter. But You, Lord, rejected that notion. You lived every moment to the fullest in the light of eternity. The outward circumstances were characterized by persecution, hatred, and lying, but those things, real as they were, paled in comparison to the splendor of God's word. Even at Your point of greatest conflict, You could say to Peter, "Shall I not drink the cup My Father has given me?" (John 18:11). You rejoiced at God's word (verse 162), loved God's word (verse 163), received peace from God's word (verse 165), hoped in God's word (verse 166), and kept God's word (verse 167). That was Your life, precious Lord—one of utter devotion to God, His will, His word; a life fully set upon God and His word.

And how am I to have such a life? It can only be as I live my life fully transparent before God. "For all my ways are before You" (verse 168). This is not just the outward deeds, but it is more so the inward life. Am I willing to lay before You all my thoughts, desires, aspirations, and motivations and bring them captive to the obedience of Christ? (II Corinthians 10:5) And what was the obedience of Christ? Nothing less than total surrender to the will of God.

Psalm 119
My Soul Lives (TAU)

Vs. 175—Let me live that I may praise you, and may
your laws sustain me. (NIV)

You cried out to the Father to let Your soul live and He answered
with the resurrection. In Gethsemane, You asked if the cup could
pass by You, and He answered with Calvary. For You, Lord, the
only path to life was through death so that now in resurrection, in
the power of an endless life, You serve in the heavenly tabernacle.
From the cross You cried *"Eli, Eli, lama sabachthani"* and Your
Father heard. Your supplication came before Him, "Father, forgive them, for they know not what they do," and He has forgiven.
Your lips did praise Him when You could utter, "It is finished."
You have done it all for Him and He answered by rending the veil,
thereby honoring You by giving free access to all through the veil
which is Your flesh.

Truly, Lord, it is only because Your soul lives that my soul has life,
You live in the power of an endless life and have imparted to me
in redemption by Your Spirit Your very life. As Paul wrote, "I am
crucified with Christ, it is no longer I who live but Christ liveth in
me" (Galatians 2:20). He also writes, "When Christ who is your
life" (Colossians 3:4). Lord, in resurrection power You now live
and it is that kind of life I am to live now "that I might know Him
and the power of His resurrection and the fellowship of His suffering being made conformable to His death" (Philippians 3:10).
Now that is really living!

Psalm 120
I Am for Peace *A Psalm of Ascent*

Vs. 1—I call on the LORD in my distress, and he answers me. (NIV)

Having seen so clearly the life Jesus lived while in the flesh here on earth, but now exalted at the right hand of the Father, and having become a partaker in that life which He now has, then how am I to now live my life in the flesh in this fallen world? I see that I am to live a life of upward progress in growth, maturity, and understanding of the things of God, and those lessons and that growth will be learned in the school of affliction. Why must that be, Lord?

Oh, I see; there is nothing in this world that encourages spiritual growth; all is opposed to it. Those things I used to enjoy and bask in are now a source of affliction to me. Those lies and deceptions of this world I used to live in are now opposed to my new life. Whereas I once dwelt in Meshech (the extreme north) and Kedar (the extreme south) and was glad to be distant from God, now I want nearness. I dwelt in a world at enmity against God and His Kingdom, which hated the idea of making peace with God, for that would mean confronting and confessing its lost condition before God. But I have been brought nigh to God by the blood of Jesus shed upon the cross, and He is seeking by the gospel to reconcile the world to Himself. So, though I carry the gospel of peace to the world, the world prefers its enmity, its war with God.

Psalm 120
I Am For Peace *A Psalm of Ascent*

Vs. 7—I am for peace; but when I speak, they are for war. (NIV)

God is both the God of peace and the one who can give true peace. It is man who is at enmity against God; it is man's rebellious heart that refuses to submit to His Lordship. In our sins, we have been alienated from God. It is He who wants and seeks us out, not the other way around. Look at Adam and Eve in the garden after the Fall; God came into the garden in the cool of the day seeking fellowship with them, but they fled and hid themselves. Did they call out to God in their need, fall at His feet in confession and repentance? No. Sin had already done its evil work in their heads. They feared God, covered up their shame, blamed the other, and justified themselves. And even though God had to speak the curse upon them and over the earth, He spoke of the future seed, which would bring peace and redemption. Where the fault was 100% on man's side, the remedy in redemption would be 100% on God's side.

Jesus made peace by the blood of the cross to bring reconciliation to man. Christ has come and we, by faith, have accepted his death at Calvary and have peace with God; we can experience the peace of God. Jesus told us, "In this world you shall have tribulation." But oh, how sweet the peace of Jesus, to know and experience the presence of God, to have His favor resting upon you, to feel peace even amid the storm. The peace of God passes understanding—it is not based upon circumstances but upon faith in God. Then you have the peace of God. Others may be at war with God, but let you be for peace through the gospel.

OCTOBER 26

Psalm 121
My Help *A Psalm of Ascent*

Vs. 1, 2—I lift up my eyes to the mountains—where does my help come from? My help comes from the LORD, the Maker of heaven and earth. (NIV)

You know, Lord, what it is to live in this world in which everything is opposed to the reign of God. So, to what, to whom do I look for the help I need? You showed me clearly that it is to God that I look for help, not within myself or to those around. So, why is it so difficult to do? Because it takes faith and requires full confidence in the love of God that He will not allow anything to come into my life that His grace cannot handle. First, this Psalm shows me God's sovereignty—He is the maker of heaven and earth. This also reminds me of His omnipotence—that as creator, He is all-powerful to be able to accomplish anything He wills. Once I am grounded in His power, I am taken to His love—He keeps me, He perpetually watches over me, He preserves me.

So this is the God that I have, one that is all-powerful and all-loving. Lastly, I am to rest in His providential care—He will not allow, and that is in perpetuity. God has all the power He needs to bring about providentially any and everything that His love ordains. Now if that were all there was to it, I would be the most joyous and peaceful of people upon earth, but such is not the case. In my ascent toward greater union with Christ, having the life of Christ and the resources of heaven at my disposal is wonderful, but only by faith are they activated in my life.

Psalm 121
My Keeper *A Psalm of Ascent*

Vs. 7—The LORD will keep you from all harm—he will
watch over your life... (NIV).

Lord, You have shown me what it is to be kept by You. Though I
live amid circumstances that oppose me and often pose threats,
You are watching over me. You preserve me both in physical safety
and also in emotional stability. Where fears assail. You bring me
peace. When doubts arise, You give me confidence. You remind
me that it is not up to me, but it is up to You. You orchestrate my
life and my very circumstances. When evil men conspired against
me to try to compromise my health and safety, to provoke me into
rash retaliation, Your calming Spirit kept me back from precipi-
tous action. It is only by leaving matters in Your hands that I find
peace and strength.

Whenever I take the reigns of control and try to direct my life *my*
way, then anxiety and dread come in. Forces are too powerful and
too numerous for me, but not for You. Lord, guard me both from
the schemes of the enemy and rashness on the part of my flesh. As
I consider all that You are and all that I am in You, how could it be
that I could ever doubt? Yet I do. Though the sun shines by day
and the moon rules the night, Your word teaches me that they shall
not smite me, shall not oppress me. The common circumstances
of daily life do not need to be a source of anxiety for me, for You
protect me both before I enter into those circumstances and after
I leave them. Teach me to rest, to rely on Your love, to trust in Your
care, to live in the assurance of Your keeping.

Psalm 122
Being in God's House *A Psalm of Ascent*

Vs. 1, 2—I rejoiced with those who said to me, "Let us
go to the house of the LORD." Our feet are standing
in your gates, Jerusalem. (NIV)

Not only have I been brought to Christ by faith in His shed
blood, but I have also been brought into a fellowship of believers, a household of faith, and the family of God. As a member of
God's family, He welcomes me into His house with "Christ as
a son over His own house, whose house we are" (Hebrews 3:6,
NKJV). How wonderful to have been brought into this relationship with God through Christ.

If all one sees of salvation is the obvious—deliverance from
judgment and condemnation—then he has missed the real
blessedness of it. "For Christ suffered...that He might bring us
to God" (I Peter 3:18, NKJV). So, I rejoice and am glad that You,
Lord, have invited me to come up to Your Father's house. And
what do I find? That You have prepared a room for me in that
house, a place for me to abide in and enjoy the Father's fellowship. In this house is also intimacy, to be able to sit around the
Lord's table and to enjoy the meal You have prepared for us, bread
and wine, feeding on Your body and blood. Paul writes, "...how
you ought to behave yourself in the house of God, which is the
church of the living God..." (I Timothy 3:15, KJV). The pathway
to the Father's house is always upward, the journey begins with
conversion, new birth. Order and discipline become the Father's
house, as well as love and intimacy. Thus we are exhorted to walk
in the Spirit as sons of the Father and grow.

Psalm 122
Pray for Peace *A Psalm of Ascent*

Vs. 7, 8—"May there be peace within your walls and security within your citadels." For the sake of my family and friends, I will say "Peace be within you." (NIV)

Lord, You have brought me into a fellowship of believers. Together we are Your body, Your temple, Your household of faith. We are to learn together, worship as one, serve you in unity, and praise you as your people. We are not to see ourselves as individuals only but also as members together of Your body. Together we are built up. We minister to each other. None of us can get along in a spiritually healthy way without the interactions and involvement of others. Your word exhorts me to "keep the unity of the Spirit in the bonds of peace" (Ephesians 4:3, KJV).

For years, I lived in a self-imposed emotional isolation, pretending that all was well when it was not. There was not inner peace in my life, but a restless struggle with bitterness and resentment. How much better would it have been to reach out to others in the body of Christ! Then I could have had Christ ministered to my heart and begun to experience peace in my heart. "Peace be within [my] walls ..." would have been the result. Through the death of Christ and my faith in Him I have peace **with** God, but it is only as the Spirit ministers Christ to my suffering heart that I feel the peace **of** God. "For the sake of my brethren and companions I will now say, 'Peace be within you.'" Together may I, may *we* all prosper in the things of God as we are joined in fellowship around Him.

Psalm 123
Our Eyes are Looking *A Psalm of Ascent*

Vs. 1—I lift up my eyes to you, to you who sit enthroned
in heaven. (NIV)

On my upward journey, You would have me lift up my eyes. You
want to give me a higher, broader perspective as I journey to the
New Jerusalem, the place of my eternal abode, the place that You
are even now preparing for me and all of Your beloved ones (John
14:2). This place will descend from heaven to alight upon the new
earth (Revelation 21:2), the movement is always upward, always
an ascent. You had proceeded from the Father, had come to earth,
had descended into the lower parts of the earth, were going back
to the Father, and have given to us an upward calling (Philippians
3:14). This upward call of God in Christ Jesus is to take us spiritually (in regeneration), morally (in sanctification), and physically
(in resurrection) out of this world and this realm into the bosom
of God.

As servants upon earth, our eyes look to You, for only from You do
we receive direction; only in You are we transformed from glory to
glory; only to You do we look for that perfect example of a life fully
lived for God. What a privilege we have to be sons in Your house
and servants upon earth just as You were. So, when I experience
the scorn and contempt of the world, I know it is just a continu-
ation of the hatred that had been directed at You, so I know I can
count on Your mercy and grace to sustain me on my journey to
Jerusalem.

Psalm 123
Have Mercy on Us *A Psalm of Ascent*

Vs. 3—Have mercy on us, LORD, have mercy on us,
for we have endured no end of contempt. (NIV)

Jesus, you know how difficult life is in this fallen world. You learned firsthand what pangs of hunger and thirst are. You know what it is like to lose a loved one. You suffered the taunts and rejection of people; even your own brothers laughed and made fun of You. At one time, they even thought You were crazy and wanted to take You away. Your neighbors in Nazareth were so enraged by the things You said there on that day that they tried to kill You by pushing You off the cliff. The Pharisees, who knew the word and were in the best position to judge what You said and did was true, were in the lead to destroy You. The Romans, who really couldn't have cared less, turned You over to be crucified even though they knew You were innocent.

This is a harsh, cruel, unfeeling world, and You felt it firsthand. Yet You were never hardened by it. Even from the cross itself, You could say, "Father forgive them for they know not what they do." We are weak and frail creatures. In us, that is in our flesh, dwells no good thing. We owe all that we are for you to your grace and goodness. We are hated by this world just as this world hated You. It does not want You or want Your truth. Give us the strength to testify to it about You, and give us Your mercy and compassion to endure in the face of opposition.

Psalm 124
If It Had Not Been the Lord *A Psalm of Ascent*

Vs. 2, 3—…if the LORD had not been on our side when
people attacked us, they would have swallowed us alive
when their anger flared against us… (NIV).

Do I have an adequate knowledge of the grace of God? Do I know
how all-encompassing and overarching is His goodness and care?
Do I live my daily life in the moment-by-moment consciousness
of His favor resting upon me, or do I just go blithely on my way
without acknowledging Him? This Psalm, Lord, stops me in my
tracks; it arrests my motion, my automatic living, and causes me to
see reality as it is. As Paul would write, "By the grace of God I am
what I am." Only eternity and the Judgment Seat of Christ will
fully declare the fullness of His grace, but now I am called to the
conscious acknowledgment of it.

There are enemies arrayed against me, enemies far more powerful than I and more ruthless than I can imagine who would love
to have me to destroy me, to rise up and swallow me whole, but
God will not have it so. When waters of circumstance could
have easily overwhelmed me, He made a way through the floods.
Principalities, powers, and rulers in high places would seek to
bring me to shame, but God has forgiven and sustained me. As
Jesus said to Peter, "Satan has desired to have you that he may sift
you as wheat." And we know that Satan was granted his request.
But, "I have prayed for thee that your faith fail not." Do I know
that my High Priest is praying for me, supplicating for me? How
much I owe You, Lord, daily for all Your favor toward me!

Psalm 124
Blessed is the Lord *A Psalm of Ascent*

Vs. 6, 7—Praise be to the LORD, who has not let us be torn by their teeth. We have escaped like a bird from the fowler's snare, the snare has been broken, and we have escaped. (NIV)

Lord, how powerless I really am. So much of my life I have lived a delusion of believing that I had some control or power over my life. Little did I understand that it was You all the time working out your providence, even amid my self-willed existence. How wonderful You truly are. Why did it have to be that only when I finally came to the end of my resources that I began to see You? But now I understand. You are showing me that I have no resources apart from You so that I can begin to draw upon You for wisdom and strength from the very beginning. Then, rather than striking out on my own, failing, and then calling upon You, I have come to see that I can call upon you from the outset.

Lord, in all of my vain attempts at handling my life on my own, You have preserved me from being eaten up by circumstances and those powers which are arrayed against me. How many traps could I have avoided; how many snares could I have never been caught in! Yet You were always with me to deliver me from my own self-willed foolishness. And why do You do this? Surely, it is all motivated by your love for me, but primarily it is for your great name's sake, that all creation would bring You praise for the great things You have done.

Psalm 125
Surrounded by the Lord *A Psalm of Ascent*

Vs. 2—As the mountains surround Jerusalem, so the LORD surrounds his people both now and forevermore.
(NIV)

What a wonderful blessing to be surrounded by God's protection, but how do I know it is there? It is solely by faith. Do I take God at His word or not? If I do, then that is all the proof that I need. But if I don't, then no amount of evidence will give peace. When Elisha was beset by the Syrian army, his servant would cry out in desperation. But Elisha prayed that his eyes would be opened to see God's provision (II Kings 6:17). Elisha didn't need to have his own eyes opened, only the eyes of unbelief. Satan knew very well the hedge that was around Job so that he could not oppress Job (Job 1:10). So, Satan dares God to remove this hedge so he can attempt to prove to God Job's hypocrisy.

As in all things dealing with the Christian life, it must be grounded in faith. This Psalm is a very real challenge to us. Shall we take God at His word? Shall we believe what He says and rely upon His sovereignty or our own machinations? Are we grounded securely in His love, taking strength knowing that God will make all things work together for our good and not complain against His providence as the children of Israel did in the wilderness? True, the forces of evil do not rest; Satan and his hosts do not slumber. There is no let up in the spiritual warfare, but they shall not prevail against faith. "And this is the victory that overcomes the world—our faith" (I John 5:4).

NOVEMBER 4

Psalm 125
Doing Good *A Psalm of Ascent*

Vs. 4—LORD, do good to those who are good, to those
who are upright in heart. (NIV)

The Psalmist asks for you to do good to those who do good, but
what about me? There is so much that I have done that is not
good! The prophet wrote that you are of purer eyes than to behold
evil, yet we make you behold so much evil; we fill the world with it.

There is not a man who could stand in your presence and receive
what he deserves and live. I know I am not good, that no good
thing dwells within me; that is my flesh. Yet you have taken residence within me by your Holy Spirit. How wonderful it is to
know that I do not stand before you in my own merits but those
of Jesus Christ. So, any good you do to me will be the overflow
of the good you do because you are so pleased with your Son. It
is humbling to realize that I do not deserve good from you, but
so secure to know that your grace gives me good things because
of your love for Your Son. He has been made unto me wisdom,
righteousness, and sanctification. By new birth, I have been given
a new heart, and I seek to live through that new life I have been
given through faith.

Psalm 126
He Has Done Great Things *A Psalm of Ascent*

Vs. 3—The LORD has done great things for us, and we
are filled with joy. (NIV)

There is no greater captivity, no crueler taskmaster than that of sin. "For when you were slaves of sin, you were free in regard to righteousness" (Romans 6:20, NKJV). Such was my natural state as a son of Adam, born in sin and a slave to it to fulfill its passions and lusts. Then, I had no choice but to be in my sin, enjoying and captive to it, and alienated from God. From this bondage, God has set me free, "having been set free from sin, and having become a slave to God" (Romans 6:22, NKJV). I am to have fruit unto righteousness. And herein lies my shame that having been set free, I still find in myself the flesh, drawn to, attracted by, and enticed to sin. Having sown to my flesh often, I have reaped from it sin and shame; having sown seeds of anger, bitterness, and resentment, I had reaped sadness, sorrow, and loss.

But God has done a great thing in that He broke down the walls I had erected, the self-imposed prison of my flesh, and delivered me into His liberty of the Spirit. Much sowing in tears, much prayer and brokenness came to repentance and restoration. The tears are not primarily due to the consequences in my own life, but the harm done to the honor and glory of God's name. The consequences of sin can sadden any unbeliever, but only the believer sees how God's reputation has been harmed by his actions. But to come out of it in restoration and have your life handed back to you with many of the pieces put back together ... that is joyful reaping. You have brought back my captivity; may I ever judge the flesh in Your presence and live in liberty in which I stand by Your grace.

NOVEMBER 6

Psalm 126
Sowing in Tears *A Psalm of Ascent*

Vs. 5, 6—Those who sow with tears will reap with songs of joy. Those who go out weeping, carrying seed to sow, will return with songs of joy, carrying sheaves with them. (NIV)

How hard it can be to just keep going on! Our natural hearts want acclaim and some recognition, but the true test of our perseverance is to carry on through the drudgery of life. So much of life is the day-to-day activities and responsibilities that don't appear to make any difference, but God notices all of it. Jesus experienced this same thing—working as a carpenter for so many years, seemingly accomplishing little for His Father. But we can never be the judges of what the value of our life is. So often, it appears that our lives don't matter for much. Jesus tells us to just keep sowing. If we do not sow, then we can never reap. Proverbs tells us of the sluggard who never sows because he is too busy regarding the sky, too busy looking for an excuse not to be about his business.

We are called upon to sow; sow in season and out of season; sow when it is hot and when it is cold; sow when it rains and when it is dry. You may feel that the good you are doing for another person who scarcely appears to notice is wasted energy, but little do we know the harvest that can come from it. But as we sow despite all outward appearances, one day, the harvest will be joyous, and all of our efforts for Him will be vindicated. Jesus calls us to not be weary in well doing. Let us sow into the lives of others; in due time, we will rejoice at the harvest God has produced.

Psalm 127
Unless... *A Psalm of Ascent*

Vs. 1—Unless the LORD builds the house, the builders labor in vain. Unless the LORD watches over the city, the guards stand watch in vain. (NIV)

Lord, You want me to build the house. You want me to be a watchman who guards the city, to be diligent and vigilant. What You do not want is for me to act and think that it all depends upon me. So, You remind me that no matter how diligent (rising early) or how vigilant (sitting up late) I am, it avails nothing without You in it. How easy it is for me to slip into self-reliant habits and effectively cut You out to take the credit for myself. If I fall back into independence, I shall become captive to my flesh again.

Continue to teach me these lessons of dependence and humility, Lord. And where will that lead me? To spiritual warfare. I will be building my family house, I will be guarding my city, and will be able to rest in the assurance that God is there doing the part that only He can do. When the battle comes, I will have something worth defending and sons who will stand with me. Rather than shame there will be boldness against the enemy; for I have an enemy who wishes to steal my joy, kill my testimony, and destroy my hope. He is relentless and will bring the battle to me. So, I must be prepared to take the fight to him to deal with the enemy at the gate so he never gets in again.

Psalm 127
Behold a Heritage *A Psalm of Ascent*

Vs. 3—Children are a heritage from the LORD, off-
spring a reward from him. (NIV)

What a wonderful set of blessings we have received as our heritage from the Lord. We have received His word which tells us of
His great love and forgiveness, of how He has acted on our behalf
to acquire a redemption we were unable to achieve on our own.
While man's heritage is one of sin, failure, war, and hatred; God
has for us a heritage—what we have received from Him as our
birthright as being His children. There is the natural desire to
continue on. We know that death cheats and steals from us the
opportunity to carry on. Children provide the means by which
our hopes, dreams, and values become projected into the future—
a future that extends beyond our lifespan.

But Jesus is the same yesterday, today, tomorrow, and forever; it
is He who fights for me. He has met my enemy at the cross and
defeated him. It is He who has given me the armor of God so
that I can face the enemy and experience victory over Satan, the
flesh, and the world because He has ascended on high and intercedes for me before the throne of grace. How wonderful that I do
not need to live in shame or be ashamed because, when the great
accuser comes forward to accuse me before God, Jesus is there on
my behalf. What security I have in the finished work of Christ.

Psalm 128
Blessed *A Psalm of Ascent*

Vs. 3, 4—Your wife will be like a fruitful vine within your house; your children will be like olive shoots around your table. Yes, this will be the blessing for the man who fears the LORD. (NIV)

Since there is such blessing associated with the fear of the Lord, so many good things coming as a result, then why is there so little of it? Because we cannot have our cake and eat it too. We want the blessing, but not the means of blessing: obedience. I cannot claim to fear the Lord without obeying Him, nor can I claim to love Jesus without obeying His commandments. And what is the blessing? Fruitfulness. The two images of this are the vine and the olive tree. In John 15, the Lord explains the metaphor of the vine's fruitfulness: it is abiding in Christ. The branch has no life in itself; it must draw its life from the vine, which is Jesus. And what is the proof of abiding? Fruit. The vine does not "work" to produce that fruit; the fruit is the natural consequence of its abiding relationship with the vine. So, as children are the natural result of the love relationship of husband and wife, fruitfulness is the natural consequence of this "abiding" relationship with Christ.

As an olive tree matures and spreads its roots, little sprouts emerge from those roots like child plants about the olive tree. Not only is there fruit in my own life, but now there is fruit, life, evidenced in others around me, even new life as a result of my growth and maturity. This is the sort of blessing God has in store for those who trust in, abide in, and are blessed by Him.

Psalm 128
Fear *A Psalm of Ascent*

Vs. 1—Blessed are all who fear the LORD, who walk in
obedience to him. (NIV)

The world is full of so many things to excite fear within me. But
from whence comes most of those fears? Is it not that I feel out of
control of the circumstances of life? But how did I ever convince
myself that I had anything under my control? Is not that actually
a form of delusion? Is there anything that is fully under my control? Is there anything that is not fully under God's control? Does
anything happen in this world without His total understanding
and awareness; has He not incorporated it into His great unfolding plan? Do I truly believe that all things work together for good?
Do I truly believe that no good thing will He withhold from me
as one of His elect?

Have I begun to grasp the unbounded, infinite love of God, which
abides like a banner over me? Then what else is there for me to fear
other than Him? In fact, as I grow in the fear of the Lord, the fear
of other things recedes. The blessing always comes from the doing,
not from the knowing. I can know of the fear of the Lord, but if I
do not act upon it by faith, then I do not experience the blessing.
We are taught that we have all spiritual blessings in heavenly places
in Christ Jesus. With such blessings before us, let us grasp them by
faith, having no fear other than for God.

Psalm 129
The Afflictions of Faith *A Psalm of Ascent*

Vs. 1, 2—"They have greatly oppressed me from my youth," let Israel say; "they have greatly oppressed me from my youth, but they have not gained the victory over me. (NIV)

All men who live in this world will suffer, for we are fallen creatures in a fallen world. Satan, the god of this world, enjoys adding to our pain and suffering. But for us as believers, we who are no longer in that kingdom of darkness but have been translated into the Kingdom of God's dear Son, we are particularly the targets of Satan's attacks, for we represent what he hates most: the triumph of Christ over Him. Nothing fuels his hatred and mania more than the opportunity to afflict one of God's own. But in order for Him to be able to do so, he must receive permission from our Father, who will specify the extent of Satan's leeway, the limitations within which he can act.

I must always seek to understand the ways of God in my life. Some things in my life are primarily the result of being in this fallen world, and the heartaches and disappointments that come remind me that this world is not my home. Other things result from my sin and the consequences of my foolish choices; so God is dealing with me in chastisement and love. But some things are the afflictions, the result of my life of faith, which attracts the enmity of the ungodly and of Satan to oppose the truth. God allows these trials of faith to purify my life, to trim off the clutter, and prune away false growth so that only what is the result of the life of Jesus remains. No one's back was plowed like Jesus' was.

Psalm 129
The Lord is Righteous *A Psalm of Ascent*

Vs. 4—"... But the LORD is righteous; he has cut me free
from the cords of the wicked." (NIV)

May I never allow persecutions or the successes of the enemy of
my soul bring me to question the rightness of God's dealings with
me. The day will come when He will cut their cords in two and
sever them from the joys of life. He will one day put them to shame
and return all of their devices back upon their heads. He will make
all of their hopes and dreams dry up and wither away for lack of
water, depth of soil, and the scorching heat of the sun. There will
come a time when all their progress and benefits will pass away. No
blessing comes from their lips.

But if God so chooses to let them have their way for a time, let me
not questions the ways of God in my life, nor should I desire to
see their demise. I am called upon to pray for my enemies. Jesus
spoke a blessing upon those who were persecuted for His name's
sake. How can persecution be a source of blessing? Only as I see
it in relationship with Him. Jesus said that whatever is done to
the least of His own is done to Him. He is bearing the suffering
with me; He feels it as keenly as I do and identifies with me in it.
Persecution also produces a work in my soul by causing me to look
beyond myself and my own circumstances to Him, who is able to
deliver me out of it all. And He will deliver me one day either by
vindication or by death.

Psalm 130
Out of the Depths *A Psalm of Ascent*

Vs. 1, 2—Out of the depths I cry to you, LORD; Lord, hear my voice. Let your ears be attentive to my cry for mercy. (NIV)

Out of the depths of anguish, of fear, of suffering, of loneliness, out of the depths of my soul, I cried unto You, and You heard me. For the Lord, His anguish of soul was ultimately taking upon Himself the sin of the world. But for me, it was my own sin and failure and shame that I had to bring to You, those very sins for which You suffered on the cross. Truly, Father, if all You could see were my sin, if all that was marked and noticed was my iniquity, then I would have had no standing. But thanks be to God, there was more than my sin to see; there was Jesus' blood, and in the sufficiency of His offering, I could stand and, on the basis of His shed blood, find forgiveness.

If there had been no hope for forgiveness, then there would be only two options: hopeless despair or giving myself completely over to sin since there would be no point in self-restraint or holding back. But with You there is forgiveness and redemption, and that gives hope and encourages me to fear the Lord. So, now my soul waits for You, rests in You, and hopes in Your word. And this hope is not like the human hope born of chance and rooted in uncertainty; this is hope born of redemption and rooted in certainty. This is hope born of redemption and rooted in the character of God, a hope that does not bring shame. Out of the depths I cried, and in Your love, You answered.

Psalm 130
With the Lord *A Psalm of Ascent*

Vs. 5—I wait for the LORD, my whole being waits, and
in his word I put my hope. (NIV)

I can only begin to see all that there is with the Lord. With You,
Lord, there is great forgiveness. Not the grudging kind of forgiveness you get from people, the kind that lets one know that others
will never forget, never see you without your sin again, always
mindful and ready to remind one of the past. Yours is a forgiveness
that can take the sin away, that can reach down to the very core of
my being and root it out.

When speaking with Simon the pharisee, You asked such a simple
question, "Which loves more?" To which he replied, "The one to
whom more was forgiven." Now I see what I am truly forgiven
of; not only the actual sin itself, but the nature and desire that
impelled me toward it. I found with you an attentive ear that
would listen, sympathize, and deal with my sin fully. Now, with
You, I have hope. And this is not the hope of one who says, "I hope
so!" Rather, the hope of one who says, "I know so." Sin is bondage. Sin fools us into thinking that we are free to do as we please,
not knowing that with each sin we bind ourselves ever stronger to
that sin "which so easily besets us." Oh, to experience the freedom
which comes from redemption and deliverance. Now I am free to
truly love You.

Psalm 131
Calmed and Quieted *A Psalm of Ascent*

Vs. 2—But I have calmed and quieted myself, I am like a weaned child with its mother; like a weaned child I am content. (NIV)

After one goes through the experience of Psalm 130, where is he left? To what condition is he brought? This Psalm teaches me two things. Firstly, humility. Had I been humble before the Lord I would have not needed to go through what I did; but, though I didn't mind my pride, God did. He found the haughtiness an abomination in His sight. What is God to do with pride and arrogance? He must bring it down. Once lofty thoughts of self are gone, and I agree with the apostle that in me dwells no good thing by nature, then all that is good in me is what God has done through grace.

Secondly, I am calmed and quieted in his presence. Before a child is weaned, he cannot rest quietly upon his mother for he wants her breast; he wants the milk and sees the mother solely in terms of satisfying his needs. But once the child is weaned, the agitation and grasping is gone and the child can rest quietly and enjoy the security and warmth of affection. How often has prayer been seen as a means to obtain the things I want, as if God were a vending machine and blessings a transaction? How little has prayer been seen as an opportunity to meet my God, hear His voice, and rest in His love! Now everything has changed and by God's grace, I will ever be as a weaned child, calmed and quieted, resting in the assurance of relationship.

Psalm 131
Things Too Difficult for Me *A Psalm of Ascent*

Vs. 1—My heart is not proud, LORD, my eyes are not haughty; I do not concern myself with great matters or things too wonderful for me. (NIV)

When God began the process of changing me, I found that there were many things too difficult for me. As I yielded to the Holy Spirit's way in my life, of exposing and revealing what had been truly lurking in my heart, I found that it was all too difficult to face and deal with. For many days, the big success was just being able to roll out of bed, falling on my knees, and praying myself onto my feet. I still had to work—to earn money for my family, and run my business—in short, to function. What I found was that God was doing in me what only He could do so that I could do what I was able to do. I came to understand what was happening when Joshua fought the Amalekites in the valley while Moses held up the rod of God on the mountain. God was doing through Moses what only He could do so that Joshua could do in the valley what he was supposed to do.

Just because the battle is the Lord's, and the victory is His, doesn't mean that I have nothing to do. Joshua had to go out and fight the enemy. He couldn't say (in some hyper-spiritual way), "The battle is the Lord's so I don't have anything to do but sit back and watch Him win." Jesus defeated on the cross the enemy which was too powerful for me to ever face down. He has now imparted His Spirit to me to empower me to deal with the flesh. "For it is God who works in you, the willing and the doing."

Psalm 132
A Dwelling Place *A Psalm of Ascent*

Vs. 7, 8—"Let us go to his dwelling place, let us worship at his footstool, saying, 'Arise, LORD, and come to your resting place, you and the ark of your might. '" (NIV)

This Psalm speaks so powerfully, so passionately of David's desire to find a resting place for the Lord. He looked upon his own dwelling place and its opulence and had zeal for the honor and glory of God's name. And how wonderfully God responded to David's desire, for God declared His intention to build David a dynastic house, ultimately headed by Jesus Himself. But if the heaven of heavens cannot contain Him, how and where is He to dwell? God now dwells within each believer making of them, of me, a dwelling place for God by His Spirit. What an awesome privilege to have the Spirit of the living God dwelling within. The virtue of the blood of Jesus is so great, its cleansing so immense that He can make of me a vessel in which He can abide. And it is all grace.

Holiness befits His house, but I could never bring myself to the point of adequate holiness on my own. Jesus has sanctified me and set me apart for Himself, and now, by faith, I can have victory over the flesh and live holy for God. There was a time when God could walk with man in the cool of the day and enjoy fellowship with His creature. But sin came in and separated God from man, and ever since, it is God who has sought man out. You, Lord, have sought me, found me, and bought me, and I am Yours. Make Yourself fully at home, arrange the furniture, decorate my life to enhance the beauty of Your grace, and be at home. May my heart be a resting place for You.

Psalm 132
We Heard it in Ephphratha *A Psalm of Ascent*

Vs. 6, 7—We heard it in Ephrathah, we came upon it
in the fields of Jaar: "Let us go to his dwelling place, let
us worship at his footstool..." (NIV).

After 400 years of no new revelation, where God was testing and
seeking to purify His people, a cry was finally heard in Ephphrath.
And what was that cry? For Mary, there was the cry of suffering as
she bore down and pushed to give birth to her firstborn son. Then,
she could give that cry of relief and excitement that her child had
been born. For Joseph, that was a cry of relief and excitement that
the long journey from Nazareth was over and his wife was finally
delivered of her child. For the angels, there was the cry of praise
and exaltation as they announced to the shepherds that unto them
was born this day in the city of David a savior who is Christ the
Lord. For the shepherds, there was the cry of how they needed to
search for this child who had just been announced to them so they
could see and worship.

For Jesus, it was His first breath as a man upon the Earth that
He had created, culminating in Him weeping over Jerusalem and
crying out to the God who had forsaken Him. For me, it was the
realization that Christ had been born into my heart, that I was
born not of corruptible seed, but by the incorruptible word of
God. I realized that the dirty, messy, foul-smelling stable in which
He was born and the crude manger into which He was placed was
none other than my wicked, sinful life, and no matter what I did
or said, I would never be forsaken.

Psalm 133
The Commanded Blessing *A Psalm of Ascent*

Vs. 1—How good and pleasant it is when God's people
live together in unity! (NIV)

Though salvation is an individual thing, that I must confess with my mouth and believe with my heart and that no one can do it for me, faith in Christ brings me into a community of faith. I have been baptized by the Holy Spirit into the body of Christ, that this body is composed of all those who have placed their faith in Him, and that each member is uniquely suited by the Holy Spirit for some ministry in that body. Little wonder the apostle decries the spirit of sectarianism (conflict between two parties) in I Corinthians 1:12–13), which had become so prevalent among the Corinthians and was so much a reflection of their culture. We have been brought into a blessed union with Christ, a union we share with all believers, and are exhorted to "endeavor to maintain the unity of the Spirit in the bond of peace" (Ephesians 4:3, KJV).

We do not create the unity by any constitution or common consent, the Holy Spirit creates the unity; we are tasked with maintaining it—to express outwardly what He has created inwardly. And in this Psalm, we hear that it is in unity that God has commanded the blessing of life. What a source of joy and strength in the united worship and prayers of the saints. How can we "bear one another's burdens and so fulfill the law of Christ" if we do not see our destinies and fortunes bound together? When the high priest was anointed, the oil ran down from his head and onto his clothes. Our High Priest has been installed in glory, and we are blest together in Him.

Psalm 133
The Dew *A Psalm of Ascent*

Vs. 3—It is like the dew of Hermon were falling on Mount Zion. For there the LORD bestows his blessing, even life forevermore. (NIV)

When God first refashioned the Earth for mankind's habitation, it did not rain, but rather a mist rose from the earth to water the land. In this way the ground was watered so that vegetation could germinate and grow. The difference between rain and dew is immense. Dew is always gentle, condensing upon surfaces whose temperature has dropped sufficiently for water droplets to form, whereas rain can be torrential and destructive in its power and volume. Dew is essential to vegetation growth in Israel providing needed moisture for continued growth. Dew is always seen as a symbol of refreshment and blessing. God says of Himself, "I will be like dew to Israel; he will blossom like the lily."

The Lord says that unity functions like dew amongst us. Unity doesn't mean that there will be no differences or arguments, but that the relationship is more important than the differences. Unity has a calming effect. As temperatures rise and rancor grows, unity reminds us that we have more in common than we have in differences. Would anyone willingly sever one of their limbs saying: "I don't need it anymore; I can get along just fine without it?" We are members one of another, made one body in Christ by the indwelling of the Holy Spirit. Teach me, Lord, to value Your entire body of believers.

Psalm 134
Lift Up Your Hands *A Psalm of Ascent*

Vs. 2—Lift up your hands in the sanctuary and praise
the LORD. (NIV)

Lord, You have brought me to the last of the Psalms of ascent. It all began with having made peace with You by the blood of the cross, being brought into relationship by Jesus' death and the new birth I experienced through faith in Him. You have been my help, brought me into Your family, directed my gaze to Jesus, protected me, provided for me, delivered me, blessed me, strengthened my faith through affliction, brought me into Your house, and brought me into unity with other believers. And now, Lord, You call upon us all, upon me, to lift up our hands in praise and worship to bless Your name. And there is so much to praise You for, not only in Your creator glory and the wonders of the world around us, but also for the great grace You have shown toward us.

As I look over these Psalms of ascent, built upon the foundation of the life of Christ as portrayed in Psalm 119, I stand in wonder and amazement at what the cross of Christ has accomplished, not only for eternity but in this life now. "By the grace of God I am what I am," Paul could write and remind us of "the grace wherein we stand." So in Your presence we lift up worshiping hands; as priests we come into Your sanctuary to honor and praise You, to petition and thank You, to supplicate and interceded before You, for You are the author of all good things.

Psalm 134
Who Serve by Night *A Psalm of Ascent*

Vs. 1—Praise the LORD, all you servants of the LORD who minister by night in the house of the LORD. (NIV)

Do I find it humbling to serve by night in the Lord's service, to serve in obscurity with little notice or acclaim? Wouldn't I rather serve in a manner to be noticed by others? Not that I want a lot of praise, but would just a little bit really be that out of place? Then I ask myself, *Was there anyone who served in obscurity more than Jesus Himself?* For 30 years he was barely noticed. The angels announced Him at his birth, but only to shepherds. Simeon proclaimed Him at His circumcision and Anna joined in to praise him, but was anyone listening? The wise men traveled many miles to see him, only to cause Herod's paranoia to land upon the innocents of Bethlehem. The learned teachers marveled at His insight and integrity, but his parents had already learned the danger His prominence could pose. Hence, He toiled in obscurity for 30 years, far from the eyes of men, but always under the watchful eyes of God.

Were those wasted years full of missed opportunities? Evidently, the Father didn't think so. So, who am I to question my God's wisdom? If I serve in the night, may I be thankful that I serve and let my service please His heart. If He allows some light to be cast upon my simple role in His great drama, may it only be to give Him glory! Mine is not to choose the when, the what, or the where of my service, only the faithfulness of it.

Psalm 135
Whatever Pleases the Lord

Vs. 6—The LORD does whatever pleases him, in the heaven and on the earth, in the seas and all their depths.
(NIV)

How wonderful it is to praise the Lord, to be able to give thanks for all He has done. God's ways are inscrutable and beyond the pale of human reason, and by faith, we can rejoice that whatever pleases the Lord He does and whatever He does pleases Himself. Even of the crucifixion it is said, "It pleased the Lord to bruise Him." We who are believers can rest in His sovereign love and care and praise Him even though the circumstances make no sense. If I truly praise Him in the good times, only then can I praise Him in the bad (Job 2:10). If I am unable to praise Him in the bad times, then it reveals the shallowness of my praise in the good times, that it was only circumstantial and not spiritual praise.

Paul could say from a jail cell that he had learned to be content in the Lord through all circumstances. That is when I know that faith is the guiding principle of my life. I cannot wait to see what circumstances come before I am thankful, nor can I wait to see how it all pans out before I praise Him; by faith, I am thankful before it happens and praise Him, knowing that however it turns out, it will be worked by God for good. As the Psalmist looks around him and sees God's hand at work, and looks behind him to recall God's faithfulness in the past, his heart rises in faith for the present and the future.

Psalm 135
The Lord has Compassion

Vs. 14—For the LORD will vindicate his people and
have compassion on his servants. (NIV)

Your word tells me that You must judge Your people, but that judgment also includes compassion. However, there are two types of judgment: one of evaluation and another of condemnation. I believe that here is a judgment of evaluation where You seek to reveal and separate what is true from what is false. What a blessing to know that there is therefore no condemnation for those who are in Christ Jesus. You are compassionate in Your judgment, revealing, correcting, and chastening me as needed. And what did You, my God, have to show me? That I was holding onto my hurt rather than holding onto Jesus. I was making a fair show of it while all along hypocritically nursing anger, bitterness, and resentment and, in pride, refusing to let them go. Then I became ensnared in lust to try to bring comfort to my tortured soul, only torturing it more and making an idol of my lust.

Outwardly teaching Sunday School and bible study, yet I was indulging my flesh. Your word shows me that we become like the thing we idolize, and so the leaven of evil spreads through the life and permeates it more and more. So thankful, Father, that You finally cut it short. You saw that I was not going to deal with it, so You did. Such is Your love and compassion toward a wayward son. And now I can praise You for the new manner of life You have made in me. Bless the Lord, oh my soul.

Psalm 136
Our Low Estate

Vs. 23—He remembered us in our low estate *His love endures forever.* (NIV)

Have I grasped the low place that sin had brought me and the high estate that redemption will take me? In Jude 6, we read of the angels who did not keep their first estate (the realm of the spirit) and, through sin, desired to enter our estate (the realm of flesh) to enjoy the sinful pleasures of a fleshly life. When I think of the high place of privilege Adam and Eve held before the Fall and this low estate that I occupy, I am even more marveled at how Jesus laid aside all the display and trappings of deity and became flesh to redeem me from the sin that I craved. He took part in flesh and blood to suffer, bleed, and die; He entered my low estate (without sin) to bring me up out of my sin. It is said of Jesus that He made Himself a little lower than the angels on account of the sufferings of death. This is the greatest condescension of all, the great expression of love, the full display of mercy that God in Christ would take our place to redeem us from the condition we deserved.

No greater enemy there is than death, and it is the very last enemy to be destroyed (I Corinthians 15:26). At the cross, Jesus defeated Satan, who had the power of death and freed us from the fear of death which holds men subject to bondage (Hebrews 2:14, 15). Now, in this life, I experience the mercy of God daily as He cares and provides for me physically, emotionally, and spiritually. By its very nature, mercy is undeserved but flows purely from the heart and hand of God.

Psalm 136
Everlasting Lovingkindness

Vs. 2, —Give thanks to the God of gods. *His love endures forever.* (NIV)

I must never doubt that His loving kindnesses are everlasting. If I look for proof, I only need to see how marvelously He has created and ordered the universe. The world is so finely tuned and ordered that it is inconceivable that it came about through random processes. Surely all of this is by His grand design. But if that is not enough, He shows me how He has worked providentially in the circumstances of my life, making room for me, standing between me and my enemies, and giving me a place in this world to move and grow.

But what greater proof of His lovingkindness is there other than Calvary? Hasn't God shown me His total commitment to my salvation through the offering of His own Son? Hasn't He already supplied for me all that pertains to life and godliness? Hasn't He already given to me of His Spirit as down payment and seal for eternity? What more could He really do for me other than take me home now to enjoy Him? But He wants glory for Himself from my life. He has delivered me from sin (my exodus) and delivered me from the bondage of my flesh (my wilderness journey), has shown me the power of His resurrection (my crossing the Jordan), and led me to overcome the enemy in the land (my spiritual victory). There is just so much for which to give him thanks!

Psalm 137
My Chief Joy

Vs. 3—...for there our captors asked us for songs, our
tormentors demanded songs of joy; they said, "Sing us
one of the songs of Zion!" (NIV)

Do I see myself living in a foreign land, that in many ways I don't
really belong here, that my home is elsewhere, and I am merely
a traveler? John exhorts me to love not the world nor the things
that are in the world, that if I love the world the love of the Father
is not in me (I John 2:15–17). But I can't live my life negatively.
I must know where my home is, where my life is to be lived, and
what I am to love. God's word tells me that I am now seated with
Christ in heavenly places; I am told to seek those things that are
above where Christ is seated. I read that it is far better to be with
Christ, but to be here is necessary. God is preparing me here for
my life there. I am not merely to just tread water, but to swim and
make progress in my life.

While I am in this foreign world I can sing the songs of praise
and thanksgiving because I am not a captive any longer for Christ
has set me free in freedom. As a believer I have this wonderful
opportunity to experience and enjoy God as a liberated soul amid
others in bondage and lead them to freedom. One way I can do
this is through the power of attraction. What is my chief joy? Even
Jesus before the cross and on the cross had a joy set before Him.
The Father's pleasure should be my chief joy, bringing pleasure
to His heart, and He will give me His joy which no man can take
away. Even if they will not hear my message they can still see my joy.

NOVEMBER 28

Psalm 137
My Harp

Vs. 2—There on the poplars we hung our harps... (NIV).

Lord, I want my life to be Your harp upon which You can play songs of worship, love, and praise. I want You to take pleasure in what You hear coming from my life. However, I must confess that often you hear discordant notes. Many are the times when my will asserts itself against yours resulting in either disregard for your glory or rebellion against your will. At other times, I allow the circumstances of life to oppress me and the taunts and derision of the world to affect me. In those times I am like those who would hang their harps in the willow trees and refuse to sing songs to You. But then I read of how Paul and Silas could sings praises to You from their cell in Philippi, where they had been wrongly imprisoned for your Name's sake. I also read of how You had taught Paul how to be abased and how to abound. You had taught him that he could be content in whatever circumstances he was in.

Teach me to rise above the circumstances, above the stress and sorrow of this world, and to be able to have my heart sing for You regardless of what the circumstances are like. Lord, may my inward life blossom as yours did rather than wilting under the scorching heat of rejection.

Psalm 138
Praise From the Heart

Vs. 1—I will praise you, LORD, with all my heart;
before the "gods" I will sing your praise. (NIV)

What a wonderful privilege You have given to me to be able to praise You. While thanksgiving is associated more with what You have done, praise is associated more with who You are. I am exhorted by Your word to give thanks in everything, whether the circumstances appear good or bad, for all is being worked for my good and Your glory; so I rest in Your sovereign love and praise You for all Your care on my behalf.

The Psalmist doesn't specify the occasion for his praise for praise doesn't need one; it only needs an object for its praise and that object is You, Lord. The more my heart is filled with Your love, the more it overflows with praise; the more my heart is captivated the more it can fully express praise. I love how we see praise and worship so closely linked. Worship is the expression from my spirit of the greatness and wonder of God. The greater I see Your worthiness, the purer and fuller is my praise. May I never make my praise conditional, might it ever flow. And Your name is the content of much worship for Your name communicates to me something of Your nature. When Moses came down from the mountain and saw the people's idolatry, he pleaded with You on the basis of Your name—not merely Your reputation, but on the faithfulness inherent in all You do. Everything You do is consistent with Your great name. Praise has strengthened my soul.

Psalm 138
He Regards the Lowly

Vs. 6—Though the LORD is exalted, he looks kindly on the lowly, though lofty, he sees them from afar. (NIV)

No matter how high, no matter how exalted or transcendent God is, He is never too far away, never distant. We have been brought nigh to the Father by the blood of Jesus shed on the cross. His offering was accepted and now I am acceptable in Him. This is pure grace, all on its own with nothing I can do to add to it. If I would attempt to add anything of self to it, I would only mar the work of Christ. So, where is boasting? If any would boast, let him boast in Christ who has done it all. If pride comes in, it shows that my eyes are no longer fixed on Jesus but looking around me.

Thank the Lord that He regards the lowly for such I am in myself. It is pride which creates the distance. What an appeal to faith when I read that You will perfect that which concerns me. Even in the worst of circumstances and amid my failure, You are still at work to bring about into my life Your providential will to the glory of Your name. You are teaching me, Lord, that it is all about You, Your name, Your glory and not about me at all. Job had to learn that truth. He had been the object of great favor, and Satan desired to expose him as a fraud to shame God's name. Through terrible trials Job comes forth as gold and is found praying and worshiping in the end.

Psalm 138
In the Midst of Trouble

Vs. 7—Though I walk in the midst of trouble, You will revive me... (NKJV).

Lord, You told us that in this world we would have tribulation; but in the midst of that tribulation, we can be assured that You have overcome the world. I always thought of that tribulation as due solely to the hatred and opposition of this world against You, Your truth, and Your people. What am I to do when I see that my trouble is now actually the fruit of my own self-willed life—that the troubles I experience are of my own doing and that I deserve them? How do I pray when I know that I refused Your way of escape that You assured me would always be available in every temptation. But I didn't want your way of escape; I wanted my sin.

Lord, You have taught me that I am not to wallow in my misery; that I am not to wear my suffering like a garment. I am to humble myself under Your mighty hand, to confess forthrightly what I have done, to fully repent of both the deeds and the ways that led to my failure, and to embrace Your forgiveness and restoration. You know the tremendous crush of the weight of sin for there on the cross, You took upon Yourself our sin and became sin for us. Your death is able to fully deliver that saint that will only come to You in full confession; and it has. You have revived me. You have given me my life back. There are those who would have me live in permanent shame and bondage, but such is not Your way.

Psalm 139
To Be Searched

Vs. 1, 2—You have searched me, LORD, and you know me. You know when I sit and when I rise; you perceive my thoughts from afar. (NIV)

There was a time when this was a scary thought: the idea of being searched out, for fear of what would be found and of being exposed. Even though my mind told me that God knew everything anyway, yet I still sought to hide things from Him much like the child's game in which the child covers his own eyes and thinks he cannot be seen. I did not want to be exposed; the thought of all that ugliness being excavated was just too horrible to face. So, I continued to stuff it down and cover it up with another layer. Now I read those same words with freedom in my heart, liberated from the burden of hidden guilt and shame. What a comfort to realize that He who knows me best loves me most.

Now I welcome the searching light of God's Spirit to go to those nooks and crannies and search out to reveal to me those hidden thoughts and feelings that translate into shameful behaviors and root them out before they erupt in sin. What once I dreaded and feared I now welcome. This Psalm tells me of just how intimately God is acquainted with even the most mundane and least significant of activities. Lord, this is the God with whom I have to do, so why would I flee from Your Spirit? I have nothing to fear for all that You do is good and is for my good.

Psalm 139
To Be Known

Vs. 14—I praise you because I am fearfully and wonderfully made; your works are wonderful, I know that full well. (NIV)

It is You, Lord, who said, "It is not good that man dwell alone." You placed in us all an intense need to relate and communicate with one another. We want to be able to reveal to another who we really are, but we fear that if the other knew us then we would be rejected. What a relief to my soul it is to be fully known by God and still be loved and accepted by Him. You are intimately acquainted with all of my ways and idiosyncrasies and are working to conform me to the image of Your Son. Before I conceive a thought, express a word, have a feeling, perform an action You know all about it.

How much time did I spend hiding who I really was, prisoner of my Self! What freedom now I have that all is exposed, all is out, and God is able to heal the fear and shame. Who would have thought that the path to liberty was to be through this route, but God has done just that. To be known, to be able to reveal the true self, to be able to enjoy the fullness of the life in Christ unshackled by the weight and burden of sin is liberty. He knew me all along; it was I that needed to be enlightened as to my true character so God could reveal, deal, and deliver me into this glorious liberty in Christ.

Psalm 139
Why Hide?

Vs. 15—My frame was not hidden from you when I was made in the secret place, when I was woven together in the depths of the earth. (NIV)

Lord, why do I want to hide? What am I truly afraid of? Do I doubt Your love? Do I question Your ways? Is the pain just too great to bear that I do not want the light of Your gaze to be cast upon *that?* Habakkuk wrote that You are of purer eyes than to behold evil (Habakkuk 1:13), yet we force our wickedness upon You repeatedly. When I feel the desire to hide from You, it merely demonstrates how much I love my sin. Lord, You had to change my attitude toward my own sin, to learn to hate it as much as You do, to see it for what it truly was and cooperate with You in the work of rooting it out of my life. I shall always have the flesh with me until the day I die, so I shall always have to contend with it as a principle working in me.

But I am a new creature; I have a new nature. I have Your life within me. May I ever cooperate with Your Spirit's work in me to destroy those strongholds, to cast down all vain imaginations, and to bring every thought to the captivity of Christ As I am honest and open before You, this shall be.

Psalm 139
Know My Heart

Vs. 23—Search me, God, and know my heart; test me
and know my anxious thoughts. (NIV)

Lord, I need You to know my heart; I need You to reveal my heart
to me; I need You to show me what is there, for I am deceived by my
own heart. Your word tells me that "the heart is deceitful above all
things and desperately wicked, who can know it?" (Jeremiah 17:9,
KJV) I have proven that I cannot know my own heart, for I lied
to and deceived myself and others living a hypocritical life quite
successfully until You blew upon it. Your answer is, "I the Lord
search the heart, I try the reigns" (Jeremiah 17:10, KJV). And thus,
Lord, is how I desperately want it, need it. Only You can reliably
see if there is a wicked way in me. I can frequently tell if there is a
wicked thought in me, and my conscience and Your Spirit convict
me, but to find a wicked way is an entirely different matter.

When a particular sin has become a settled disposition, such as bitterness, it results in other attitudes and actions that I find my heart
justifying because of my settled disposition, my evil way. How
much jealousy, envy, resentment, racism, and vengefulness are
allowed to continue for years and even passed on to the next generation, all because they have been accepting it as *normal*. Lord, I
need you to expose this to me and lead me in Your everlasting way.

Psalm 139
Your Precious Thoughts

Vs. 17—How precious to me are your thoughts, God!
How vast is the sum of them! (NIV)

When You began this work of searching, revealing, and making
it known to me what was there in my heart, I instinctively pulled
back and resisted this work of the Spirit. It was just too uncom-
fortable, too painful to face; keeping hold of my sin is what had
become comfortable, to relish and soothe myself with those bitter,
vengeful thoughts and hideous justifications that formed a cocoon
about my heart. But You loved me too much to leave me there. If
You had not pursued me, I would never have pursued You. It was
all of Your love and grace. I did not see it that way at first, but You
have caused me to understand how precious Your thoughts are
toward me. How do I know they are precious? Because You paid
such a high price to bring them to pass. You so loved that You gave;
the price was the life and blood of Your Son upon the cross.

Nothing in all the universe is more valuable to You than Your Son;
such is the measure of the value of my soul to You. So, I now know
and have experienced how precious Your thoughts are toward me.
I can rest in the fullness of Your love, the safety of Your providence,
and the assurance of Your sovereignty that all things will work to
my good. Hallelujah!

Psalm 140
Hear My Voice, My Supplication

Vs. 6—I say to the LORD, "You are my God." Hear, LORD, my cry for mercy. (NIV)

Thank You for always being there, never hard of hearing, and always attuned to the voice of Your own. There is an intensity of feeling that You desire of me, that I approach You passionately, not perfunctorily. I must confess, Lord, that there are times that I have come to You casually, that I mouth words with little feeling, that I recite lists of needs and requests as if I were going through a pre-flight checklist. But I come to You now with supplication, with humble and earnest entreaty, acknowledging that I have nothing in myself. All resources are in Christ, all power in heaven and earth is His, and I come to You as Your child that You come to my aid and deliver me from those who are seeking to destroy me, who wish to wreak vengeance upon me. You know who they are and what they are planning, and I will leave it in Your hands.

It is not that I am above reproach, that I have behaved at all times purely, and I confess that in Your presence. I thank You that Your Son Jesus was perfect, did perfectly please You, and that I am clothed in Him as my righteousness. May I live my life as You would have it so that You would see Your Son reflected in me.

DECEMBER 8

Psalm 140
The Strength of My Salvation

Vs. 7—Sovereign LORD, my strong deliverer, you
shield my head in the day of battle. (NIV)

How I had deceived myself to *actually* think that I had any strength. How humbling it is to realize just how weak I am. As a pharisee would, I maintained an outward veneer of respectability. No one would have suspected the evil that was harbored within. *Not even did I!* The deception started with self-deception and then grew into a deception of others. How easy it is initially to maintain the outside while the inner decays. But eventually, it shall break forth. What is suppressed inwardly will eventually find expression outwardly. I found out to my shame how much easier it is to uphold the Mosaic law outwardly while violating the Law of Christ inwardly. The flesh has no strength; willpower is only the finger in the dike. And when all of my resources are gone and all of my defenses collapse, there is still You. You had been there all along, prodding and convicting, waiting for me to turn to You.

And now I see that all these other bulwarks I had erected to support my life were worthless, only refuse. It is always, only Your grace. It alone is sufficient. It has been a long, hard lesson, but it has been learned well. It is You who has saved me, You who has sustained me, and You who will gather me to Yourself. From start to finish and everything in between it is all of Your grace. There is never anything of me; it is all Your Spirit acting through the new nature that has been implanted in me. May You never be my last resort but always my first.

Psalm 141
As Incense

Vs. 2—May my prayer be set before you like incense; may the lifting up of my hands be like the evening sacrifice. (NIV)

What a beautiful image You have given of my prayers as they come before You. The incense was placed upon the fires of the golden altar, burning and producing a cloud of a sweet odor ascending to You. And where did the coals come from for the fire of the golden altar? They came from the brazen altar where the burnt offering of evening sacrifice was made. How precious to know that the incense that goes before God are the precious prayers of the saints (Revelation 5:8). This is how You value my prayers and how they are received by You. I cry unto You; this is not some bland recitation of a laundry list of requests, nor a perfunctory recitation of a set of common prayers, but the heartfelt expressions of my innermost needs.

You know better than I do how weak and feeble I am, how easily I am upset and disturbed. I need Your strength, Your stability, for in one moment I lift my hands in praise to You, and then the next moment my heart is drawn away (into an evil thought). So, I need You to watch over me, to be diligent to help me guard my tongue and bind up the loins of my mind to remain faithful to Your truth in my life. As my prayer ascends as a sweet savor to You, I want my entire life to be sweet incense to You as the life of Jesus was that fine meal offering to You.

Psalm 141
Oil on My Head

Vs. 5—Let a righteous man strike me—that is a kindness; let him rebuke me—that is oil on my head. My head will not refuse it, for my prayer will still be against the deeds of evildoers. (NIV)

How could it be that being smitten could count as oil upon my head? How could something that is for my comfort, pleasure, and enjoyment come from being smitten? Surely, Lord, You were smitten for me—smitten, stricken, and afflicted—that I might never have to bear the judgment and wrath due to me from my God. So, these smitings are not like those You endured. These, rather, are Your loving chastening that I need to be brought back to my senses and to You.

Only now can I look back and see just how gently and with such kindness you dealt with me. You did not deal with me to the level that my sins deserved. You chastened me as a son, as a son You love. What, at the time, seemed to be the worst possible outcome—to have my sin exposed, my shame laid bare, and my guilt proclaimed for all to hear—has become the very means of healing so much hurt that I had allowed to build up in my heart and create a stronghold. Truly, that root of bitterness had to be torn out before any blessing from You could be enjoyed. Amid Your chastening, I did turn my eyes toward You and took refuge in Your love, knowing that You would not allow anything in my life that wasn't for my good or that Your love could not see me through.

Psalm 142
Overwhelmed Within Me

Vs. 3—When my spirit grows faint within me, it is you who watch over my way. In the path where I walk people have hidden a snare for me. (NIV)

As the forces of evil and the hatred of men combined to destroy You, Lord, You brought Your complaint and need to the Father who knew and understood and in whose hand all was determined. I never hear a word of discouragement or self-pity from You, but that You would be completely given over to the will of God. It would have been so easy and humanly understandable to have whined about Your *lot*, but You even wept over Jerusalem. Your thought was for their welfare not Your own. And then no other place is Your heart's supplication more intense than at Gethsemane as You faced the horror of being made an offering for sin. You went all the way to death, three days and three nights in the belly of the earth—death's prison—to break forever the power of death through resurrection.

So, Lord, I know that no matter what my condition, what depth of sin to which I've descended, You have already descended further and shall deliver me out of all of it. I cry out to You, for at times my spirit is overwhelmed within me, and know that I am heard in the land of the living and shall praise Your name for all the wonders You have done for me.

Psalm 142
Who Cares for My Soul?

Vs. 6—Listen to my cry, for I am in desperate need;
rescue me from those who pursue me, for they are too
strong for me. (NIV)

Why did I not care more for my own soul? Why did I pursue my course of sin fully knowing that it would lead to my own destruction? My flesh had brought me so completely into bondage that I did not even fight that hard against the temptations surrounding me. I have learned that all sin is a form of addiction. Like the addiction, the sin at first looks attractive and seems to make life more pleasurable and pleasant, but it is a behavior which is destined to consume and destroy the life. Eventually, it wraps its tentacles around the heart and brings it into a prison of its own making.

You, Lord, cared for my soul more than anyone else—even more than I did. You showed it in Your incarnation and proved it in Your crucifixion. In resurrection, You live for me, ever making intercession for my soul in the very presence of the Father. Through sin, I had delivered myself over to Satan so that he could bring me into a bondage more cruel than death, but through Your grace, You brought me out of that prison into Your liberty.

Psalm 143
The Days of Old

Vs. 5—I remember the days of long ago; I meditate on all your works and consider what your hands have done. (NIV)

Of what value is there to look upon and remember the days of old? Am I to look wistfully upon better times and feel sentimental about how it used to be with me? No! It is not about me at all, but it is always all about God. You call upon me to remember the days of old, to recall to mind Your faithfulness, to recount Your mighty works, to think upon Your ways, and to realize that You are the same yesterday, today, and forever.

When I see evil without and fears within, I look to You, having my faith bolstered by the remembrance of Your character revealed in Your ways. Let me not be like the way we first see Gideon, who was despairing of the God who used to be, but rather the Gideon who was stirred to action by the God who is. When my soul is overwhelmed within me, and at times it shall certainly be, let my soul remember and long for You like a thirsty land that drinks in the rain like it can never get enough. Your supply is always greater than my desire; increase my desire to want more and more of You.

Psalm 143
My Spirit Fails

Vs. 10—Teach me to do your will, for you are my God; may your good Spirit lead me on level ground. (NIV)

Lord, You know how weak and frail I am. Though I may present an outward show of confidence and adequacy, inside You see the truth, and my weakness is not hidden from You. When I look around and am assailed by doubts and fear, when I look within, my spirit fails me; when I look up and call out to You, answer me speedily amid my need. You, Lord, know what it is like to be surrounded by enemies and forces determined to destroy You, and Your Father would strengthen You; so Lord, I look to You in my confusion and distress. It is You I want—to see Your face, to hear Your voice, to feel Your presence and to know Your will. All my confidence is in You, You are my Savior God and Your Spirit lives within me.

Revive me, O Lord, amid my enemies. Let them see Your strength and glory revealed through me as Your Spirit sustains me and I overcome by faith. Let it not be for me, but for the glory of Your name, for I am a mere servant. You, Lord, were the Servant, the Holy One of Israel; I am Your servant wishing only to give glory to my Lord. Be it in suffering, let me bear it; be it in poverty, let me be content; be it in plenty, keep me humble; be it in glory, let it all be Yours.

DECEMBER 15

Psalm 144
Trained for War

Vs. 1, 2—Praise be to the LORD my Rock, who trains my hands for war, my fingers for battle. He is my loving God and my fortress, my stronghold and my deliverer, my shield, in whom I take refuge, who subdues peoples under me. (NIV)

If You won the battle on the cross, why must I be trained for war? If Satan is a defeated foe, then why is he still such an effective enemy? Now, I see more clearly what Paul means when he says we have this treasure in an earthly vessel. Though I have this new life in Christ, it is still in this old body of flesh. And what do I see when I look inside my flesh? I see that in my flesh dwells no good thing; I see that sin still dwells in me. From my conversion onward, I am engaged in a battle.

But I see that I have both an internal enemy as well as an external enemy. Through Your Spirit, I am called to consider myself dead unto sin and alive unto God; I am supposed to deny myself, take up my cross (the instrument of death)—to crucify my flesh, and follow you. But I also have the enemy of my soul, Satan, who seeks to bring me into bondage through my flesh. I must be trained to put on Your armor and use Your weapons of warfare. I am engaged in spiritual warfare with an enemy who is impervious to all earthly weapons, whose intelligence is far beyond mine, whose resources exceed my natural ability to match. Teach me Lord to put on your armor, to use Your weapon of truth, and shod my feet with Your gospel so that I can engage this enemy and prevail.

Psalm 144
Sing a New Song

Vs. 9, 10—I will sing a new song to you, my God; on the ten-stringed lyre I will make music to you, to the One who gives victory to kings, who delivers his servant David. (NIV)

Lord, what is man? He is weak, feeble, changeable, and inconsistent, yet he is the focus of Your redemptive work. Had you been a God who looked only upon the outward, You would have consigned us to the destiny we had chosen by our sins. But You saw in us the creature You had made in Your own image to have fellowship with Yourself. So, You became all the things that this Psalm speaks to us about (blessed, lover, defender, protector, deliverer) to have us for Yourself. It's not for anything in ourselves, but solely what was in Your heart.

So I have a new song in my heart—a song of deliverance, a song of praise, a song of wonder at how marvelous You are. It's not that anything was wrong with the old song, but it cannot adequately express what is in my heart now. I know that if this could have been accomplished another way, it would have, but I would not let it be so. You had to deliver me over to the taskmasters and tormentors to chasten and deliver me from myself and my sin. You told Peter that Satan had desired to have him to sift him, and Satan was given permission to do so. But Jesus had prayed for him, not that Peter would be kept from the sifting, but for his restoration and the service that would follow. Lord, I am a servant; use me.

Psalm 144
Blessed People

Vs. 15—Blessed is the people of whom this is true; blessed is the people whose God is the LORD. (NIV)

Under the Law, Israel was promised many earthly blessings, but receiving them depended on their obedience. That was an obedience they could never maintain; in fact, no one could ever maintain. Rather than the Law being able to constrain the flesh, Paul writes that "... the sinful passions, which were aroused by the law..." worked death in me. Such is my sinful flesh—it never submits itself to the righteousness of God. But thanks be to God, I am not under the Law, the old covenant! I have been brought into relationship with God through the new covenant, inaugurated at the Cross through the offering of Christ. Having been risen from the dead and ascended to the right hand of the Father, Jesus now dispenses to me all spiritual blessings in heavenly places in Himself.

And what are these blessings? Sweet forgiveness—so that nothing is standing against me anymore. There is no condemnation for those in Christ Jesus. Full acceptance—because my acceptance is based solely upon the Father's acceptance of Jesus and His offering. He is my burnt offering and I am accepted in him (Leviticus 1:4). Sonship—I who was worse than the prodigal - who used this precious gift of life for my own selfish gratification and am not worthy to be called His son have been given the Holy Spirit, whereby I can cry "Abba, Father" (Romans 8:15, KJV). There is also mercy, grace, redemption, an inheritance, and the seal of the Holy Spirit as a guarantee of all this. We who are Christ's are truly blessed.

Psalm 145
God's Greatness

Vs. 2—Every day I will praise you and extol your name
for ever and ever. (NIV)

Your word declares that Your greatness is unsearchable. Does that mean that I should not search it out? That I am not able to search it out? No, but it does tell me that with all of my searching I will never find the extent of Your greatness, for it is infinite. Psalm 19 tells me of how all creation declares Your glory, and Paul tells me in Romans 1 how Your existence and invisible attributes are seen, exposed, mirrored in Your creation. And then Psalm 139 tells me of how I am fearfully and wonderfully made, how You have fashioned me in love. Your greatness is seen in part in the greatness and wonder of creation, but how much more is Your greatness seen in Calvary.

In the cross, Your perfect holiness and righteousness are met and fully satisfied by the offering of Jesus so that He would declare the work finished, and You could declare Yourself satisfied. Your demand for perfection was great, and You could not come down from it; His provision of perfection was great to expiate Your wrath fully. Now You can fully come out in grace and love to a blood bought, redeemed people. How great Thou art.

Psalm 145
Meditate, Declare, and Sing

Vs. 5, 6, 7—...I will meditate on your wonderful works...I will proclaim your great deeds. [I] celebrate your abundant goodness and joyfully sing of your righteousness. (NIV)

You have given us a wonderful progression to enjoy You and our relationship through Christ. Firstly, You call us to meditate, but this meditation is not inward-looking to connect with an inner light, guidance, or beauty. Rather, it is a meditation that takes us out of ourselves to You to contemplate Your glory, Your honor, Your majesty, and Your splendor displayed in Your works and ways. What better theme of contemplation to see the fullness of Your character other than to consider the life of Jesus and see His grace, mercy, compassion, and strength.

As we meditate on Him, we are full of thoughts and feelings of gratitude and praise and so are moved to declare Your greatness. We can declare Your greatness in worship, thanksgiving, and praise; we can declare Your greatness in teaching Your word and also in preaching Your gospel. Your goodness toward all Your creatures is manifest, but never more than at the cross where redemption for all mankind was procured. And so I sing, sing songs of praise, lift my heart in thanksgiving, and declare Your righteousness, for all You do is righteous and good.

Psalm 145
He Will Fulfill

Vs. 19—He will fulfill the desire of those who fear Him... (NKJV).

How can man be so confident that You will fulfill his desire? Is it arrogance to have such an expectation? Is it pride or ego that makes man feel that he deserves to have his desires fulfilled? No! It is a confidence based firmly upon the nature and character of God. I have reverential fear of You, Lord, because I know just how much You hate sin. Your hatred of sin is so great, so profound, so complete that nothing less than the death of Your own Son was adequate to deal with it. I may play games with sin, but You do not. And since I know the terror of the Lord, I eschew sin and seek to persuade others to repent and come to You. My reverential fear also teaches me of Your great love, power, mercy and grace; all these attributes without which I would have no hope. Apart from You, I truly am nothing and have nothing.

So, what is the overriding desire of my life? To see You glorified in my body. I want Your work in my life to yield praise to Your name. I want others to see that everything I have and am results from Your mercy and grace. I want Your goodness to be seen in my life, that You would receive all the credit for anything that comes of my life. I want to proclaim to others how great You are, how awesome Your majesty is, and that You can truly supply every need through Your riches in glory in Christ Jesus.

Psalm 146
Praise the Lord, O My Soul!

Vs. 1, 2—Praise the LORD. Praise the LORD, my soul.
I will praise the LORD all my life; I will sing praise to
my God as long as I live. (NIV)

How much You are worthy of praise! Why don't I do it more often? Thanksgiving seems so much easier to give, but there I have in mind all Your goodness toward me. But I can also praise You for those very things I thank You for, so may Your Spirit teach me to praise You more. In praise, my focus is much more directed to You, and I see You as the center. Praise gets focus off of myself and how I am benefiting, and places it solely on You and what You have done. What You have done reflects who You are, so praise takes me there too.

When I was first saved, my appreciation centered mainly upon what God had done for me through Christ at the cross. It was only later that I slowly began to see what Jesus had done for the Father at the cross, what the work of redemption had done for God. The Psalmist says that he will sing praise while he has being, while he still lives. I understand that to mean a continual life of giving praise, of seeing God at work around me and acknowledging that, rather than living life and punctuating it with praise occasionally. This is my desire, too, to be in an attitude of praise at all times, to be able to rejoice in the Lord always, and to pray without ceasing.

Psalm 146
Freedom to a Prisoner

Vs. 7—He upholds the cause of the oppressed and gives food to the hungry. The LORD sets prisoners free... (NIV).

Do I have any real notion of how much of a prisoner of sin I truly was? I know what it is like to be a prisoner of sin. I know what it is like to have sin bind me and take me where I do not want to go, to have my freedom taken away from me because of my sin. But God's word tells me, "Do you not know that to whom you present yourselves slaves to obey, you are that one's slave whom you obey, whether of sin leading to death or of obedience leading to righteousness?" (Romans 6:16, NKJV)

Adam, in the garden, was a free man, free to act without compulsion, free to serve in God's garden, free to enjoy the life and the wife God had blessed him with. As soon as he sinned, Adam exchanged his freedom for bondage. No longer was he free to act, but from then on, he had an inner compulsion to sin, and his flesh became a slave to that sin nature. Without Christ, man walks this earth as a slave to sin. In Christ, indulging my flesh, I brought myself into bondage and was sin's prisoner, but thanks be to God he has set me free. Now I am a prisoner of Christ, I am no longer sin's prisoner.

Psalm 147
The Beauty of Praise

Vs. 1—Praise the Lord. How good it is to sing praises to our God, how pleasant and fitting to praise him! (NIV)

Praise is the language of the redeemed heart. Praise sets before our eyes the God of redemption, the One who has brought us into relationship with Himself. It is good not only to be occupied in praise, but to be filled with a spirit of praise. It has the effect of bringing pleasure to our hearts as we bring pleasure to God's. Just think about the word pleasant: pleasing, agreeable, enjoyable, giving pleasure. All this is for the heart of God! What an inestimable privilege God have given to us, Lord, that we could bring pleasure to Your heart.

And what, above all things, gives You pleasure? "This is my beloved Son in whom I am well pleased." As the life is full of Christ, emptied of self, the image of Jesus is reflected in us and the Father is pleased. My heart, mind, and will, every desire and expression bring praise to You through the life of Your Son in me. And You are pleased, soothed, comforted, eased. How pleasing to Your senses and attractive to Your eyes is the life centered on Christ. Such is the beauty of praise as it springs forth from a heart fully devoted and undivided for Jesus.

Psalm 147
The Lord Takes Pleasure

Vs. 10, 11—His pleasure is not in the strength of the horse, nor his delight in the legs of the warrior; the LORD delights in those who fear him, who put their hope in his unfailing love. (NIV)

Do I want to give God pleasure? God created the universe, both the spiritual and physical one, to please Himself. He created sentient beings, both angels and man, to give Him pleasure, to respond to Him, and have relationship with Him. God, who needs no one or anything in order to be complete, created all things just to please Himself. And who gave pleasure to the heart of God like Jesus Himself! And what was the one distinguishing feature of Jesus' life? "He humbled Himself" (Philippians 2:8, NKJV). "Humble yourselves, therefore, under the mighty hand of God and He will exalt you in due time" (I Peter 5:6, NKJV).

Your strength, Lord, is made perfect in me through my weakness. As long as I am looking to my abilities, endowments, or resources, I cancel out the benefit of Your grace in my life. You take no pleasure in those things of merely human nature, but rather in those who fear You. Only as I see You as You truly are, the infinite God, do I have that godly fear that so pleases You. This fear has a positive side in that I have awe, respect, wonder, and love for You. But it also has a negative side, for You are a jealous God and one who exacts justice and executes vengeance. Let my hope be in the God of mercy.

Psalm 148
Exalt His Name

Vs. 4, 5—Praise him, you highest heavens and you waters above the skies. Let them praise the name of the LORD, for at his command they were created... (NIV).

Your name, Lord, entails so much and is so important in our understanding and experience of You. When You spoke to Moses in the wilderness, his first question proposed to You was to know Your name. Prior to that, titles had been used to identify You and identify places with You. But You were about to do a new thing and fully identify Yourself with a people, a nation, and that requires a personal connection through a name (Exodus 6:3). Your name did not just convey Your own eternal, abiding existence, but also conveyed Your eternal, abiding presence. As this Psalm praises You in creation glory, it reminds us that wherever we go Your creation screams out to us of Your presence.

Your presence is what Moses will greatly experience on the mount and will desire most of all at the great crisis of the golden calf (Exodus 33:14). And so Moses asks for and sees the glory of God as the Lord passes by and proclaims His name. And what has the apostle Paul written to us? That God has given Jesus a name above every name to which every knee shall bow (Philippians 2:9–11), and Peter said that there is no other name under heaven, given among men, by which we must be saved (Acts 4:12). It has been Your consistent desire to have a people near to You; so may we cleave to You and let praise bring us nigh to you.

Psalm 148
His Glory is Above

Vs. 13—Let them praise the name of the LORD, for his name alone is exalted; his splendor is above the earth and the heavens. (NIV)

God is greater and more glorious than His entire creation. Pantheism would teach that all things are part of God and that God is in all things. The Bible is clear that God is separate and apart from His creation, that His existence alone is eternal. "All things were created by Him and without Him was not anything made that was made." God alone is infinite whereas all other things are finite and limited in both their duration and scope. Paul wrote in I Timothy 6:6 that God alone is immortal (that is, He Himself as the only self-existing one) and dwells in unapproachable light.

For any created being to exist God must create an environment suitable for them. For the angels, spiritual beings, He created the highest heaven. It is there that they commune with God and exalt Him. But Solomon himself declares that "the heavens, even the highest heavens cannot contain Him." So great is our God that He exceeds all of His creation. For man, He created the earth and the physical heavens (atmospheric and spacial) as the suitable environment for our habitation. And everything is a song of praise to our God. It is only man in his wicked sinfulness which seeks to withhold the praise that He is due. May I, through the Spirit worship, praise Him in spirit and in truth.

Psalm 149
Be Joyful in Glory

Vs. 3, 4—Let them praise his name with dancing and make music to him with timbrel and harp. For the LORD takes delight in his people; he crowns the humble with victory. (NIV)

Praise brings joy to the heart of God, but it also rebounds in joy to us. Your call to me, Lord, is an unqualified call to praise. I can, in the Spirit, give You praise in the good circumstances as well as the unpleasant, when life makes sense and when nothing in life is sensible, in life and in death, in plenty and want (Philippians 4:11–12). If I cannot give praise in the hard times, then my praise in the good times doesn't mean much.

For I have a new song, a song of redemption, of reconciliation, of belonging that expresses a fullness of relationship that I have with God through Christ. My praise can be in word, in song, in music, or in dance, for God has made me a whole being, alive in spirit, soul, and body, and all of me can express praise to the Lord. And He desires to have pleasure in us! As a loving father takes pleasure in his child's joy, so does God take pleasure in the joy of His people. "Let the saints be joyful in glory" (verse 5). My glory is in the Lord. May I never glory in myself, but in Him who loved me and gave Himself for me. He is my glory, my joy, the lifter of my head. Jesus desired for His joy to be in us and His joy to be complete. I rejoice in Your joy and glory in Your salvation.

Psalm 149
The Lord Takes Pleasure

Vs. 4—For the LORD takes delight in his people; he crowns the humble with victory. (NIV)

Lord, it is so humbling to realize that you take pleasure in me. You have imparted to me Your nature; I have been born again. You didn't seek to rectify my old nature, to try to unravel in it the perversion that sin had wrought. You imparted to me Your nature and granted me Your Spirit through which I exercise that new nature. There was nothing in me by nature that would commend Your love toward me; it was all by Your grace.

You alone can take this wretchedness and change my garments of filth to give me garments of salvation. You are able to take pleasure in me because You don't see me in my sin but in the perfection of Your son. When Satan brings an accusation against me before Your throne, Jesus steps forward to intercede on my behalf. No longer an object of Your wrath, I am an object of Your favor. And I am clothed in the perfection of Christ's work. Such is my beauty in Your eyes. Father, You are so satisfied with Your Son that You see His glory and not my wretchedness.

DECEMBER 29

Psalm 150
Let Everything Praise the Lord

Vs. 6—Let everything that has breath praise the LORD.
Praise the LORD. (NIV)

All creation owes its existence to God. Without Him, there would be no creation, no other being, no other life. God would not be lonely; He has no needs, nor would He be diminished in any way whatsoever. It is only the impetus of His love that He chose to create so that He could share Himself with a creature. And so that creation, in appreciation of His sovereign act, displays the glory of God, and we His creatures, made in His image, are privileged to praise Him.

We have so much to praise Him for, so many opportunities for praise, and so many ways to express it. Therefore, I praise Him for life, for another day to enjoy His love and goodness. I praise Him for this beautiful creation, which is such a pleasure to behold. I praise Him for my life in Jesus, who bought me and brought me to God. I praise Him for all His blessings, both temporal and spiritual. In Christ, I have forgiveness, reconciliation, union, peace, joy, sonship, fellowship, love, redemption, justification, righteousness, inheritance, and so many other spiritual blessings in heavenly places in Christ (Ephesians 1:3). May we be employed in praise daily; may we be ever conscious of all that surrounds us and is in us for it is all due to You, to direct our praise to You.

Psalm 150
How Shall I Praise Him?

Vs. 2—Praise him for his acts of power; praise him for
his surpassing greatness. (NIV)

How shall I praise you? How do You want me to praise You? This
Psalm tells me. You want me to praise You with every part of my
being. You want me to praise You with my hands as I serve You
through serving Your people and ministering to needs. You want
me to praise You with my lips as I tell of Your greatness and glory
and share Your gospel with a lost and dying world. You want me
to praise You through my heart as I meditate upon You and Your
attributes of love, grace, mercy, and compassion. As I experience
Your great heart for me, I can express the greatness of Your heart
to others, for I have Your Spirit living within me and Your nature
at work in me. You want me to praise You with every talent that
I have. You have made me this way; everything that I am is a gift
of Your grace, and You want to express Your nature through me.

Shall I sing? Shall I dance? I can even praise you and give you glory
through the most mundane, simplest of tasks such as eating and
drinking. You want every expression of my being to be a living,
breathing testimony to You. When John the Baptist said, "He
must increase but I must decrease " (John 3:30, NKJV), it had to
do with more than the relative strengths of the ministries. What I
am in the flesh must decrease so that the indwelling life of Christ
may increase in me and redound to Your praise and glory.